Ethics and the Environment

What is the environment, and how does it figure in an ethical life? This book is an introduction to the philosophical issues involved in this important question, focusing primarily on ethics but also encompassing questions in aesthetics and political philosophy. Topics discussed include the environment as an ethical question, human morality, meta-ethics, normative ethics, humans and other animals, the value of nature, and nature's future. The discussion is accessible and richly illustrated with examples. The book will be valuable for students taking courses in environmental philosophy, and also for a wider audience in courses in ethics, practical ethics, and environmental studies. It will also appeal to general readers who want a reliable and sophisticated introduction to the field.

DALE JAMIESON is Director of Environmental Studies at New York University, where he is also Professor of Environmental Studies and Philosophy, and Affiliated Professor of Law.

Ethics and the Environment

An Introduction

DALE JAMIESON
New York University

CAMBRIDGE
UNIVERSITY PRESS

CAMBRIDGE UNIVERSITY PRESS

Cambridge, New York, Melbourne, Madrid, Cape Town, Singapore, São Paulo, Delhi

Cambridge University Press
The Edinburgh Building, Cambridge CB2 8RU, UK

Published in the United States of America by Cambridge University Press, New York

www.cambridge.org
Information on this title: www.cambridge.org/9780521682848

First published 2008

Printed in the United Kingdom at the University Press, Cambridge

A catalogue record for this publication is available from the British Library

ISBN 978-0-521-86421-3 hardback
ISBN 978-0-521-68284-8 paperback

For Béatrice

"One of the real mistakes in the conservation movement in the last few years is the tendency to see nature simply as natural resources: use it or lose it. Yet conservation without moral values cannot sustain itself."

George Schaller

Contents

Preface

Environmental philosophy is a large subject that involves epistemology, metaphysics, philosophy of science, and history of philosophy, as well as such obviously normative areas as ethics, aesthetics, and political philosophy. The main focus of this book is environmental ethics, but I discuss the normative dimensions of the subject generally, including issues in aesthetics and political philosophy. My hope is that this book will be used in classes in environmental philosophy, but I also hope that it finds a wider audience in courses in ethics proper or in environmental studies. In addition, I hope that it will be read by philosophers, environmental scientists, environmental policy specialists, and others who simply want a reliable and relatively sophisticated introduction to the field.

Over the past twenty-five years I have taught courses on environmental philosophy to thousands of students at six different colleges and universities on three continents. Ultimately, this book is the product of these courses. More proximately, it is based on lectures that I gave at Princeton University in spring, 2005. It is a pleasure to thank Princeton, and particularly the University Center for Human Values, for inviting me to spend the academic year 2004–5 as Laurence R. Rockefeller Visiting Professor for Distinguished Teaching. I am especially grateful for the personal warmth and intellectual vigor of my colleagues, both in the Center and in the Princeton Environmental Institute. I expanded and rewrote the lectures the following summer while living in France. I thank Béatrice Longuenesse and her family for making this such a happy and joyful time. I completed the book in New York under less favorable circumstances, and I am grateful to my sturdy community of scattered friends who would drop everything at a moment's notice to help me through the hard times. My home institution, New York University, has been consistently generous in granting me the leave that allowed me to take up the Princeton professorship, providing the sabbatical during which I revised the lectures, and assisting me in various other ways both personal and professional. I am especially grateful to Dean Richard Foley for his unwavering support.

That this book exists at all is due to Hilary Gaskin's kind (and persistent) invitation to contribute to the series in which it appears. That it is better than it would have been is due to the kind (and again persistent) interventions of many friends and colleagues including Phil Camill, Ned Hettinger, Béatrice Longuenesse, Jay Odenbaugh, Reed Richter, Sharon Street, Vicki Weafer, and Mark Woods. I am especially grateful to the (formerly anonymous) reader for Cambridge University Press, Steve Gardiner, for many helpful suggestions. While there are further acknowledgments in the notes, I am certain that I have forgotten to thank some who will find echoes of their ideas or marks of their influence in the text. For this I apologize in advance.

In the interests of precision I have used some technical terms and adopted various conventions. I use italics for book titles and for non-English words. I use single quotation marks when discussing words, and double when reporting words and for other related purposes. For example, the *Oxford English Dictionary* defines 'environment' as "the objects or the region surrounding anything." I indent and number sentences whose uses I wish to discuss. I capitalize these sentences, but in most cases I punctuate them as if they were simply part of the text. However, when these sentences are exclamations or questions, I use double punctuation. For example, I say that on some views a perspicuous reading of

(1) It is wrong to eat animals

is

(2) Do not eat animals!.

Finally, when discussing the divisions that rend our planet, I talk about the rich and poor countries, the north and south, and the first and third worlds. I dislike all of these contrasts but I think it is clear what I'm talking about when I use these terms.

Although I have tried to be precise in ways that matter, this book is intended as an introduction and I have attempted to rein in my tendency to be pedantic. I have focused on ideas and controversies rather than on authors or cases. Among other advantages, this has allowed me to get quickly to the heart of various views, but often at the cost of oversimplifying them and not properly crediting those whose work has advanced the discussion. When it comes to references, I have sometimes cited passages as they are quoted by other authors. While I disapprove of this as a scholarly standard, I think it is permissible in a book of this type. Those who go on in the subject will find the original sources; those who do not go on will not care. I offer a similar justification for often referring readers to websites rather than texts that are stored in libraries.

I have been selective in the topics that I discuss. For example, although I mention some themes broached by deep ecologists and ecofeminists, I have not discussed their work in detail. This omission does not imply a judgment about the value of this work, but is only a concession to the finitude of life, books, and attention spans.

Returning to the source, I thank the students to whom I have taught this subject over the years. Whatever hope I have for the future rests to a great extent on their energy and enthusiasm. I also want to acknowledge the love and support of my parents, which lingers beyond the grave: anything that I do that is of any use was made possible by their sacrifices. Finally, I would like to thank two Pauls: one for teaching me how to do philosophy, and one for showing me something about life.

Dale Jamieson
New York

1 The environment as an ethical question

1.1 Nature and the environment

What is the environment? In one sense the answer is obvious. The environment is those special places that we are concerned to protect: the Arctic National Wildlife Refuge in Alaska, the Great Barrier Reef in Australia, the Lake District in Great Britain. But the environment is more than these special places. It is also Harlem and Brixton, as well as the Upper East Side of Manhattan and the leafy suburbs of Melbourne. It is even the strip malls of Southern California. The environment includes not just the natural environment, but also the built environment.

Indeed, we can even speak of the "social environment." The term 'environmentalism' was coined in 1923, to refer not to the activities of John Muir and the Sierra Club, but to the idea that human behavior is largely a product of the social and physical conditions in which a person lives and develops.[1] This view arose in opposition to the idea that a person's behavior is primarily determined by his or her biological endowment. These environmentalists championed the "nurture" side in the "nature versus nurture" debate that raged in the social sciences for much of the twentieth century. They advocated changing people by changing society, rather than changing society by changing people.

While the scope of the environment is very broad, contemporary environmentalists are especially concerned to protect nature. Often the ideas of nature and the environment are treated as if they were equivalent, but they have quite different origins and histories. The *Oxford English Dictionary* defines 'environment' as "the objects or the region surrounding anything,"

---

[1] John Muir (1838–1914) founded the Sierra Club in 1892 and is one of America's great environmental heroes. For more about his life and work, visit <http://en.wikipedia.org/wiki/John_Muir>.

and traces its origin to an Old French term, '*environner*', meaning "to encircle." The word 'nature' has much deeper roots, coming to us from the Latin *natura*. While disputes about the environment have occurred mostly in the twentieth century and after, arguments about the meaning and significance of nature are as ancient as philosophy.

That these terms, 'environment' and 'nature', are not identical in reference and meaning can be seen from the following examples. The *boulangerie* (bakery) on the corner of my street in Paris is part of the environment, but it would be strange to say that it is part of nature. The neurons firing in my brain are part of nature, but it would be weird to say that they are part of the environment. Finally, had the contemporary environmentalist, Bill McKibben, written a book called *The End of the Environment* instead of the book he actually wrote, *The End of Nature*, it would have had to be a quite different book.

Sorting out the reasons for these disparate uses would be good fun. Perhaps it is a necessary condition for something to be part of our environment that we think of it as subject to our causal control, while no such condition applies to what we think of as nature. So the moon, for example, is part of nature but not part of our environment. On this view the end of nature might be thought of as the beginning of the environment.[2]

Whatever the explanation of their use, having alerted us to some of the complexities involved, I will now do my best to ignore them. Although there are important differences between the idea of the environment and the concept of nature that will sometimes have to be acknowledged, many of the themes expressed by using one term can also be expressed by using the other. In the next section we discuss some examples.

1.2   Dualism and ambivalence

The expansiveness of the environment is reflected in the contemporary environmental movement by the concept of holism. The First Law of Ecology, according to Barry Commoner in his 1971 book, *The Closing Circle*, is that "everything is connected to everything else." This holistic ideal resonates in the common environmentalist slogan that "humans are part of nature." This slogan is often used to imply that the "original sin" that leads to

---

[2] For further discussion see Sagoff 1991.

environmental destruction is the attempt to separate ourselves from nature. We can return to a healthy relationship with nature only once we recognize that this attempt to separate ourselves is both fatuous and destructive.

The thirst for "oneness" runs throughout much environmentalist rhetoric.[3] Indeed, one way of rebuking someone in the language of some environmentalists is to call them a "dualist." Dualists are those who see the world as embodying deep distinctions between, for example, humans and animals, the natural and unnatural, the wild and domestic, male and female, and reason and emotion. "Monists," on the other hand, deny that such distinctions are deep, instead seeing the items within these categories as continuous or entwined, or rejecting the categories altogether. Despite the attractions of monism, it is difficult to make sense of many environmentalist claims without invoking dualisms of one sort or another. The trick is to figure out when and to what extent such dualisms are useful.

Consider the idea that humans are part of nature. If humans and beavers are both part of nature, how can we say that deforestation by humans is wrong without similarly condemning beavers for cutting trees to make their dams? How can we say that the predator–prey relationships of the African Savanna are valuable wonders of nature while at the same time condemning humans who poach African elephants? More fundamentally, how can we distinguish the death of a person caused by an earthquake from the death of a person caused by another person?

Aesthetically appreciating nature also seems to require a deep distinction between humans and nature. Aesthetic appreciation, at least in the normal case, involves appreciating something that is distinct from one's self. Perhaps it would be possible to appreciate some aspect of oneself aesthetically, but that would require a strange sort of objectification and appear to be a form of vanity.

Some might say that this is no great loss, since viewing nature aesthetically is a way of trivializing it. As we shall see in section 6.4.2, this claim rests on a false view of the value of aesthetic experience. Moreover, it is a plain fact that environmentalists often give aesthetic arguments for protecting nature, and these arguments are extremely powerful in motivating people. For anyone who has spent time in such places as the Grand Canyon, it is easy

---

[3] The rejection of monism is in different ways a theme of both "deep ecologists" and "ecofeminists." For overviews of these positions, see Jamieson 2001: chs. 15–16.

to see why. The view from the south rim is an overwhelming aesthetic experience for almost anyone. Jettisoning aesthetic arguments for protecting the environment would greatly weaken the environmentalists' case.

This ambivalence between seeing humans as both part of but also separate from nature is part of a larger theme that runs through environmentalism. Under pressure, environmentalists will agree that Harlem is as much a part of the environment as Kakadu National Park in Australia, but it is a plain fact that protecting Harlem is not what people generally have in mind when they talk about protecting the environment. Moreover, much of the history of environmentalism has involved distinguishing special places that should be protected from mundane places that can be used for ordinary purposes.

Consider an example. The contemporary environmental movement is often dated from the early twentieth-century struggle of John Muir and the Sierra Club to protect the majestic Hetch Hetchy Valley, in the recently created Yosemite National Park, from a proposed dam intended to provide water and electricity to the growing city of San Francisco. Muir had no trouble suggesting alternative water supplies for the city, going so far as to say that "north and south of San Francisco . . . many streams waste their waters in the ocean."[4] Hetch Hetchy was special, according to Muir, and his arguments against the dam appealed, in quasi-religious terms, to its unique character and majesty. This idea that there are special places that deserve extraordinary protection is part of the historical legacy of environmentalism, and reflects an attitude going back at least to our Neolithic ancestors.

As these examples suggest, there are deep ambivalences in environmental thought and rhetoric. On the one hand, judging human action by a standard different from "natural" events requires distinguishing people from nature, but convincing people to live modestly may require convincing them to see themselves as part of nature. Aesthetically appreciating nature involves seeing ourselves apart from nature, but this is supposed to be the attitude that gives rise to environmental destruction in the first place. The environment is everything that surrounds us, but some places are special.

Someone who is unsympathetic to environmentalism might reject my polite but vague description of these cases as expressing "ambivalences."

---

[4] From a 1909 pamphlet by John Muir, available on the web at <http://lcweb2.loc.gov/gc/amrvg/vg50/vg500004.tif>.

Such a person might say instead that environmentalism is a view that is enmeshed in paradox and contradiction, and for these reasons should simply be given up. This, however, would be the wrong conclusion to draw. I agree that we take different perspectives on nature and the environment on different occasions, and sometimes, perhaps, even simultaneously; and that it is a challenge to understand these phenomena and to bring them together. In my opinion, however, this is not peculiar to our thinking about the environment, but reflects deep tendencies in human thought. What for some purposes we see as the setting of the sun, for other purposes we see as a relation between astronomical bodies. What from one perspective we see as a man who is a predictable product of his environment, from another perspective we see as an evil person. We live with multiplicity; the trick is to understand it, and to deploy our concepts productively in the light of it.[5]

Consider, for example, the stances that we take towards our fellow humans. We are almost never single-minded about them, nor are our attitudes serial or linear. We live with multiple views and perspectives, often held simultaneously, sometimes with quite different valences. Imagine a colleague who is excellent at his work, narcissistic in his behavior, an emotional abuser of women, but a charming and intelligent social companion. I might happily work with him on a project, but I would not introduce him to a female friend. I might enjoy going to the movies with him, but I would not open my heart in a conversation over dinner. I would say that such complexity in human relationships, rather than plunging me into inconsistency is the stuff of everyday life.

Our relationships to nature are no less complex. Consider my relationship to the Needles District of Canyonlands, part of the American wilderness system. I have hiked and camped there, experiencing the sublimity of Druid Arch and the luminescence of the full moon over Elephant Canyon. In searching for water I have felt myself to be part of the natural system that orders and supports life in this desert. I am irate about proposals to open this area to off-road vehicles. Such a policy would be unjust to backpackers and wilderness adventurers, who would lose the silence and solitude that make their wilderness experiences possible. I also mourn for the wildlife that would be destroyed or driven away by such a policy. I find the idea of

---

[5] For a celebration and defense of this attitude see Goodman 1978.

people treating this place as if it were some desert speedway both vulgar and disrespectful. My attitudes towards this area embody multiple perspectives: a recognition that who I am is defined, at least in part, by my relationship to this place; a desire for the aesthetic experiences that it affords; and most of all, a passion that those who love and inhabit this place be treated justly. The moral psychology of my attitudes is complex, but it should not be surprising that our attitudes towards nature can be as complex as our attitudes towards our conspecifics.

1.3   Environmental problems

Even if there were no environmental problems, there would still be a place for reflecting on ethics and the environment. However, what has given our subject its urgency and focus is the widespread belief that we are in the early stages of an environmental crisis that is of our own making. Many biologists believe that the sixth major wave of extinction since life began is now occurring, and that this one, unlike the other five, is being caused by human action. Atmospheric scientists tell us that we have set in motion events that will take more than a century to play out, and that the result is almost certain to be a climate that is warmer than humans have ever experienced. Many other examples could be given.

Some doubt the seriousness of this crisis because they are skeptical about the science. They think that scientists exaggerate their results in order to obtain more research funding. Or they are put off by the methodologies used in environmental science that often involve "coupling" highly complex computer models, and using them to produce forecasts or "scenarios" on the basis of data sets that are often seriously incomplete. Of course, the same concerns can be raised about other sciences, including those that inform the management of the economy. The defense in both cases is the same: there is no better alternative than to act on the basis of the best available science, recognizing that it is the nature of scientific claims to be probabilistic and revisable. Of course, it may turn out that the skeptics are right and that environmental science is mostly a bunch of hooey. But then, I may also win the lottery.

Every so often a book is published which largely accepts the findings of environmental science, but views the glass as half full rather than half empty. According to these critics, environmentalists focus only on the "doom and gloom" scenarios and ignore the good news. Life expectancy, literacy, and wealth are increasing all over the world.[6]

It is certainly true that we have made progress in addressing some environmental problems. One of the best examples of a success story is the improvement in air quality in many of the cities of the industrial world. In December 1952, air quality was so bad in London that it killed thousands of people over a four-day period. Today, the levels of most pollutants in London's air are about one-tenth of what they were in the 1950s, and the number of deaths they cause is measured in the hundreds per year rather than in the thousands in a single week. However, some cities in the developing world have much higher levels of air pollution today than London did in the 1950s. For example, in 1995 air pollution in Delhi, India, was measured at 1.3 times London's average for 1952, and the air pollution in Lanzhou, China, was measured at an astounding 2.7 times greater than London's 1952 average.[7] While there has been progress in addressing some environmental problems, it has been patchy and incomplete.

Some people deny the seriousness of environmental problems, not because they believe that we are making great progress in addressing them, but because they believe that the changes that we have set in motion will have limited or even positive impacts. They have an image of nature which views it as resilient, almost impervious to human insults. Sometimes this vision is inspired by the "Gaia hypothesis," put forward by the British scientist James Lovelock in the 1970s. According to Lovelock, Earth is a self-regulating, homeostatic system, with feedback loops that give it a strong bias in favor of stability. From this perspective, it would be surprising if the actions of a single species could threaten the basic functioning of the Earth system.[8]

Others, especially many environmentalists, view nature as highly vulnerable and planetary systems as delicately balanced. In their view, people have the ability to disrupt the systems that make life on Earth possible. While

---

[6] Lomborg 2001 is the latest book in this vein to receive a great deal of media attention. Before that it was Easterbrook 1996. For critical reviews of Lomborg, visit <www.ucsusa.org/ssi/resources/the-skeptical-environmentalist.html>. For critical reviews of Easterbrook, see <http://info-pollution.com/easter.htm>.

[7] Brennan and Withgott 2005: 326.

[8] Recently, however, even Lovelock (2006) has become pessimistic about the human impact. Generally on Gaia, see Volk 2005.

once people needed to be protected from nature, today nature needs to be protected from people.

Both of these views have more the character of an ultimate attitude or even a religious commitment than of a sober scientific claim that can be shown to be true or false. However, even if those who are most skeptical about the existence of an environmental crisis are correct, this would not obviate the need for reflecting on the ethical dimensions of environmental questions.

Suppose that it is true that environmentalists dwell on the dark side, and that, however implausible this may seem, things are really getting better all the time. Even if this were true, an improving situation is, by definition, not the one that is best. So long as one innocent person dies unnecessarily because of environmental harms caused by others, there is a need for ethical reflection.

Suppose, as do those who are inspired by the Gaia hypothesis, that Earth's systems are resilient. It would not follow from this that environmental problems are not worth taking seriously. Even if Earth systems successfully respond to our environmental insults, there may still be a high price to pay in the loss of much that we value: species diversity, quality of life, water resources, agricultural output, and so on. Through centuries of warfare, European nations demonstrated their resilience, but millions of people lost their lives and much that we value was destroyed. Moreover, even if it is highly unlikely that human action could lead to a collapse in fundamental Earth systems, the consequences of such a collapse would be so devastating that avoiding the risk altogether would be preferable. Just as it is best not to have to rely on the life-saving properties of the airbags in one's car, so it would be best not to have to rely on the resilience of Earth's basic systems.

Environmental problems are diverse in scale, impact, and the harms they threaten. They can be local, regional, or global. They can involve setbacks to human interests, or they can damage other creatures, species, or natural systems. These features of environmental problems will be discussed in the next two sections.

1.4   Questions of scale

Many environmental problems are local in scale, and people confronted them before the word 'environment' existed. For example, the common practice in medieval Europe of tossing sewage into the street caused an environmental problem that was largely local in scope. My neighbor who insists on playing heavy metal music at all hours also causes a local environmental problem. Noise is ubiquitous in modern life, and we do not often think of it in this way, but it has many of the hallmarks of a classic pollutant. It causes people to lose sleep and to stay away from home, and it generally degrades their quality of life. There is evidence that persistent exposure to high levels of noise can even raise blood pressure and serum cholesterol. Noise pollution can spread out from being a matter of one household affecting another, to being a serious urban problem, as anyone who has ever lived in a large metropolitan area such as New York City can testify.

Another local environmental problem that is often not viewed in this way is the exposure to tobacco smoke. This is a much more serious problem than noise pollution, claiming thousands of lives each year. Local environmental problems can affect quality of life or seriously threaten life itself.

Some environmental problems are regional in scope. In these cases people act in such a way that they degrade the environment over a region, thus producing harms that may be remote from the spatio-temporal location of their actions. Rather than involving one event that simply produces another event in the same locale, they involve complex causes and effects spread over large areas. Air and water often provide good examples of regional environmental problems since they follow their own imperatives rather than political boundaries. Floods and other water-management issues involve entire watersheds, and air quality involves the dynamics of the troposphere.

For example, when I drive in the Los Angeles Basin, pollutants discharged by the tail pipe of my car mix with other pollutants and naturally occurring substances to produce harmful chemicals that are transported over the entire basin by prevailing weather patterns. My behavior, when joined with that of others, produces serious health risks to, and even the deaths of, many people.

The catastrophic floods that occurred in China in 1998 provide another example of a regional environmental problem. For decades deforestation has been occurring in the upper elevations of the Yangtze River Basin. When extremely heavy rains occurred in June and July of that year, runoff was much more intense and rapid as a result, leading to floods that affected more than 200 million people and killed more than 3,600.

In recent years global environmental problems, such as climate change and stratospheric ozone depletion, have captured a great deal of attention. These are problems that could not have existed without modern technologies.

Ozone depletion is caused by chlorofluorocarbons (CFCs) – a class of chemicals that was invented in 1928 for use as refrigerants, fire extinguishers, and propellants in aerosol cans. CFC emissions, through a complex chain of chemistry, lead to the erosion of stratospheric ozone, thus exposing living things on Earth to radically increased levels of life-threatening ultra-violet radiation.

The climate change that is now under way is largely caused by the emission of carbon dioxide, a byproduct of the combustion of fossil fuels. The massive consumption of fossil fuels which fed the Industrial Revolution and continues to support the way of life of industrial societies is causing the climate change that is now under way. The Earth has already warmed 0.6°C (more than 1° Fahrenheit) since the pre-industrial era, and the emissions that have already occurred commit us to at least another 0.4–0.6°C (0.72–1.08°F) warming. Since emissions of carbon dioxide and other climate-changing gases continue to increase, we are bequeathing to future generations the most extreme and rapid climate change to have occurred since the age of the dinosaurs. Although this problem has been mostly caused by the residents of the industrialized countries, to some extent everyone has contributed. However, it is non-human nature and the descendants of today's poor people who will suffer most from this problem.

1.5   Types of harm

Environmental problems inflict many different types of harm. For example, some environmental problems primarily affect the quality of life for human beings. The harms caused by my heavy-metal-loving neighbor are an example of this sort. No one will die nor will a species be driven to extinction by his boorish behavior, but the quality of life of his neighbors will be compromised.

Other environmental problems threaten human health. Indeed, the protection of human health is the primary rationale for most of the regulations issued by the United States Environmental Protection Agency. Regulations controlling pollutants in air and water, and levels of pesticide residues, are examples. Some statutes do require that other values be taken into account, but it is not too much of an exaggeration to say that over the years the United States Environmental Protection Agency has increasingly evolved into a public health agency.

Some environmental problems affect mainly non-human nature. While arguments have been made for why there is a human interest in protecting species diversity, for example, it is difficult to deny that blanket prohibitions against driving species to extinction presuppose values that are deeper than considerations about human health or quality of life. The American Endangered Species Act, for example, first passed in 1973, evinces a concern for species themselves that goes beyond considerations of human health or quality of life.

Economists call such goods that make no essential reference to human interests "pure environmental goods." They find a place for them in their calculations through such concepts as "existence value." The idea is that driving the Spotted Owl to extinction (for example) harms me even though it is not a threat to my health, life, or quality of life. I am harmed because I value the very fact of the Owl's existence, even if I were never to experience the Owl directly. It is this existence value that is lost when the Owl becomes extinct.

There are reasons to be dubious about this way of accounting for the loss of value caused by species extinctions. Value does not easily translate into harms and benefits to the valuer. While it is true that a poor egalitarian liberal may benefit from the realization of her values, a rich investment banker who shares these values may be harmed by their realization. There are further difficulties that will be discussed in section 6.4.1 about how we are supposed to compute the value of rare species. The main point here, however, is that environmental problems cause a wide range of harms.

1.6   Causes of environmental problems

There are many reasons for wanting to know what causes environmental problems. Understanding history is interesting in itself, and can provide general guidance for how to think about the future. It can also be important in determining how to distribute responsibility, blame, and even punishment.

Sometimes knowing the cause of a problem is a direct line to identifying its solution. If I know that my stereo isn't working because it is not plugged in, the solution to the problem immediately presents itself: plug it in. When I plug in the stereo, I fix the problem by removing its cause. However, in some cases there are more elegant solutions to problems than removing their causes. For example, if I am late for an appointment because I'm stuck in traffic, teleconferencing is a better solution than trying to remove the problem by fixing the traffic jam. Still, it is generally good advice that when facing a serious problem, one should try to understand its cause.

Another reason why it is important to understand the causes of environmental problems is that people respond quite differently depending on how they are caused. A classic example concerns lung cancer deaths caused by inhaling cigarette smoke compared to those caused by radon exposure. Cigarette-smoking is the leading cause of lung cancer in the United States, killing about 160,000 people per year, while inhaling naturally occurring radon gas is second, killing about 21,000 people per year, seven times as many as die from breathing secondhand smoke.[9] Yet despite the comparative risks, people are much more motivated to regulate secondhand smoke than radon exposure. Our moral psychologies and reactive attitudes are geared to what we do to each other, rather than to what nature does to us even when this is mediated by human agency.

In the debate over climate change there have been several stages of denial: first, climate change isn't happening; then climate change is happening, but it is natural; finally, climate change is happening and partly caused by people, but on the whole quite a good thing. Implicit in the second stage of denial is the view that if climate change is a naturally occurring phenomenon then no one can be held responsible for its toll. Tell this to the people of New Orleans who were victimized by human agency, whether or not Hurricane Katrina was a product of climate change or naturally occurring weather patterns.

1.7 The role of technology

There are many theories about the cause of environmental problems. Perhaps the most influential at present centers on technological failures and

---

[9] <www.epa.gov/radon/healthrisks.html>. Generally on this issue see Edelstein and Makofske 1998.

solutions. This view claims that we are victims of our success. We suffer from environmental problems because we have become rich and mobile so quickly that we have overwhelmed the technological systems that enabled these successes to occur. When few people had automobiles it did not matter very much that they were highly polluting. When everyone has an automobile they become an environmental problem. When few people can afford furniture made from tropical hardwoods, gathering the materials does not harm the environment. When many people buy furniture made from tropical hardwoods, the problem of deforestation occurs. This kind of story can be told for many environmental problems.

The solution, on this picture, is a new round of technological development. Previous generations of technologies were developed to solve problems and reduce labor in a world in which environmental costs were not significant. Now that they are very important, a new generation of technology is needed that performs these labor-saving functions, but with much greater sensitivity to the environment. Thus, some people (including President Bush) propose as a solution to climate change a new generation of hydrogen-powered cars. We could still zip down the highway to our local shopping mall, but the impact on the atmosphere would be greatly reduced. Other leaders and opinion-makers are calling for new technologies for decarbonizing coal, or even technologies that would allow us to geo-engineer the climate.

Technological approaches are popular both with politicians and with the public because they promise solutions to environmental problems without forcing us to change our values, ways of life, or economic systems. Moreover, for many people who came of age in the post-World War II period, the image of the scientist as the "can-do" guy who can solve any problem remains quite potent. Thus it should not be too surprising that politicians of various stripes advocate buying our way out of environmental problems through scientific research and technological development, though there is often considerable vagueness about what these new technologies should be or what they might actually accomplish. Whatever potential such high-tech solutions may have for ameliorating the environmental problems most on the minds of the rich people of the world, they seem almost entirely irrelevant to the needs of the poorest of the poor, who often are locked in a day-to-day struggle with life-threatening air and water pollution.

1.8   The economic perspective

Economists tend to be skeptical of technology-driven approaches. Simply talking about the need for new technologies or subsidizing their development will not guarantee that they will actually come into existence, much less that they will be widely adopted. In many cases, alternatives to environmentally destructive technologies already exist but are not widely used.[10] The real solution to environmental problems lies in restructuring the system of economic incentives that has led to environmental destruction, and replacing it with a system that creates incentives for environmentally friendly behavior, including the development and use of "green" technologies.

Environmental problems, from the perspective of economics, concern the allocation of two types of scarce resources: sources and sinks. Things as different from one another as oil, elephants, and the Grand Canyon can be seen as sources that provide opportunities for consumption. Oil is consumed, in refined form, by burning it in our automobiles. Elephants are consumed by killing them and using their ivory, or even by photographing them. We consume the Grand Canyon by using it for backpacking or hiking, or by viewing it from airplanes and helicopters. Sinks provide opportunities for disposing of the unwanted consequences of production and consumption. A river is used as a sink when a factory dumps wastes into it. The atmosphere is used as a sink when I drive my car to the supermarket, emitting nitrogen oxides, carbon monoxide, carbon dioxide and other chemicals from the tailpipe. Some of the most serious environmental problems occur when the same resource is used both as a source and as a sink: for example, when the same stretch of river is used both as a water supply and as a sewer; or when the same region of the atmosphere is used as a source of oxygen to breathe and as a sink for disposing of various pollutants. Using the environment as a source or a sink typically degrades its ability to function. Thus, opportunities to use the environment in these ways can be viewed as scarce resources.

The fundamental economic question regarding the environment involves determining the most efficient allocation of these scarce resources.

[10] For example, Pacala and Socolow (2004) show that we could satisfy a large fraction of global energy demand over the next fifty years while limiting atmospheric concentrations of CO_2, using only existing technologies.

'Efficiency' (like 'consumption') is used as a technical term by economists: an efficient state of affairs in this vocabulary is one in which no one can be made better off without making at least one person worse off. The allocation of environmental goods is typically inefficient for a number of reasons, the most important of which is that environmental goods have many of the characteristics of public goods.

Pure public goods are typically defined as goods which are "non-rival" and "non-excludable." They are non-rival in that one person's consuming the good does not diminish another person's consumption. They are non-excludable in that they are available to everyone. The paradigm of a pure public good is national defense: it is available to everyone and its value to each person is not diminished by its availability to others.

Environmental goods such as sources and sinks have some but not all of the properties of public goods: in many cases they are relatively non-excludable, but significantly rivalrous. Everyone can use them but each use slightly degrades them.[11] It is difficult to allocate such goods efficiently because people use them, diminishing their value to others, without paying the full costs of their use.

Consider the following example. Suppose that I want to buy your car. You have a right over the use of the car, and you won't transfer it to me unless I give you something in return that you value more, typically a particular sum of money. If we can agree on a price for the car, then at least by our own lights the transaction makes us both better off. You would rather have the money than the car, and I would rather have the car than the money. We have reached, in the economist's sense, an efficient outcome. So, cheerfully, I drive away in my new car, spewing out of the tailpipe a noxious brew of chemicals that contributes to climate change and also to various forms of air pollution that kills many innocent people, including senior citizens, asthma patients, and people with heart disease. While I had to pay your price in order to obtain the right to drive the car, there is no one I have to pay in order to obtain the right to dump these pollutants into the atmosphere. The consequence is obvious. Markets may allocate private goods to their highest valued uses, but public goods such as the atmosphere will be over-exploited

---

[11] Such goods are sometimes called "common pool resources," but there is no harm for our purposes in calling them public goods, so long as we recognize that they typically do not have all the properties of pure public goods to the fullest extent.

because they are free to those who use them. The result will be diminishing resources and increasing pollution. Welcome to the environmental crisis.

To put the point a little more formally, the costs of consuming private goods are "internal" to the good: they are borne by the owner, and reflected in the price. The costs of consuming a public good, on the other hand, instead of being internal to the good, are "externalized" over the entire community. Thus, the full cost of using a public good is not reflected in its price. The solution, from this perspective, is to privatize public goods, or create policies that mimic the outcomes that a properly functioning market would deliver.

The obvious objection to the first approach is that there is a reason why markets have not developed for many environmental goods: they simply do not have the characteristics of private goods. Consider again the example of my newly purchased automobile. When it comes to cars, it is not difficult to distribute enforceable property rights, but what would it mean to create such rights to the atmosphere? Similar problems occur with other environmental goods such as the biological resources that constitute biodiversity. Of course we can imagine various ways of trying to implement such a privatizing program, but they often seem like a joke. However, the fact that privatizing environmental goods is somewhere between improbable and impossible has not prevented powerful figures from advocating this policy, including some in the United States government. It has even been suggested that the way to save endangered species is to auction them off to the highest bidder. If they are really worth saving, the story goes, then they will be purchased by environmental groups who will protect them. Anyone who harms these animals would then be violating a private property right and could be prosecuted or sued.

The mainstream in environmental economics has advocated a more sensitive mix of policies involving taxes, subsidies, and regulations that would mimic the results that would be produced by a well-functioning market in environmental goods. The problem with this "kinder, gentler" approach is that it does not respond to the most fundamental objections to the economic perspective. How can we protect the interests of entities that do not themselves participate in markets? What happens if the optimal economic approach is not to save the whales, but rather to harvest them as quickly as possible and invest the returns in high-yielding junk bonds? How can

future generations be represented in present transactions that will affect
them when they do not yet exist?

Ultimately, on this approach, entities that do not participate in markets
have no recognized welfare that the economic system is in a position to promote. Whatever value attaches to the Grand Canyon, Polar Bears, and clean
air is solely in virtue of the preferences of people who do participate in
markets. If people value these things highly, then they are highly valuable;
if they do not, then they are not. But people's preferences for environmental goods are highly contingent and historically variable, and there is little
reason to believe that a purely economic approach, even one that reached
efficiency, would produce any long-standing policy of environmental preservation. Consider, for example, how preferences regarding the environment
of North America have changed since white settlement began. When the
Puritans wrote their relatives in England and told them that they were living in a "wilderness," they meant this as a term of abuse. What today we
designate by the neutral term 'wetlands' were 'swamps' only a generation
ago.[12] The great seventeenth-century philosopher, John Locke, whom many
credit as the foremost influence on the American constitution, saw uncul-
tivated land as a "waste," utterly without value.

For many preferences it matters little that they are skittish and volatile.
One generation values short skirts and primary colors while the next goes
for earth tones and "granny" dresses. From a global point of view it matters
little which we prefer, and anyway we can be sure that in due course the
preferences will be reversed. But as we shall see in chapters 5 and 6, there are
important non-economic reasons for supposing that some environmental
goods have importance in their own right. Moreover, some preferences are
such that they are not reversible. If the goods in question fall out of favor
and are eliminated, then unlike short skirts or "granny" dresses they can
never be recovered. All it takes is one generation that values the return from
junk bonds or a world without predators more than marine mammals or
wolves, and we can be sure that whales and wolves will never again inhabit
the Earth, regardless of what preferences future generations might have in
this regard.

---

[12] Ecologists have recently tried to rebrand 'swamp' as a term referring to a particular
  kind of wetland. I am tempted to say that these efforts have been "swamped" by the
  older connotation.

This leads to the next problem: how to adequately value the preferences of future generations. The standard practice in economics is to "discount" the value of the future impacts of any policy that is adopted in the present. This practice can be rationalized on a number of grounds. First, there are probabilistic reasons: the present is certain and the future is not, however likely it may be; and even if the future does come to pass, the predicted consequences may not. The second reason for discounting is that people and economies are dynamic and productive. It makes sense for me to borrow money at an agreed rate of interest because, if I use this money wisely, when the loan comes due I can pay the principal and the interest and still make a profit.

However, it is quite common in public decision-making to apply a discount rate to extremely long-term benefits and costs on the basis of rather vague considerations such as the belief that future people will be better off than present people because of capital investment, technological innovation, and continued economic growth. While there may be some empirical basis for such beliefs, they are largely expressions of faith. Even if one is sympathetic to this faith, it is still not easy to see how these beliefs translate into some specific rate for discounting the future. For this reason it is easy to see how this attitude can slip into "pure time preference": preferring present benefits to future benefits simply because of their location in time. Even without pure time preference, the power of compound interest has the unwelcome consequence that costs deferred to the further future are worth almost nothing at present. Worse still, the future damages entailed by some present policies may not be compensable at all.

Table 1 brings out the power of compound interest, and its interactions with the choice of particular discount rates.[13] Once one understands the consequences for the further future of even modest discount rates, it is easy to see why some economists think that preventing the worst impacts of a global warming that will be felt over centuries is not worth sustaining even a small loss to the economy today.

Even more importantly, the negative effects of environmental destruction are often not costs that can be compensated for at all. If someone takes my bank account or even my house, there is a sum of money that would allow me to replace them. If someone takes my best friend or my companion,

---

[13] Adapted from Cowan and Parfit 1992.

Table 1. *Estimated number of future benefits equal to one present benefit based on different discount rates*

Years in the future	1%	3%	5%	10%
30	1.3	2.4	4.3	17.4
50	1.6	4.3	11.4	117.3
100	2.7	19.2	131.5	13,780.6
500	144.7	2,621,877.2	39,323,261,827	4.96×10^{20}

there is nothing that can replace them. What are we to say of actions that completely eliminate Mountain Gorillas, wild nature, a stable climate, or clear skies?

Some people find the economic perspective on the environment inherently distasteful. They reject the idea that pollution is inevitable and that the goal of public policy should be to ensure that it occurs at the "optimal level." They point out that such a policy implies that pollution will be allocated to regions and populations where the costs are lowest; in other words, that poor people will suffer most from pollution. Some years ago a memo attributed to Lawrence Summers, then an economist at the International Monetary Fund, was published in the British magazine, *The Economist*. The memo stated that the problem with pollution in the developing world is that there is not enough of it, and that an optimal allocation of pollution would bring more of it there where costs are low, and less of it to the tonier parts of the developed world. At various times Summers has denied that he was the author of the memo and claimed that it was a joke.[14] Despite the outrage that many people felt, it certainly did not hurt his career. He subsequently served as the United States Secretary of the Treasury and as president of Harvard University. For our purposes what is important is that the memo clearly states a plausible implication of the economic view of the environment, and it is precisely this implication that many people find repugnant.

Other critics of the economic perspective grant that it brings into focus a very powerful and important set of instruments that can be used to protect

[14] Versions of the memo are widely available on the web. See, e.g., <http://en.wikipedia.org/wiki/Summers_memo>.

the environment, but object that it does not go far enough in analyzing the causes of our problems. If it is true, as most economists would agree, that we have created an economic system that provides incentives for environmental destruction, this fact too stands in need of explanation. Why have we created such a system? Why is it so difficult to reform? Almost every attempt to create a more rational system of incentives, by imposing carbon taxes, for example, or even raising the mileage standards for automobiles, meets ferocious resistance from a population that overwhelmingly considers itself "green." What does this tell us about ourselves, and the political systems that we have created? These important questions about behavior are not easy to answer from within the economic perspective itself.

1.9   Religion and worldviews

In 1967 Lynn White Jr., a historian from the University of California at Los Angeles, gave a lecture to the American Association for the Advancement of Science that had an enormous impact on the subsequent discussion of the causes of environmental destruction. The article, originally published in *Science*, has been reprinted dozens of times. In the hundreds of books and articles in which it has been discussed, it has been vilified as much as praised. Essentially what White claimed was that the environmental crisis is fundamentally a spiritual and religious crisis, and that its ultimate solution would itself have to be spiritual and religious.

White located the source of the environmental crisis in the exploitative attitude towards nature that is at the heart of the dominant strand of the Christian tradition. As a historian of science and technology, White did not underestimate their importance to the environmental crisis. However, he saw them as proximate rather than ultimate causes. On his view, science and technology themselves are expressions of the dominant tendencies within Christianity.

White granted that environmental problems occur all over the world, even in those regions that we do not think of as part of the Christian world. Yet even there Christianity is ultimately responsible for the environmental crisis through her progeny, science and technology, and her heresies, such as Marxism.

What is special about Christianity, according to White, is that it is the most "anthropocentric" of world religions. At the center of the traditional

Christian story is God becoming man in the figure of Jesus. This idea is blasphemous from the perspective of other Near Eastern religious traditions such as Judaism and Islam. Rather than "anthropocentric," these traditions are fundamentally "theocentric." In both Judaism and Islam, God is utterly transcendent. He is as radically distinct from humans as he is from nature. Both humans and nature are his handiwork, but they are not in any way divine. In the traditions of the Far East – Buddhism, Hinduism, and Jainism, for example – the idea of the divinity of Jesus would not come as big news. For in these traditions divinity is seen as manifest among all living things. Indeed, within these traditions the goal of spiritual practice is often seen as the realization of the divinity within oneself. In contrast to Christianity, what all of these traditions share is the rejection of anthropocentrism. It is this anthropocentrism, which White believes is unique to the dominant form of Christianity, that gave rise to the development of modern science and technology, which in turn has led to the environmental crisis.

White tells his story in some detail. For him, the development of new forms of plowing, irrigation, and logging in the late medieval period mark the beginning of the rise of modern science and technology. The introduction and widespread adoption of these technologies also mark the beginning of the modern view of the world. On this view, nature is there to be managed by humans for their benefit. White points out that the use of these technologies was often opposed by those who clung to a minority tradition within Christianity, one that sees the human transformation of the Earth as an expression of the sin of pride. This minority tradition emphasized that the role of humans is to live in partnership with nature, rather than to dominate it. The twelfth-century saint, Francis of Assisi, is emblematic of this tradition. White believes that any real solution to our environmental crisis will have to draw on such minority Christian traditions, as well as on traditions from Asia and those found in indigenous cultures.

Whether or not White is correct in the details of these claims, what is most important in his account is that, for him, religions and worldviews can have profound consequences for human behavior, society, and ways of life. It is no exaggeration to say that he sees the environmental crisis as the ultimate product of how we view the world. This is in stark contrast to those who view the environmental crisis as the product of material forces or relations.

Because Marxism these days is widely seen as a discredited theory, it is worth noting how complete its victory has been in some areas of thought. Many of those who reject Marxism's particular economic theories still accept its economic determinism. On this view, social change is fundamentally driven by economic facts. Marxist economists used to say that environmental problems were caused by privatizing environmental goods and the solution is to socialize them. Today economists say the reverse: environmental problems are caused by "socializing" environmental goods and the solution is to privatize them. Both agree that environmental problems are caused by the distribution of property rights and incentives. They disagree about exactly what is the correct explanation, but they agree about the terms. For both of them, the correct explanation of environmental degradation is one that is fundamentally economic in character. This view is as congenial to Nobel Prize-winning economists and distinguished legal theorists as it was to those who held professorships of "dialectics" in the old Soviet Union.

White's assertion that ideas have consequences is a rejection of both economic and technological explanations of environmental problems. This rejection was extremely important to the environmental movement, and White's influence was felt in the attraction to Native American proverbs, Buddhist references, and the New Age tenor of some environmental thought. Perhaps it is not too surprising that an emerging social movement such as environmentalism would be attracted to a view in which people's beliefs, values, and commitments really matter. It was one of the many untenable consequences of Marxism that the revolution was supposed to be inevitable, but nevertheless people were supposed to commit themselves to fight and die to make it happen. And while the contemporary economic paradigm may inspire people to go into real estate or investment banking, it does not provide the inspirational fabric required for a social movement. Henry David Thoreau, Aldo Leopold, and Rachel Carson are the sort of writers and thinkers that do move people to action. They are the heroes of the contemporary environmental movement.

1.10   Ethics, aesthetics, and values

In the previous section we examined several different accounts of the causes of environmental problems. We interpreted them in their extreme forms as providing single-factor, ultimate explanations. Each of these accounts is insightful, but none is very convincing as the whole story – the one that we should accept to the exclusion of all others. For our purposes, it is sufficient to view these different accounts as providing resources that can be used for understanding aspects of particular problems and the range of possible solutions. There is no need for us to struggle for a single, unified theory of environmental problems. Indeed, no such account may be forthcoming.

Normally, we think of environmental problems and their possible solutions as multidimensional. If we are concerned with air pollution, for example, we may adduce a host of considerations in discussing why it is bad, what its causes are, and what may be the solutions. We may talk about the health and economic effects of air pollution, the loss of aesthetic values it entails, such as the erosion of clear skies and big views, its impacts on natural systems, and a wide range of other consequences. In explaining its causes we may mention the perverse incentives that encourage the use of private automobiles rather than public transportation, the inappropriate technologies involved in heating and cooling, and the attitudes of people who put their own shortsighted interests above everything else. We may consider possible solutions ranging from public campaigns to change attitudes, to carbon taxes, congestion pricing, and the development of alternative technologies. We may disagree about the comparative importance of various factors, but it would be strange to think that any one of them is beside the point, irrelevant, or completely out of bounds.

In short, we are pluralists about the nature of environmental problems, their causes, and solutions. In both public and private decision-making we are not primarily motivated by a concern for theoretical rigor or ultimate explanation, but by what will contribute to solving our problems. We adopt the vocabularies that are useful, that connect with how we and others think about these problems, and the kinds of considerations that move us and others to action. When it comes to environmental problems it is clear that these include scientific, technological, and economic considerations, but they also include considerations about ethics, values, and the aesthetic dimensions of the environment. Perhaps one day we will discover that this vast array of concerns can be reduced to a single concept, but whether or not this is the case is of little relevance to addressing our current problems.

Consider an example. Suppose that I have a friend who has difficulty completing projects, and this leads to all sorts of problems in both his professional and his personal life. Indeed, these are interconnected: his difficulty in completing projects inhibits his professional advancement, which puts serious pressure on his marriage, and makes it difficult for him to care properly for his children. As his friend, how should I think about his problems? What I should not do is to spend very much time wondering whether there is a single explanation for everything that is wrong with his life. Consider the vast array of candidates. Perhaps birth-order is the answer, his having been weaned too soon, the negative reinforcement he got at school, his tendency to daydream, or his feelings of worthlessness. Perhaps the problem is in his genes, his brain chemistry, or his failure to make authentic, autonomous decisions or to act on the basis of the moral law. As his friend, I should worry about causes in order to help think about interventions, not because I am interested in providing an elegant explanation of his problems. The interventions that might help are quite diverse, ranging from quietly encouraging him to complete his projects to assisting him in seeking medical attention. They may involve taking his side in disputes in the workplace, giving him tips on how to do his job more effectively, or even encouraging him to change jobs. Sympathetically interpreting his behavior to his colleagues and even to his wife may help. So may encouraging both him and his wife to undertake marriage counseling. Even taking his kids to the ball game might help to alleviate some of the pressure. This is not elegant, but it is the stuff of real-life problem-solving. Even if there is one unifying explanation for my friend's behavior, I am not likely to know what it is, nor do I need to know in order to try to help him with his problems. The fact that I take one particular approach to trying to help him does not require me to reject all the others. We do what we can, when we can. As his friend, I will try different approaches at different times, trying to find something that works in understanding his behavior and helping him with his problems.

My claim is that much the same is true of environmental problems. On their face, they are complex and multidimensional. They can be described in different vocabularies and can be explained in various ways. Perhaps someday we will have an explanation of them that will show that they are really "such and such" and can best be solved by doing "so and so." However, it is far from certain that such explanations exist and, if they do, we are very far from having them at our disposal. At any rate, the entire question is of little importance to us now. My purpose is not to insist that environmental problems are really ethical, rather than economic, technological, or whatever, but rather to suggest that these problems present themselves to us as having important ethical dimensions. They can be thought about and discussed in these terms, and rather than trying to explain this away, we should follow the thread and see where it leads.

In the remainder of this book that is exactly what I shall do. I will assume that among their many dimensions, environmental goods involve morally relevant values, and that environmental problems involve moral failings of some sort. To state my purpose more grandiosely: I will explore the idea that environmental problems challenge our ethical and value systems. If I am right about this, our thinking about the environment will improve by thinking about it in this way, and our moral and political conceptions will themselves become more sophisticated as a result of their confrontations with real environmental problems. Now, on with the show.

2   Human morality

2.1 The nature and functions of morality

Many people react badly to the very idea of morality. It seems too closely associated with religion, and guilt seems to be the god that it is most interested in serving. Morality seems to be mostly about obeying the rules promulgated by parents or other authorities, no matter how pointless or stupid they may be. The very language of morality seems absolutist and dogmatic. At best it has the mustiness of an old attic; at worst, it is dangerous.

Having grown up in a Lutheran boarding school, I have a great deal of sympathy for this reaction. Indeed, the dangers posed by the language of morality are becoming more apparent every day. Too many political leaders see the world in terms of absolute good and evil, and identify these with their own religious beliefs. They exploit people's fears and prejudices with categorical assertions of "our" virtue and simplistic denunciations of "their" venality. Shabby moralizers seek power and domination through fiery condemnations of those whose sexual practices are different from theirs, or have different views about when life begins, or what it means to die with dignity.

In my opinion, the best way to remedy this appropriation of morality is not to give the language away to its abusers, but to go back to the source and examine the concepts and institutions of morality from the ground up. Such a thoroughgoing investigation will not only shed light on why it is sensible to think about the environment from an ethical point of view, but also help to liberate us from stereotypes about morality that prevent us from thinking ethically about many of the distinctive problems of our age.

What, then, is morality? Of course different accounts can be given, but let us begin with this one. As a first approximation, morality is a behavioral system, with an attendant psychology, that has evolved among some social animals for the purposes of regulating their interactions. Such systems are characteristic of social animals living under certain conditions, such as scarcity, because in these circumstances relentless self-seeking behavior on the part of each individual can lead to disaster for everyone.

This was compellingly demonstrated by the seventeenth-century philosopher, Thomas Hobbes, in his description of what he called "the state of nature." In this state no one engages in productive work, for they cannot be sure that they will capture the benefits of their labor. As a result,

> there is no place for industry, because the fruit thereof is uncertain: and consequently no culture of the earth; no navigation, nor use of the commodities that may be imported by sea; no commodious building; no instruments of moving and removing such things as require much force; no knowledge of the face of the earth; no account of time; no arts; no letters; no society.

When faced with such a "war of all against all," it is in each person's interest to strike first, before they themselves are struck. Even those who prefer peace have reason to attack preemptively, since they can be sure that less peaceable people than themselves will attack first if they have the chance. Thus life in the state of nature, according to Hobbes, is "solitary, poor, nasty, brutish, and short."[1]

Hobbes believed that the only solution is to form a state ruled by an absolute monarch. Whatever we may think of this proposed solution, it seems clear that establishing a moral system can at least help in solving the problems posed by the state of nature.[2] Since moral systems regulate and coordinate behavior by systematically rewarding some and informally sanctioning other behavior, they can complement (or serve as alternatives) to social control by the direct exercise of power or authority. It is thus not surprising that moral systems exist among all known human societies. Whether such systems exist among other animals is controversial, but it is

---

[1] Quotations are from Thomas Hobbes, *Leviathan*, chapter 13, available in many editions, and on line at <http://oregonstate.edu/instruct/phl302/texts/hobbes/leviathan-c.html#CHAPTERXIII>.

[2] Hobbes himself denied this for reasons having to do with his conception of morality, but this detail cannot be pursued here.

clear that precursors of such systems exist among many species of social mammals, including the other Great Apes and canids.[3]

There are various building blocks that figure in the construction of existing moralities, including sympathy, empathy, generosity, and the ability to appreciate the situations of others. The ability to control one's own behavior by suppressing impulses and desires is important as well. The disposition to reciprocate behavior, a trait that is very deep in our nature, is especially important. Taken together, such abilities and dispositions have the potential to bring us from Hobbes's state of nature into cooperative societies that can accomplish great things.

Imagine a population of organisms in which each individual, when confronted by strangers, either randomly cooperates or not. If strangers meet and initially cooperate, then it is up, up, and away towards establishing a pattern of behavior in which cooperation becomes increasingly likely. My cooperating with you makes it more likely that you will cooperate with me, which makes it more likely that I will cooperate with you, and so on. This is the behavioral infrastructure that makes social institutions possible. Compare this with organisms that do not have the tendency to reciprocate. They may experience random incidents of cooperation, but since these will not increase the probability of cooperation, these organisms will not reap the benefits of sustained, mutually reinforcing cooperation. Those who behave only in immediately self-interested ways will do even worse. They will be stuck in the state of nature in which life is "nasty, brutish, and short."

We can see why Mother Nature would favor children who have tendencies to cooperate and reciprocate, as well as a tendency to pursue their own interests. Under many sets of conditions, including those that are most characteristic of human life, these children will do better than those who do not have these tendencies.

Much more needs to be said about how this story of the construction of morality goes, but we can already see its basic outline. Kindness begets kindness, which begets kindness, which begets kindness, and so on. From here, it is onwards and upwards towards full-blown morality.[4]

---

[3] See De Waal 2006 for discussion.

[4] For more on the evolution of morality see Jamieson 2002: ch. 1, and the references cited therein.

Once moralities are off and running, like many other institutions they have a tendency to become autonomous. Sympathetic identification and the disposition to reciprocate make moralities possible, but once they come into existence moralities have the power to strengthen their own hands. Our sympathy becomes increasingly vivid, and as our expectations grow, reciprocity becomes normative. Reason also gets into the game, perhaps initially as an instrument for working out the details of implementing reciprocity, but later as a device for imposing order and consistency. These developments make it possible, and in some cases almost irresistible, for us to care about others who are in no position to reciprocate our behavior. Since reason, normative reciprocity, and vivid sympathetic identification make demands on us as well as on others, morality becomes aspirational and critical in a way that other systems of social control are not. It gives rise to the following sorts of questions: What kind of person should I be? In what sort of society do I want to live? Am I doing as well as I can? How can my society be better? These are also the resources that allow us to make trans-historical and trans-cultural judgments, to project ourselves out of our present situation, and to make claims about how we should act, were we in another set of circumstances. We ask children how they would feel if they were treated as they have treated others. To an acquaintance we point out that it would not cost much to visit a sick parent, and that it would do the parent a world of good. We condemn a friend for not acting as a friend.

Once we have reached this point, we are in the domain of full-blown moralities like our own. We have a particular system of social control that embodies the resources for creating personal standards. It also encompasses the possibility of its own critique, and contains the materials for projecting our judgments outward across space and time. Unlike other systems of social control, such as custom, when it comes to morality the demand for reasons is always in order. Thus we can say that morality always involves doing what we have good reason to do.[5]

At this point we are tottering on the edge of what can be said generally about morality, and there is a warning here that we should heed.

[5] Does it always involve doing what we have most reason to do? Some philosophers such as the eighteenth-century German philosopher, Immanuel Kant, would declare affirmatively. Other philosophers, such as the eighteenth-century Scottish philosopher, David Hume, would say that I radically exaggerate the importance of reason to morality.

Philosophers have a tendency to import their own views of a controversial matter into the very definition of the subject under investigation. For example, those who theorize about justice often define the very concept in terms of their favored theory rather than arguing for its normative or factual superiority over alternative theories. They define justice as some version of reciprocity, equality, or mutual advantage, rather than arguing on substantive grounds that one of these theories of justice is superior to the others. I have no wish to gain by definition what should be obtained only through hard work and honest argument, though some might say that I have already attempted to do this in characterizing morality in the way that I have. At any rate, it is important to leave open a wide range of questions that can be debated by proponents of various moral theories. For example: What counts as a reason? Must reasons be impartial? Is there a class of distinctively moral reasons? Are moral reasons decisive? Different responses to these questions will follow from various moral theories, and they should be evaluated generally on the basis of how plausible these various theories are. These are the sorts of questions that we will investigate in the next two chapters. First, however, we need to respond to some challenges to morality.

2.2   Challenges to morality

In the previous section I outlined a plausible view about the nature and functions of morality. This, in itself, will not be enough to put at ease those who find morality distasteful. Indeed, we are now in a better position to sharpen the vague, inchoate challenges to morality evoked at the beginning of this chapter. I will refer to these new improved versions as the challenges from amoralism, theism, and relativism.

It is important to recognize at the outset that I attach specific meanings to these terms. While I have my doubts about amoralists, it is clear that many theists and some relativists would not challenge morality in the ways that I suggest. What I mean by 'theist' in this chapter is not just a religious person who believes in God, but someone who has a quite specific view about the relations between her religious commitments and morality. Clearly, not all theists share this view. Similarly, there are many relativists who do not fall into the traps that I discuss. These caveats should be borne in mind in considering my responses to these challenges.

2.3 Amoralism

An amoralist is someone who listens to what I have said about the nature and functions of morality and says that what this story really shows is that there is no such thing as right and wrong. He accepts my account of why moralities have emerged in human societies, but he sees no reason why he should be bound by any of them. He can understand morality just as he can understand the religion of the Atztecs or the science of the Babylonians, but thinks there is no more reason to feel bound by morality than to worship the Aztec gods or believe that the laws of Babylonian science are true. The amoralist chooses to opt out of morality altogether. He refuses to have any part of it. It has nothing to do with how he is going to live his life. He is going to do exactly as he pleases, and not worry about the state of nature, moral rules, or any of that stuff. As far as he is concerned, nothing that I have said gives him any reason to pay attention to morality, much less shows him why he must.

Initially, amoralism seems romantic. It conjures up the image of an existential hero living his own life, according to his own lights, paying no attention to what "square" society might think. He is James Dean rejecting his parents in *Rebel without a Cause*; Bonnie and Clyde robbing banks in the American south, then making love on the side of the road; or the misunderstood Mafia don, Joey Gallo, as portrayed by Bob Dylan in his album, *Desire*. Yes, these are romantic images, and in some moods, especially after a particularly tedious faculty meeting, I'm tempted to go for them myself. However, rather than being amoralists, these characters are all really moralists. An amoralist is someone who rejects the idea that there is any such thing as right or wrong. All of these figures have a morality, though it may be one that is at odds with the morality of those around them.

James Dean is a frustrated romantic. His beef with his parents and square society is that they are hypocrites who do not live up to their own standards. He has integrity; they do not. He stands up for his friends; they abandon their children. Bonnie and Clyde are basically hedonistically motivated Robin Hood figures. They rob banks because it is exciting, pays for the good times, and lets them give money away to those who need it. Killing people is part of the fun, but generally they are willing to let the little guy get away, unless he is a cop who takes his job too seriously, or someone who really needs killing. They have a loyalty to each other that goes all the way to the grave. Bob Dylan's Joey may do a "hit" on a member of another crime family or rough up a gambler who owes him money, but that is just business. You can be sure that he is a loving son, kind to his children, and loyal to his family. The church also probably benefits from his largesse.

These characters all have moralities. They think that certain things are right, others are wrong, and still others are of no real importance. They believe that it matters what kind of people they are. They want to exemplify a certain set of virtues. Far from being amoralists, they are more like existentialist heroes who place a high value on authenticity. Bonnie and Clyde, and Joey, all have their own codes of conduct. They rob the rich and help the poor, but what really matters to them is their own integrity as they understand it. They want to be true to themselves. It is with such people in mind that Bob Dylan wrote in another song that "to live outside the law you must be honest." It is this concern for honesty that most vividly separates these characters from parents, cops, and other authority figures.

Who, then, is an amoralist? Since it is difficult to name a famous amoralist, let us invent one called "Dirk," and describe what he would have to be like in order to be a real amoralist. Dirk is someone who does not think that any facts about other people's interests or even their suffering provide reasons for him to act one way rather than another. When Dirk sees a man on the side of a road who has just been run over, it is a matter of indifference to him whether he helps him, kicks him in the head, or just walks away. At any particular moment he may feel like doing one thing or another, but he does not feel that one is the right response, or that he should be consistent in what he does. Indeed, he might initially feel like helping the man, and then decide to kick him instead; or the other way around. It doesn't really matter which. Even if the man is Dirk's father or his best friend, he still does not see that he has a reason for acting one way or another. If he were to think or feel that he really ought to help his father, then Dirk would have a morality. It would, perhaps, be a clannish morality of "filial piety" that is not very attractive or plausible, but if Dirk is really an amoralist he does not even have that. Indeed, it is not even clear in what sense Dirk could have a friend as opposed to someone he has hooked up with for some particular purpose. Suppose that it is Dirk who is lying on the side of the road having been beaten and robbed. Between episodes of excruciating pain he can regret that he is in this condition, that he took this road rather than another, that he did not shoot first, and so on. But what he cannot feel is that he was treated unjustly or that his assailants did something wrong in beating and robbing him. Indeed, even if they tortured him for their own amusement, Dirk cannot consistently resent them, fault them, or hate them for it, for these are moral emotions that are unavailable to Dirk if he is truly an amoralist.[6] If Dirk has these emotions, then he has a morality. He may be deeply immoral in that he has these feelings only about himself and not others, or that he does not act on these feelings. But if Dirk is a consistent amoralist, then he has no place for such feelings at all.

As we fill in the picture of Dirk, amoralism becomes increasingly less attractive. Rather than being the portrait of an existential hero, it begins to look like the sketch of a sociopath. We also begin to see how difficult it is to choose amoralism and opt out of morality. The very ties that bind us to a society entangle us in a morality. Morality is ubiquitous; amoralists are rare. Indeed, one wonders whether they exist outside of the classroom.

2.4 Theism

Like the amoralists, some theists understand my story about the nature and functions of morality but say that it has nothing to do with them. Unlike the amoralists, they say this, not because they reject morality, but because they reject my conception of morality. Morality comes only from God, they say, and God has no place in my story. As I have explained it, morality is a human construction that emerges in a world controlled by natural selection. Whatever this human construction is, it cannot be a morality. For God alone is the author of morality.

This view is extremely common in America, from the current President on down. In fact, outside of a few pockets in which Enlightenment ideals continue to thrive, it is probably the dominant view in the world. The twentieth-century philosopher Jean-Paul Sartre stated the challenge posed by this view when he wrote that "if God is dead, then everything is permitted."[7]

---

[6] But isn't there some notion of "blind" or "animal" hatred in which individuals can hate the cause of their suffering, without this in any way implying that their suffering is unjustified? If so, then in this sense Dirk can consistently hate his torturers.

[7] These words are from Sartre's 1946 lecture "Existentialism is a Humanism," available on the web at <www2.cddc.vt.edu/marxists/cd/cd2/Library/reference/archive/sartre/works/exist/sartre.htm>. Interestingly, Sartre falsely attributes these words to the nineteenth-century Russian novelist, Fyodor Dostoyevski, though it is true that the thought is Dostoyevski's.

There are two distinct reasons why someone might think that without God, everything is permitted. The first reason is that without God, morality would have no content. The second reason is that without God, we would not be motivated to act morally.

Consider the second reason first. Why might someone believe that if we are not motivated to act morally then everything is permitted? The argument might go like this. Suppose for the sake of argument that

(1) The content of morality is a set of requirements R; everything else is permitted.

Now suppose that

(2) We are not motivated to do R,

where "doing R" is shorthand for something like "obeying the requirements included in R." If

(3) It is a necessary condition for doing R that we are motivated to do R,

then, given (2),

(4) We cannot do R.

If

(5) It is a necessary condition for being required to do R that we can do R,

then, given (4),

(6) We are not required to do R.

But if (6), then

(7) R is an empty set.

But if (7), then, given (1),

(8) Everything is permitted.

The reasoning in this argument is valid: if we are not motivated to act morally, then everything is permitted. However, for the theist's challenge to morality to succeed, a further assumption, reflected in step (2), must also be true: that without God, we are not motivated to act morally. It is this premise that I wish to deny.[8]

Notice first, that this claim is ambiguous. It may mean:

(9) If God does not exist, then we are not motivated to act morally;

or

(10) If we do not believe in God, then we are not motivated to act morally.

If (9) were true, then an atheist would certainly be committed to the view that everything is permitted. However, there is little reason to believe that (9) is true because it is difficult to see how the sheer fact of God's existence can affect people's motivations.

Imagine the following cases. In the first case, what I will call "the baseline,"

(11) God does not exist and no one believes that he does.

In the second case,

(12) God exists, but no one believes that he does.

In the third case,

(13) God does not exist, but everyone believes that he does.

It is difficult to see why there would be greater prevalence of moral motivation in (12) than in the baseline, (11). People's beliefs are the same in both cases, though the facts about the universe are different. It is difficult to see how facts about the universe engage people's motivation, except through psychological states such as their beliefs. Indeed, the power of people's beliefs to affect motivation is highlighted by (13). It seems reasonable to suppose that there would be a greater incidence of moral motivation in (13) than in (12), precisely because there is greater prevalence of belief in God in (13) than in (12), even though God exists in (12) but not in (13). For it does seem plausible to believe that there is some positive correlation between belief in God and the existence of moral motivation. Indeed, if Russian novelists and American presidents are reporting their own cases

---

[8] Some might also challenge premise (3). How successful this challenge would be depends exactly on what one means by 'doing' and 'motivated'. Even if this challenge were to succeed, the argument could be revised in such as way as to meet it.

accurately and not just speculating about other people, then we have some testimonial evidence for the existence of this correlation.

So, let us grant that the incidence of moral motivation may be higher in societies like ours when people believe in God than when they do not. Does this show that if we did not believe in God, then (2) would be true? No. In a society in which people did not believe in God, some of us still would be motivated to act morally while some of us would not be so motivated. As I will explain in detail in the next chapter, moral beliefs are distinct from moral motivations. Indeed, this helps explain why there are so few real amoralists among us, despite the apparent popularity of the view. For present purposes what matters is that this "mixed" case, in which some people would be motivated to act morally in the absence of belief in God while some would not be so motivated, is not strong enough to support the truth of (2). The fact that some of us would be motivated to act morally even if we believed that God did not exist shows that (2) cannot be true in the sense needed to support (4).

Why should we believe that many of us would be motivated to be moral even if we believed that God did not exist? Because it is a simple fact that many people today do not believe that God exists, yet are motivated to be moral. Indeed, many moral philosophers fall into this category. For this reason (and others), there is reason to believe that the moral motivation of at least some of those who believe in God would not flag, even if they lost their faith. Perhaps they could be brought to see the connections between moral motivation and other things that they care about, such as their own long-term interests, their families, and their societies, as well as other goods that they value. Morever, as we saw in our discussion of Dirk, the amoralist, it is quite difficult for someone who lives in a society to escape the tendrils of morality, however much he might claim to do so. Immorality is ubiquitous, but amoralism is rare.

It is the other version of the theistic challenge that has historically been influential.[9] On this version, it is God who gives content to morality through his divine commandments. What is right is obeying his commands and what is wrong is disobeying them. Thus, without God, there can be nothing that is right or wrong.

[9] The *locus classicus* of this discussion is Plato's *Euthyphro*.

This view, too, is ambiguous. Obeying God's commandments may be right because

(14) Actions are right in virtue of being commanded by God,

or because

(15) God commands us to do only those actions that are right independently of his commands.

On the view that is expressed in (14), that obeying God's commandments is right because the actions that he commands are right in virtue of his commanding them, rightness is constrained by nothing but God's will. Murder, rape, torture, or whatever, is right so long as God commands it. This is not the view of nice religious people but of Jihadists, Crusaders, terrorists, and cultists who engage in horrifying acts in the name of following God's commandments.

The natural response is to say that these awful people are wrong about what God commands. But how do we know? Religious people disagree about what God commands, and almost every imaginable atrocity has been committed somewhere, sometime, in his name. We are finite creatures who have little grasp of the mind of God. How can any one of us claim more insight into his commandments than anyone else?

This leads to a second response, which is not any better. Since God is good, the nice religious person says, he cannot command us to do evil. Thus we do not have to worry about God commanding us to do horrific things. True enough, we do not have to worry about God commanding us to do evil, but this does not rule out his commanding us to do things that we regard as horrific. On the view under consideration, the goodness of God's commands is secured by definition. Since whatever God commands us to do is right in virtue of his commanding it, if he commands us to commit acts of genocide it would follow that such acts are just as right as most of us now think that it is to feed the hungry. Indeed, if God commanded us not to feed the hungry, then it would be wrong to do so. The appeal to God's goodness has no independent force, since goodness is defined by whatever he commands. Rather than consulting any independent conception of goodness, we are thrown back on our ignorance of the mind of God to find out what is good.

One casualty of this view is the traditional idea that it is an important, substantive truth about God that he is good. Yes, God is good, but this is true by definition, not in virtue of God's substantive behavior conforming to any normal understanding of goodness. Finding out that God is good, on this view, is like discovering that the standard meter bar is a meter in length, or that an ounce of gold weighs an ounce. This is hardly a relief for those of us who might wonder about God's nature.

There are other unwelcome consequences of this view, but the worst is this. Suppose that God commands us to carry out the most horrific acts imaginable. That we would be compelled to carry them out is bad enough. But worse still is the idea that, in virtue of his command, these horrific acts would somehow be transformed from evil deeds into acts of goodness. If we were certain that our universe were ruled by such a creature, the right thing to say would be not that God is good, but that we are in the hands of an omnipotent genocidal maniac, or even, perhaps, an evil demon.

Consider the alternative view, (15), that God commands us to do what is right according to a standard that is independent of his commanding it. On this view, it is the independent standard of rightness, not God's commands, that gives morality its content. God conforms his commands to morality; he does not shape morality through his commands. What is right is independent of God, just as it is independent of us. Even if God exists and commands us to do what is right, it is still up to us to find out what that is. God, on this view, rather than providing a challenge to the conception of morality that I have sketched, is himself bound by it. His most important role is to provide a little extra motivation to be moral for those who believe in him. Thus, the second version of the theistic challenge goes down to defeat, whichever way we understand it.

2.5   Relativism

The third challenge to morality is different in kind. The two previous challenges have amounted to saying that while they agree that there is a ubiquitous institution of social control of the sort that I have described, they reject the idea that this institution has authority over them. The theist denies that the social institution that I have described is in fact morality, though she accepts the authority of morality. The amoralist grants that the institution that I have described is morality, but rejects its authority.

The relativist is different from either of them. She accepts both the claim that what I have described is morality, and that morality has authority over her. What she rejects is one important aspect of my conception of morality: the idea that morality embodies resources for critically assessing the views of ourselves and others, and indeed, on some occasions, can project its judgments across times and societies. What the relativist denies is the possibility of moral claims transcending the moral system of the speaker's own society. Relativism is a challenge to morality as I understand it because it threatens to deprive morality of its critical edge, thus assimilating it to other social practices whose ambitions are much more modest, such as "folkways," "customs," or "standards of etiquette." By making cultures the locus of morality, relativism not only threatens our ability to make moral judgments that range across communities and times, but also diminishes the autonomy and responsibility of individuals, features that are also important to morality.

Relativism grows from the simple recognition that different societies and historical epochs judge different actions as right or wrong. Examples of this are legion, and can be found in such diverse areas as sexual morality, judgments about killing, and the treatment of animals and nature. Food preferences, which are often highly moralized, will do as an example.

Most Americans think that it is strange to eat goats, disturbing to eat horses, wrong to eat dogs and whales, and downright ghastly to eat gorillas and chimpanzees. On the other hand they see nothing strange, disturbing, wrong, or ghastly about eating cows, pigs, chickens, sheep, fish, shrimps, and various other sea creatures. Europeans would largely share these views, though their category of the animals that can be eaten without comment might be somewhat more expansive, including, for example, horses and snails. Religious Jews and Muslims are horrified at the idea of eating pigs, but have little trouble with most of the other animals on the list. Hindus and Jains would object to eating any of these animals, especially cows. Most East Asians see little difference between eating any of these animals, and many Africans consider the flesh of gorillas and chimpanzees to be a delicacy.

When faced with such diversity, enlightened people are often inclined to think that this shows that moral rules have sway only over particular societies at particular times. This view is bolstered, it might be thought, by the picture of morality that I have presented. Since, on my view, morality is mainly directed towards regulating a community's behavior, there is little reason to think that the same set of prescriptions and proscriptions would be appropriate for all communities in all circumstances. According to the relativist, someone who claims that his morality is right and the morality of other communities is wrong fails to grasp the essential relativity of moral judgments. It is one thing for a speaker to report the moral standards of his own society; it is quite another for him to condemn the moral standards of other societies. Worse still is any attempt to impose his own morality on others.

What do we say of people who try to impose their moralities on others? One natural thing to say is that they are immoral, but this is tricky terrain for a relativist. For the tendency to export one's morality may be intrinsic to the morality of those who are doing the exporting, as certainly was the case with the Victorian morality of nineteenth-century England and arguably is the case with the prevailing, Christian-inflected morality of contemporary America. Indeed, it is obvious that many Americans think that that they have a moral obligation to "share" their morality with others. But if the tendency towards exporting one's morality is part of one's culture, then denouncing such attempts as immoral seems to require the same sort of trans-cultural moral judgment that the relativist enjoins us not to make. But what is the alternative? If we cannot denounce attempts to impose one's morality on others in moral terms, what can we say about them? Criticizing such attempts in non-moral language – as rude, insensitive, or tasteless – seems grossly inappropriate to the offence. Saying that a missionary who tries to get a tribal people to worship Jesus, adopt western standards of marriage, and behave like proper Englishmen is "insensitive" is like saying that Hitler had a problem with his aggressive impulses.

The relativist seems trapped by her own theory. The point of her challenge is to prevent us from trying to impose our morality on others. But insofar as this attempt is an expression of one's own culture, it would appear that the relativist is stopped by her own theory from morally denouncing it.

She could try the following maneuver. Just as imposing Christian morality on the natives was an expression of the morality of Victorian England, so the relativist's denunciation of this is an expression of the tolerant, secular morality of her culture. In other words, when it comes to trans-cultural judgments, everyone, including the relativist, is allowed "to do their own thing," so long as it is an authentic expression of their own culture and does not claim any universal privilege, except, of course, from within their own point of view.

This gambit amounts to a sophisticated surrender on the part of the relativist, for it puts her objection to imposing morality on others on the same level as the attempt itself. Each is an equally authentic expression of the morality of the culture in which the impulse originates. What started as a noble, if misguided, attempt to use moral language to prevent dominant cultures from imposing their moralities on others has, under pressure, degenerated into the view that when it comes to moralizing we should let a thousand flowers bloom, acknowledging that insofar as they are all authentic expressions of a culture, no view has any special claim to acceptance beyond the culture in which it originates. What has been lost is any principle, method, insight, or approach for deciding when culturally transcendent claims are appropriate, insightful, true, or right. Instead, we are left with a clash of competing cultures, with no guidance about how to resolve it. This kind of relativism ceases to be a serious challenge to anything. It has transformed its own critique into just another provincial voice, with no claim to anything more than local interest.

In addition to this theoretical objection, there are serious difficulties in implementing the relativist view in the highly globalized world in which we live. Relativism takes cultures as the primary locus of moral authority, but it is not easy to determine people's cultural membership and thus identify the standards by which their behavior should be assessed. The following case brings this out clearly.

In 1996 a seventeen-year-old girl, Fauziya Kassindja, arrived in the United States from Togo and asked for political asylum.[10] She had fled in order to escape an elaborate ritual which marks the onset of adulthood in young females in her tribe. Part of this ritual involves a procedure that is variously called "excision," "female circumcision," "female genital cutting," or "female genital mutilation." There is much to say about such cases, but the question I wish to raise here is quite limited. Which is the society whose moral standards are supposed to take precedence in this case? Is it the standards of Kassindja's tribe, those of urban Togo, those of West Africa, those of Africa generally, or those of the United States, where she came to seek asylum? It is clear that each of these societies has different attitudes towards this procedure and would produce different moral judgments about this case. My point here is not to argue any particular view, but rather to

---

[10] I borrow this example from Rachels 2003.

point out how difficult it is in the contemporary world to assign people to the cultures that are supposed to have moral authority over them.[11]

Indeed, putting the matter in this way brings out how relativism points in the wrong direction when it comes to locating the grounds for moral judgments. What is central to moral judgments are reasons for action that reflect a host of concerns involving the interests that are at stake, the harms that would be caused, the precedents that would be set, and so on. Cultural membership may bear indirectly on how we assess these considerations, but in itself it is not of central moral importance. By making cultures the locus of morality, relativism turns us away from the reasons that ground and justify moral judgments.

There are other problems with relativism. With its emphasis on cultures as the locus of moralities, it seems to have little place for moral disagreement within cultures. This risks putting horrendous acts of racism and brutality beyond criticism, so long as they occur within a society rather than across societies. For example, what do we say about people who oppose theocracy, slavery, or patriarchy in societies in which these practices are widely accepted? If the content of morality is determined by the moral standards of the society, then these people are just wrong. On the other hand, someone who simply conforms to his society's prevailing morality would be doing the right thing, however horrendous the morality he would be upholding. On this view, an abolitionist in a slave society would be wrong about the morality of slavery while a slave-owner would be right. But surely it is not the abolitionist who is wrong, but the relativist. Every society has cranks, deviants, and rebels, and they are often the revolutionaries who make moral progress possible. Yet relativism seems committed to their moral condemnation. One wonders whether moral progress is possible on such a view, and if so, what its engine might be.

Still there is something to relativism, and before moving on we should make sure that we understand what it is. Certainly one of the gifts of relativism is that it attunes us to the fact that there is a great deal more diversity in moral practices than people were once in a position to recognize, and a great deal more than many people today are willing to accept. Even so, it is easy to exaggerate the extent and depth of moral diversity.

---

[11] Sen (2006) argues strongly that it is immoral to assign people such identities, even when it is possible to do so.

Consider, for example, traditional Eskimo society, in which female infanticide was widely practiced and accepted. Perfectly healthy female infants were sometimes killed at birth. Before jumping to conclusions about the profoundly different moralities of traditional Eskimo and contemporary American societies, consider the circumstances of traditional Eskimo life. The environment was harsh, food was in short supply, and the margin of safety was small. In this society, mothers nursed for many years, thus limiting the number of children who could be supported at a given time. Traditional Eskimos were nomadic, and infants were carried while the mother did her work. Food was primarily obtained by hunting, and this was extremely dangerous under Arctic conditions. Men were the primary food-providers, and they were often in short supply because of premature death. In traditional Eskimo society, female infanticide was not a first but a last resort, often carried out only after attempts at adoption failed. However, it has been estimated that without the practice of female infanticide, an average Eskimo group would have had 50% more females than food-producing males.[12]

What should we say about the moral differences regarding infanticide between traditional Eskimos and contemporary Americans? Surely there are such differences, for one can say, however superficially, that contemporary Americans believe that female infanticide is wrong while traditional Eskimos did not. But if one tries to say anything deeper or more precise, things become quite murky. Neither society approves of murder; neither society approves of the gratuitous killing of innocent people; neither society believes that children are disposable; neither society believes that, everything else being equal, males should be preferred to females. While contemporary Americans and traditional Eskimos would disagree about what general rules they would assent to with respect to infanticide, it is not clear that they disagree about any deep moral principles or even that they would disagree about particular cases. People and communities find themselves in different situations, and achieving common purposes sometimes requires different strategies.

It should not be surprising that in the most general way there would be widespread agreement about morality across societies. Humans form a single species and they face common problems of survival; morality is an

---

[12] My account of Eskimo infanticide is based on Rachels 2003, who in turn relies on Freuchen 1961 and Hoebel 1954.

institution whose role it is to help solve those problems. However, humans are extremely adaptable and live in a broad range of environmental conditions, and in societies characterized by very different forms of social organization. It is thus not surprising that there is diversity in their moral expressions, especially with respect to "middle-level" principles.

Even though the extent of relativity is often exaggerated, there is no denying both the fact and the importance of diverse moralities. Despite the fact that awareness of diversity and difference is supposed to be part of the common knowledge of our epoch, there continue to be ignorant and arrogant attempts to remake the moral fabric of ancient societies. States whose weaponry far outruns their respect for others behave in ways that are almost as crude as their imperial predecessors. It is difficult to fully appreciate the moralities of others, and there is generally enough work to be done in reforming one's own society for even the most committed of moral crusaders. The facts of relativity should make us humble about our ability to understand, much less improve, the morality of others.

Moral relativism is a doctrine that can be educative, but as a challenge to morality it fails. Relativism errs when it goes beyond a set of observations about the diversity of cultural practices and begins to promulgate an ethic of its own. This failure is located precisely at the point at which it moves from a description of how morality is exemplified in the world to the normative view that a society's morality cannot be morally criticized. It commits the fallacy of deriving an "ought" from an "is" – of drawing a normative conclusion from a set of descriptive premises. In its crudest form, it borders on inconsistency. In its more sophisticated versions, it remains implausible, while its claim to be a challenge to morality recedes.

2.6   What these challenges teach us

There is a lot to learn from these challenges to morality. They include the following. Morality is ubiquitous and difficult to escape for even the most hard-bitten of men (e.g. Dirk). Morality does not need the support of God in order to have content or to be motivating. Morality is not culture-bound.

At the same time nothing has been said to suggest that there is a single, true morality, and the facts of moral disagreement should make us sensitive to the difficulty of interpreting and assessing the views of others. Moreover, there is no requirement in morality or any other domain that requires us to have a judgment about everything. Nothing has been said that suggests that belief in God is inconsistent with morality, or that rules out the idea that belief in God may even be supportive of morality. Finally, the amoralist's challenge highlights the fact that the conflict between morality and individual desire is ongoing, though it is generally a conflict within morality rather than a challenge to morality.

Having thus characterized human morality and responded to some challenges, we can turn our attention to some substantive questions in ethical theory.

3 Meta-ethics

3.1 The structure of the field

Ethical theory is conventionally divided into two major fields, meta-ethics and normative ethics. Meta-ethics concerns the meaning and status of moral language. Normative ethics is divided between moral theory and applied or practical ethics. Moral theory is concerned with what sorts of things are good, which acts are right, and what the relations are between the right and the good. Practical ethics is concerned with the evaluation of particular things as good and bad, and of various acts, practices, or institutions as right or wrong.

The distinctions between these fields can be illuminated by an example. Consider the sentence

(1) It is wrong to kill animals for food.

If we ask whether this sentence asserts a claim or only expresses an attitude, we are asking a meta-ethical question. If we wonder what sorts of theoretical considerations might give us reason to accept or reject such a sentence, we are concerned with moral theory. If we want to know whether the practice of killing animals for food is right or wrong, then we are concerned with a question in practical ethics.

While this account is not bad as a first approximation, there are many complications.

We might wonder how we know what counts as moral language. The occurrence of words such as 'right', 'wrong', 'good', 'bad', 'cruel', 'kind', 'arrogant', 'generous', 'liar', 'crook', 'hero', 'coward' are often tell-tale signs of moral language. But language is a resourceful instrument; context and intonation can sometimes effectively cancel the moral connotations of apparently moral words, and can also allow us to say something of moral significance using only apparently non-moral words.

Surprisingly, perhaps, there are also questions, not just about the moral/non-moral distinction, but also about what aspects of language we are concerned with. (1) is a sentence. When I say (1), an utterance occurs. When I utter (1) sincerely, I perform the speech-act of asserting. The distinctions between sentences, utterances, and speech-acts would be trivial, perhaps, were it not the case that they have different properties. Sentences are timeless abstract entities, while utterances occur at a time and place. Speech-acts are finely individuated human actions, while utterances are only utterances and sentences are not human actions at all. Important fish swim in these waters, but they will be left to swim freely.[1] Rather than trying to give a full account of moral language I will only say that, as with art, we know it when we see it (at least most of the time).

Another complication is that the distinctions between meta-ethics and normative ethics are not always sharp. Most of the great figures in ethical theory moved effortlessly between topics in meta-ethics and normative ethics, often without observing these distinctions.

In addition to the fact that particular questions do not always fall neatly into one category or another, reasons for accepting views in one area may depend, in part, on views in other areas. For example, if a view in meta-ethics fails to explain what we know to be the case about our practical moral disagreements, then this would be a reason for rejecting it. Similarly, if one side in a practical moral argument relies on a consideration that our best understanding of moral theory suggests is irrelevant, then this should lead us to reject the force of that consideration.

Questions about the exact relationships between meta-ethics and normative ethics can be quite fraught. Many environmental philosophers believe that there are important connections between meta-ethics and normative

---

[1] Two minnows may be worthy of brief comment. First, some would deny that sentences are timeless, since they are created by people. What are timeless, they might say, are the propositions that sentences express. Second, some theorists might say that utterances, like speech-acts, are actions; others would say that they are not actions at all, but rather events. These are among the host of metaphysical questions that cannot be pursued here.

ethics.[2] They think (as do some religious fundamentalists and others) that false views in meta-ethics lead to false views in practical ethics. As we will see in section 3.5, debates about intrinsic value are often the site of such disagreements. But this is getting ahead of our story.

Meta-ethics is concerned with the meaning and status of moral claims. This involves questions in philosophy of language, metaphysics, and epistemology.

Generally, meta-ethical questions that flow from philosophy of language concern the meaning of moral language, and whether it is assertive, cognitive, and "truth-apt." Consider again sentence (1). On its face, it is a declarative sentence, declarative sentences are typically used to make assertions, and assertions are true or false. But, for reasons that we will discuss in section 3.3, some have held that whatever the surface grammar may suggest, moral sentences are really disguised imperatives and thus are not truth-apt. On this view, a perspicuous reading of (1) is

(2) Do not kill animals for food!.

The metaphysical issue at stake can be stated grandly as the question of whether there exists anything that can be called "moral reality"; and if so, whether it consists in a domain of distinctive moral facts. The same issue can be approached more soberly in the following way. Assuming that moral assertions are true or false, what are the "truth-makers" for such assertions?

The epistemological questions in play can be stated in terms of the possibility of moral knowledge, the threat of moral skepticism, and so on, but they too can also be stated more soberly. Assuming that moral sentences are used to make claims, we can ask what counts as evidence for such claims and what the conditions are for rationally accepting or rejecting them.

Having slogged through some preliminaries, we can now turn to some substantive views in meta-ethics.

3.2   Realism

Realism is roughly the view that moral language states facts about the world rather than only expressing the attitudes of speakers. Since the birth of environmental ethics, there has been a strong tendency to embrace

[2] E.g. Rolston III 1988.

realism.[3] In order to understand why, it is helpful to recover some of the historical context.

In the 1970s, when the first environmental ethics courses were being taught, the field of ethics was dominated by discussion of such issues as the dignity of persons, the importance of obeying rules, and the meaning of the word 'ought'. Animals and the rest of nature were almost entirely invisible. This was especially galling because the post-World War II period had seen radical increases in consumption that were resulting in unprecedented levels of environmental destruction. There were also massive increases in the number of animals being used in factory farms, with virtually no concern for their welfare. The growing environmental and animal rights movements were questioning the practices that were giving rise to these consequences, but there was scarcely an echo in philosophical discourse. Moral philosophers, it seemed, were more concerned with whether it was permissible to walk across a lawn than with the ethics of clear-cutting entire forests.

In these circumstances, embracing realism about the value of nature seemed to be a natural response for two reasons. First, realism seemed to offer the most secure possible foundation for our duties to nature. Second, if realism was considered a plausible view about the value of humans, then it seemed reasonable to many environmental philosophers that it should also be a plausible view about the value of nature.

Realism has a strong claim to being the "default" position in meta-ethics because it takes moral language at face value. Consider, for example, the following sentences about Mountain Gorillas.

(3) Mountain Gorillas are vegetarian.

(4) Mountain Gorillas are valuable.[4]

Grammatically, both of these are declarative sentences, and it is natural to think that the job of such sentences is to state facts about the world, that they are true when they succeed in doing this and false when they fail, and that their "truth-makers" are properties or states of the world.

A realist can be thought of as someone who believes that moral language is characteristically assertive, thus true or false, and, indeed, often true.

---

[3] E.g. in the work of Rolston III (1988).

[4] Sentence (4) is ambiguous between different kinds of value (e.g. economic and moral value). For our purposes I will take (4) as a paradigm of moral language.

Moral language is true when it adequately reflects the state of the world and false when it does not. So we might say that (3) states a fact about the world, in this case about the diet of Mountain Gorillas, and similarly that (4) states a fact about the world, in this case about the value of Mountain Gorillas. On this view (3) and (4) are alike in that they are characteristically used to make assertions that are true if they adequately reflect the way the world is, and false if they do not.

Complications arise when we begin to think about how exactly we can determine whether (3) and (4) adequately reflect the way world is. It is easy to answer this question with respect to (3). We make observations about the feeding behavior of Mountain Gorillas, the structure of their teeth, their digestive systems and so on. It may be difficult to gather such information, but we can agree on the facts that would make (3) true. We also know what would count as showing that (3) is false. If we observe a Mountain Gorilla feeding on a monkey or sneaking off to McDonald's, then we can be sure that (3) is false. When it comes to (4), however, the problem is not only that it might be difficult to gather the relevant information, but that there is ample room for disagreement about exactly what information we should be gathering. We can imagine two people agreeing on some set of facts about Mountain Gorillas – their behavior, evolutionary history, social relationships, ecological roles, etc. – and still disagreeing about whether or not (4) is true. In the case of (3) the question is whether the truth-makers obtain; in the case of (4) there is the additional question of what constitutes the truth-makers in the first place.[5]

Realists have given two kinds of answers to questions about what count as truth-makers for moral sentences. On one account they are "natural" facts, while on the other they are "non-natural" facts. Realists can hold various complicated views about what makes something a truth-maker for a moral sentence – whether it is a single simple property, or whether it is a large disjunctive set of complex properties, for example. Philosophers make their living navigating the logical space of possible views, and sorting out the complex relationships between facts, concepts, properties, states of

---

[5] Of course, even complications can have complications. There is room to disagree about what the truth-makers are for some non-moral sentences as well. Consider, e.g., 'John is an avid sportsman.' Does watching snooker on TV count as a truth-maker for this sentence? Despite the fudginess in the middle, the main point I'm making here is true.

affairs, propositions, and other abstract entities. We need not go there for our purposes.

A realist who is a naturalist believes that there is some natural fact in virtue of which something is good. Consider a simple version of such a view.

Hedonism is an ancient doctrine that in the modern world is associated with the eighteenth-century philosopher, Jeremy Bentham. There are many questions about how exactly to formulate this doctrine, but let us say for present purposes that hedonism is the view that

(5) Goodness is pleasure.

If we assume that

(6) Gambling is pleasurable,

then it follows that

(7) Gambling is good.

Putting aside various complications about the relations between goodness, being pleasurable and causing pleasure, we can say that the truth of (4), on this view, turns on whether Mountain Gorillas are the sort of thing that produce pleasure. If they do, then they are valuable.

Hedonism, at least in this simple form, is not a very plausible view, but I want us to look beyond this and see why naturalism generally fell into disrepute at the beginning of the twentieth century. There were a number of reasons, but the most important is that it was thought to succumb to the "open question argument" put forward by the Cambridge philosopher G. E. Moore (1903). Moore thought that claims that identified moral properties with natural facts were importantly different from claims that identified non-moral properties with natural facts. There is always an open question about the former claims that there is not about the latter.

Consider the following trio of sentences.

(8) Triangles are three-sided figures.

(9) John's sculpture is in the shape of a three-sided figure.

(10) John's sculpture is in the shape of a triangle.

If (8) and (9) are true, then there is no question about (10). It would be absurd for someone to say, "Yes, I understand that John's sculpture is in the shape of a three-sided figure, but is it really in the shape of a triangle?" That question is closed by the identity stated in (8). In the case of (5), (6), and

(7), however, someone may accept that goodness consists in pleasure and that gambling is pleasurable, but still wonder whether gambling is good. Even after the putative identities have been stated, the question about the goodness of gambling seems open in a way that the question about the shape of John's sculpture does not. It seems meaningful to ask whether a particular instance of something that is pleasurable is really good, while it does not seem meaningful to ask whether a particular three-sided figure is really a triangle. Perhaps this is because it seems possible that an instance of pleasure is not good, while it does not seem possible that a three-sided figure is not a triangle.

Moore thought that this argument could be used to refute all forms of naturalism because any attempt to identify moral properties with natural properties would invariably leave such an open question. However, Moore did not budge from realism. Given that realism is true, if naturalism is false, then it follows that non-naturalism must be the correct view. The truth-makers of moral sentences, according to Moore, are not natural facts, but non-natural facts. On this view, there is a moral reality which is distinct from the reality that science investigates.

For many people, this is just too much to swallow. The idea that there is a domain of facts beyond the possibility of scientific investigation violates basic assumptions about nature that have been widely shared by both philosophers and scientists since the Enlightenment of the eighteenth century.

Moreover, if there were a domain of moral facts distinct from ordinary facts, then it would seem to require some special epistemological apparatus for accessing it – something over and above our ordinary abilities to reason, perceive, and so on, that puts us in touch with the natural world. It is difficult to imagine what such an apparatus would consist in. Stranger still is imagining that we have this apparatus and use it in our daily lives without being aware of it. Most of us are convinced that we know something about what is good, right, and so on, even though we are clueless about having such a special faculty and ignorant about what it could be like. Moreover, we justify our moral claims, not by appeals to non-natural facts, but by reference to everyday considerations. If someone asks us why we think that Pedro is a good man, we talk about the time that he devotes to supporting community organizations, the money he contributes to Oxfam, the love he shows for his friends and family, and so on. If moral properties were really as otherworldly as Moore suggests, it is difficult to see why they should track with such everyday facts as these.

Whatever one thinks of Moore's own view, many people find the open question argument compelling. However, there is a way for the naturalist to escape its clutches, at least in the form in which we have discussed it. The argument rests on an assumption that a naturalist need not accept.[6]

The open question argument supposes that naturalism is a thesis not only about what moral properties consist, but also about the meanings of moral terms. Hedonism, for example, is understood as asserting not only

(5) Goodness is pleasure,

but also

(11) The word 'goodness' means 'pleasure'.

It is because such sentences about the meaning of moral terms are false that all attempts to identify goodness with natural properties seem to fail.

Return to the comparison between goodness and triangles. The truth of (8) rests on the semantic fact that

(12) 'Triangle' means 'three-sided figure'.

Because (12) is true, questions about whether actual triangles, such as the shape of John's sculpture, really are three-sided figures are closed. Anyone who thought that such questions were open would not understand the meaning of the words. However, questions about whether something that is pleasurable is good remain open because hedonism is a substantive claim about the identity of pleasure and goodness, not a semantic claim about the meaning of 'pleasure' and 'goodness'. It is always possible to deny substantive claims.

The difference between a substantive and a semantic claim can be brought out by considering an example from chemistry. Compare the substantive claim,

(13) Water is H_2O,

with the semantic claim,

(14) 'Water' means 'H_2O'.

---

[6] Brink (1989) and Railton (2003: Part 1) are two contemporary naturalist realists who avoid Moore's clutches in roughly the way described below.

The term 'water' is one of the oldest words in the English language, yet only since the work of Cavendish in the late eighteenth century has it been known that water is identical to H_2O. For centuries people used the term 'water' in much the way that we do despite their ignorance of its chemical structure. Indeed, probably a great many people today are ignorant of the truth of (13), but this does not threaten their linguistic competence. This is because (13) and (14) are not equivalent. The non-equivalence of (13) and (14) is also indicated by the fact that we cannot substitute 'H_2O' into every sentence in which the word 'water' appears. At best it is a joke to say

(15) I want a glass of H_2O,

or

(16) There is H_2O damage to my house as a result of the flood.

Not only are substantive identity claims not equivalent to semantic claims, but (13) is true though (14) is false.

Inspired by such examples, some contemporary naturalists have claimed that identifying goodness with a set of natural properties is like identifying water with H_2O.[7] It is a "theoretical" identity, rather than one underwritten by the conventions of language. On this view, the word 'goodness' does not mean the same as any word that refers to a natural fact, but nevertheless goodness is identical to what is referred to by some words that refer to natural facts.

The inspiration behind this idea is the realization that meaning and reference are distinct. Instead of construing naturalism as a thesis about meaning, the naturalists construe it as a thesis about reference. 'Water' and 'H_2O' refer to the same thing, even though they are quite distinct in meaning. There is a set of facts that are the truth-makers both for sentences about water and for sentences about H_2O. As the open question argument reminds us, identities that are not grounded in meaning can be contested. But it does not follow from the fact that an identity can be contested that it does not obtain. The identity of water and H_2O was established not by semantic intuition but by empirical investigation. This is the model that is being suggested for thinking about the identity of moral properties.

---

[7] E.g. Boyd (1988).

At this point, the going gets tough for the naturalist. What makes the case for the identity of H_2O and water is the scientific theory in which the claim is embedded and the virtues that this theory displays with respect to explanation, prediction, and so on. But what is the comparable case for the identity of moral and natural properties? Rejecting the identity of H_2O and water would mean throwing away a lot of good chemical theory. In the case of moral properties, it is not even clear what the proposed identities are supposed to be, much less what theories are supposed to support them. Indeed, in the case of ethics, there do not even seem to be counterparts to the procedures and methodologies that lead to theoretical identifications in science. It is far from clear how we are supposed to establish such theoretical identities in ethics, much less what they are supposed to be.

Even more importantly, some think that even this version of naturalism fails to escape the main import of the open-question argument. On this view, what is characteristic about moral claims is that they are practical: they express motivation and are directed towards action. What the open question argument really brings out is that we can accept a set of natural facts and still ask why this should in any way motivate us to act.

This should especially concern environmentalists who have been attracted to realism because it seems to provide the basis for a deep ecological position in which nature's value is seen as just a brute fact about the world, like any other. Even if this were true as a matter of metaphysics, it is not obvious why it should lead anyone to act on nature's behalf.

Consider the practical import of realism in its natural home in the sciences. When we learn facts about the world, whether it is the structure of a chemical reaction, the geography of Asia, or the number of stars in the universe, we don't think of this as motivating us to respect, protect, or promote the chemical reaction, Asia, or the universe. What, then, is supposed to be the link between believing that the Arctic National Wildlife Refuge is valuable and acting to protect it? If moral facts are natural facts, why should they be any different from other natural facts in their power to motivate?

In response, it could be denied that there is any special relation between moral language and action. It could be pointed out that moral sentences can be used ironically, sarcastically, and in various other ways that do not involve an intention to produce action. Or I might morally praise someone who is long dead and whom you've never heard of as a way of imparting information to you, rather than in the hope that you will begin raising money to build a monument to him. Or, taking another tack, it could be claimed that all language, not only moral language, is in some way practical. When I tell you, for example, that

(17) Moscow is the capital of Russia,

I could be viewed as guiding your actions in those contexts in which you are inclined to say things about Russia or Moscow. Against this, it could be said that this view conflates language being practical with someone acting on the basis of a belief.

None of these responses would be graciously received by environmental ethicists, who believe that environmental problems present deep moral challenges, and that correctly characterizing them in moral terms should naturally lead people to action. Moreover, although the practical import of moral language can be nullified or cancelled and other forms of language can be used practically, there does seem to be a special connection between moral language and action that realism fails to capture. Indeed, there is a neurological disorder in which patients are capable of making what appear to be conventional moral judgments, but do not feel in any way impelled to act on them.[8] The fact that this is regarded as a disorder shows how deep our commitment is to the idea that moral language is in some way practical.

The fundamental problem that realism faces in this regard is that it is desires that motivate; beliefs about the world are inert, or at least this is how it appears. Of course it is open to the realist to try to make the sort of case discussed above, or to claim that moral facts, even if they are natural facts, are different from other facts in that they happen to be motivating. They are peculiar in just this way. This, however, is no explanation, only more mystery. Serious work would have to be done to make such a view plausible.

3.3   Subjectivism

Realism's claim to be the default position in meta-ethics is based on the fact that it takes moral language at face value. However, subjectivists think that claims about the existence of a moral reality – whether natural or

---

[8] Such cases are discussed by D'Amasio 1994.

non-natural – are unconvincing. They also think that there are important differences between sentences such as

(3) Mountain Gorillas are vegetarian

and sentences such as

(4) Mountain Gorillas are valuable.

The most plausible interpretation of such sentences as (4), according to subjectivists, is that rather than attributing properties to Mountain Gorillas, they express or report speakers' attitudes. While sentences such as (3) are about Mountain Gorillas, sentences such as (4) are about the speaker who utters the sentence.

Subjectivism can roughly be characterized as the view that moral language expresses the attitudes of speakers rather than stating facts about the world.[9] Subjectivism's success in explaining the connection between moral language and motivation – an important weakness of realism – is the single most powerful consideration on its behalf. Since subjectivism's basic claim is that moral language functions primarily as a vehicle for expressing approval or disapproval, the connection between moral language and action is straightforward. If I approve of something, I want to protect or promote it. If I disapprove of something, I want to discourage or suppress it. On the subjectivist view, moral language is practical, aimed at action rather than belief. Thus, when someone utters (4), she expresses an attitude towards Mountain Gorillas that finds its natural expression in action on their behalf.

Now things start to become complicated. It is one thing to have a basic insight; it is another thing to formulate a defensible meta-ethic that successfully captures it. The attempt to do this has led to the development of several versions of subjectivism.

Simple subjectivism claims that sentences such as (4) are best understood as sentences such as

(18) I approve of Mountain Gorillas.

Ironically, simple subjectivism turns out to be a version of realism, albeit an especially implausible one. Like other forms of realism, it takes moral

---

[9] The eighteenth-century philosopher, David Hume (2000) is generally considered to be the godfather of such views. Contemporary versions are typically known as expressivism, and are powerfully developed in Blackburn 1998 and Gibbard 1990. The leading exponent of this view in environmental philosophy is Elliot (1997).

sentences to be declarative sentences that are truth-apt: their truth-makers are states or properties of the world. However, in this case, it is properties of speakers that are the states of the world that are the truth-makers of moral sentences.

Despite the elegance of simple subjectivism, it is not a plausible view. The accounts it gives of moral sentences do not respect reasonable constraints on truth and meaning.

Suppose that someone asserts (4) and we want to know whether what he says is true. What we need to investigate, on this view, is the speaker's sincerity, not anything about Mountain Gorillas. Rather than asking why the speaker thinks that Mountain Gorillas are valuable, what we need to know is whether he really approves of them.

The implausibility of this view becomes apparent if we imagine Sean and Kelly having an argument over whether Mountain Gorillas are valuable. Suppose that Sean asserts (4) and Kelly denies it. Both of their utterances could be true, so long as they are sincerely reporting their attitudes. Indeed, if they were both sincere, there would be no disagreement between them despite the fact that the sentences they utter are contradictory.

Another odd consequence of this view is that so long as speakers are sincere in reporting their attitudes, they are morally infallible. Some people really do disapprove of Mountain Gorillas, wilderness preservation, and endangered species protection. Therefore, they are right when they say that these things are not valuable. Strangely, when people with the opposite attitudes say the opposite thing, they too speak truly. Sincere speakers are infallible, even when they contradict one another.

The fundamental mistake of simple subjectivism is that it confuses the truth of a moral claim with the sincerity of a speaker's assertion. Thus it fails to respect the fundamental function of moral language, discussed in 2.1, which centers on the roles it plays in resolving disagreements and enabling cooperation.

A second version of subjectivism, emotivism, escapes some of the objections to simple subjectivism by completely abandoning the idea that sentences such as (4) are truth-apt.[10] According to emotivism, sentences such

[10] A simple version of emotivism was put forward by Ayer (1946: ch. 6), and a more sophisticated version by Stevenson (1944).

as (4) are best construed as sentences such as

(19) Hurrah for the existence of Mountain Gorillas!.

Emotivism escapes the infallibility objection by denying that moral sentences are truth-apt. One cannot be infallible when uttering sentences that are not true or false. Emotivism also escapes the objection to simple subjectivism that sincere speakers do not disagree, even if they utter sentences that are in direct contradiction, by providing an explanation of how there can be real disagreement in morality. If Sean expresses his approval of Mountain Gorillas and Kelly expresses her disapproval, then they have a real disagreement. Their disagreement is a disagreement in attitude, not about the truth of a particular claim as realism would have it, but it is a real disagreement nevertheless.

Moral utterances are meant to claim the attention of others, and to a great extent they succeed in attracting it, but this remains to be explained by the subjectivist. Why should I care that you go around saying "hurrah" for this or that? We can try to fill in the story in this way. I might be concerned about your attitudes because I'm concerned about you – either because I like you or because I fear you. But often we are interested in what people say about morality even if we are not interested in them. For example, I hope that you, the reader, are interested in what I say in this book, though you have little reason to like me, much less to fear me.

A third version of subjectivism, prescriptivism, responds directly to this concern.[11] Prescriptivists understand moral sentences as imperatives, thus (4) is best understood as

(20) Promote the existence of Mountain Gorillas!.

On this view, moral sentences are of interest to their audiences because they are disguised imperatives. When someone addresses us in moral language, they are telling us what to do in the guise of making a claim about the world.

One objection that has been brought against every meta-ethical theory that abandons the idea that moral sentences are truth-apt is that they

---

[11] A simple version of prescriptivism was put forward by Carnap (1937: 23–4, 29), and a more complex version by Hare (1952). Generally on the views discussed in this section visit <http://plato.stanford.edu/entries/moral-cognitivism>.

cannot account for moral reasoning. The classic version of this objection comes from the twentieth-century philosopher, Peter Geach (1965: 463).

Geach asks us to consider the following, obviously valid, argument:

(21) If tormenting the cat is bad, getting your little brother to do it is bad.

(22) Tormenting the cat is bad.

Therefore,

(23) Getting your little brother to torment the cat is bad.

The conclusion follows because (21) is a conditional of the form: if X then Y, and (22) states that the antecedent, X, is true; thus Y inexorably follows. But if prescriptivists or emotivists are right, then (22) is really an imperative or the expression of an attitude. Since imperatives or the expressions of attitudes are not truth-apt, (22) cannot be true or false on this view, and without the truth of (22) we cannot infer (23). Thus it appears that neither emotivism nor prescriptivism can make sense of even simple cases of moral reasoning.

A great deal of work in recent years has been devoted to solving this problem.[12] Even if a technical solution can be found, this objection highlights a problem that haunts all forms of subjectivism. This problem concerns how language, thought, and action fit together in practices that we recognize as distinctively moral. We can see this problem by returning to the comparison between realism and subjectivism.

According to realism, moral language is constrained by the facts about the world that moral language aims to report. But if subjectivism is true and moral language is fundamentally a vehicle for expressing attitudes, then it looks like almost anything goes. What I like or dislike, or what I might issue an imperative about, is not constrained by what we would ordinarily consider good reasons or by facts about the world. When queried, I may produce reasons or supply explanations for why I have the attitudes that I do, but these may be quite idiosyncratic. For example, I may dislike Mountain Gorillas because they remind me of my father, or because I once saw one behaving in a way that struck me as vulgar. While such concerns might motivate me to express attitudes or issue imperatives, they are not what we would ordinarily consider moral reasons.

---

[12] For a survey visit <http://plato.stanford.edu/entries/moral-cognitivism>.

Since subjectivists cannot look to the world for constraints on what we do or say, they must find them in the agent, the language, or the act that is performed. The twentieth-century philosopher, R. M. Hare, tried to solve this problem by claiming that what distinguishes moral from other kinds of imperatives is that they are universalizable. When a speaker issues a moral imperative it must apply to everyone who is in a relevantly similar situation, herself included.

Such a constraint is plausible, but it is difficult to formulate in a way that does the required work. Being able to universalize an imperative is surely not sufficient for its being moral. I can universalize the imperative that one should avoid stepping on cracks in the sidewalk, for example, but that does not make it a moral imperative. More seriously, there are imperatives that clearly have moral content that some may be willing to universalize that are in fact immoral. Consider a Nazi who is willing to universalize his anti-Semitism, even applying it to himself should he discover that he is Jewish.[13]

Let us take stock. A plausible moral theory must provide an account of what matters morally. If moral language is to fulfill its role, such an account must in some way be one that everyone can share. It is difficult to see how any form of subjectivism can satisfy this condition, since the core of subjectivism is the belief that moral language is fundamentally about the speaker rather than about the world. Thus, whatever constraints subjectivism can find must be located in the agent, and it does not seem plausible that they would be strong enough to mark out the moral domain in the way that we ordinarily understand it.

Bringing our discussions of realism and subjectivism together, we can see clearly the fundamental challenge in meta-ethics. On the one hand, moral language seems to have some of the characteristics of fact-stating discourse while on the other it seems to have some of the characteristics of expressions or imperatives. It seems that moral sentences are truth-apt and that moral claims are constrained by reasons, yet it also appears that moral

---

[13] Hare specifically discusses this case (1963: ch. 9). Generally his meta-ethical views developed from a relatively unconstrained strong prescriptivism (1952) to one strongly constrained by a particular understanding of universalizability (1981). He took this latter meta-ethic to imply a particular normative theory, utilitarianism, which will be discussed in section 4.2. Thanks to Peter Singer for helping me get clearer about Hare's views.

language is practical and underdetermined by facts. Moral sentences have a special connection to motivation and action that ordinary fact-stating language does not have. While moral reasons are constrained and relevant, no set of reasons implies a moral judgment. Thus two people may be confronted by the same set of facts, yet have different, internally defensible, moral evaluations. The fundamental challenge of meta-ethics is to provide an account that can explain this strange set of features that seems to characterize moral language.

3.4   The sensible center

That moral language displays features that are difficult to reconcile has been known for centuries. Attempts to solve this problem were central to the meta-ethical work of the great eighteenth-century philosophers, David Hume and Immanuel Kant. Even twentieth-century realists and subjectivists made efforts to honor the insights of their opponents while retaining the clarity of their own initial insights.

In the 1950s, philosophers known as "good reasons" theorists tried to bypass technical questions in philosophy of language and metaphysics by focusing directly on the reasons that we take to support moral claims.[14] The idea was that this approach would uncover a "logic of moral discourse" that would illuminate our moral concepts. For example, a careful analysis of

(24) Jones is a bad man

would show that, when challenged, someone can support this claim by uttering sentences such as

(25) Jones is a habitual liar,

(26) Jones manipulates people,

(27) Jones cheats when he thinks he can get away with it,

(28) Jones is cruel to other people,

and so on. While none of these sentences is necessary or sufficient, each supports (24).

---

[14] For examples of such views see Baier 1958, Falk 1986, and Toulmin 1948.

The contemporary philosophical landscape has spawned many ingenious attempts to develop a meta-ethic that honors both the insights of realism and of subjectivism. These views parade under such names as "constructivism," "quasi-realism," "realist-expressivism," "internalist naturalistic moral realism," and "sensible subjectivism."[15] Although there is no good name for this family of views, I call it "the sensible center," since it lies between the extremes of realism and subjectivism. Such views have been influential among philosophers who have given up heavy-duty realism but seek to retain some kind of view that might be thought of as "realism lite."[16] Whether this space is really tenable remains to be seen. Such views are subtle and varied, and I cannot do justice to them here. However, in order to give some sense of what these centrist views are like, I will briefly discuss one version of such a view (which is itself a family of views) known as "dispositionalism."[17]

Dispositionalism draws its inspiration from the seventeenth-century distinction between the "primary" and "secondary" qualities of objects. Primary qualities, such as mass and position, can be characterized independently of the responses of observers. Secondary qualities, such as color and sound, can be characterized only in reference to observers. Primary qualities are straightforward features of objects that can be described in physical theory, while secondary qualities are often thought of as powers that objects have to produce experiences in creatures with appropriate sensory apparatus. Despite this important difference, both kinds of qualities are typically regarded as real qualities of objects.

Consider how this distinction works with respect to the planet, Mars. Where Mars is located and what size it is are primary qualities of the planet; that it has these qualities has nothing to do with us or any other creatures. That it is the "red planet," however, does depend on the experiences of creatures like us. For if our sensory systems or the distribution of light were different, Mars would not appear red to us. Despite the fact that color has

---

[15] For examples of these views, see Korsgaard 1996, Blackburn 1993, Copp 1995, Smith 1994, and Wiggins 1998. They and their followers would probably deny that they have much in common.

[16] In environmental ethics such views are exemplified by Callicott 1989.

[17] Generally on dispositionaliism in value theory see McDowell 1985 and the symposium in the *Proceedings of the Aristotelian Society*, supplementary volume 63 (1989), with papers by David Lewis, Mark Johnston, and Michael Smith.

this "subjective" dimension, we have no hesitation in saying that it is a fact that Mars is the red planet, just as it is a fact that snow is white and grass is green.

Here comes the punch line. If moral properties can be thought of as (importantly like) secondary properties, then we may be able to explain why realism is plausible while subjectivism seems inescapable. Realism is plausible because our moral responses are caused by the world; subjectivism is inescapable because it is our responses that are the currency of morality.

The meta-ethic inspired by such observations is one that holds that sentences such as

(4) Mountain Gorillas are valuable

are true in virtue of a characteristic response Mountain Gorillas elicit in valuers. While this appears to be an important insight, it is not easy to say exactly what the characteristic response is in virtue of which Mountain Gorillas are valuable. It might be thought that the problem is the strained and artificial nature of (4). However useful such sentences are for the purposes of philosophical discussion, normally those who believe (4) are more likely to say such things as

(29) Mountain Gorillas are awesome!,

(30) Mountain Gorillas deserve our respect,

(31) Mountain Gorillas are sacred.

But the same problems arise with these responses as well.

In the case of color, by contrast, it is not difficult to specify generally what we mean by a characteristic response that underwrites the truth of the claim that Mars is the red planet. The red planet is red in virtue of some statistical generalization about human color experiences caused by sightings of Mars. There is room, of course, both for greater precision and for unending controversy, since Mars does not appear red to us under all lighting conditions, some people are color-blind, and so on. Nevertheless, it seems clear what sort of information underwrites the truth of such claims as that Mars is the red planet: straightforward facts about the color experiences that people have in response to sightings of Mars.

In the case of moral language, however, it is not clear that such descriptive generalizations will do. Let us use 'X' as the name of the generic response, whatever it is, that makes (4) true. This might encompass such specific responses as thinking warm thoughts about Mountain Gorillas, reading books about them, donating money and time to protect them, and so on. But what if it turns out that most people do not respond to Mountain Gorillas in this way? Would it follow then that Mountain Gorillas are not valuable? Would sentences such as (4) be false? What if some communities had the X response to Mountain Gorillas but other communities did not? What would we say if most people did not have a positive response to world peace, honesty, or racial equality? If moral sentences are true in virtue of descriptive generalizations about people's responses, then it looks as though the moral relativism that we tried to put to rest in 2.5 has reappeared. Moreover, if morality is like color, then it is hard to see how we can argue people out of their relativism. For when it comes to colors, people either get it or they do not; argument is beside the point.

These considerations suggest a dilemma. Suppose that the truth-makers for sentences such as (4) are non-moral; that they are, for example, the facts about people's responses to the things in question. If this is the case, then we are plunged into relativism and it is difficult to see how we can make convincing claims that sexists, racists, and animal-abusers are wrong about morality. But the alternative seems to be that the truth-makers for moral sentences are themselves morally freighted. Indeed, some philosophers have accepted this alternative. They say that the response that is relevant to underwriting (4) is not the responses that people actually have to Mountain Gorillas, but rather the responses that are "merited," "appropriate," or "deserved."[18] But which ones are those? One fears that they are just those responses that involve valuing Mountain Gorillas. One worries that the realist insight is no longer being honored. Like the emotivist, we are in danger of spinning off into a world of untethered moral responses that are no longer responsible to the world. Notice how different this is in the case of color. We don't say that Mars is red in virtue of the fact that people ought to have red experiences when they look at this planet, or that such experiences are merited, deserved, or appropriate. Rather we say that Mars

---

[18] Something like this view is endorsed by McDowell (1985).

is the red planet because people do as a matter of fact see the planet as red when they look at it.[19] When we move to moral language in specifying the ground of (4) in an attempt to defeat relativism, we break the analogy between moral judgments and judgments about color. What then are we left with? We seem to face the following dilemma. If the truth-makers for sentences such as (4) are non-moral, then we face relativism; if they are moral, then we face circularity.

Philosophers who are attracted to a dispositionalist account typically respond in one of two ways. One is to try to "thread the needle" between the moral and the non-moral, and to characterize the responses that underwrite sentences such as (4) as those that we would have if we were properly informed and rational. The idea is that the responses that would make (4) true are not our actual responses, but rather hypothetical responses. This dodges the threat of circularity because these hypothetical responses are non-moral. The other approach is to admit the charge of circularity, but argue that this is not really an objection to the dispositionalist account.

One thing this discussion makes clear is that it is easier to say what an acceptable meta-ethic must be like than it is to spell one out. I will conclude this section with some remarks about where, in my opinion, the search for an adequate meta-ethic should go, but will stop short of trying to develop and defend such a view here.

Dispositionalism attempts to incorporate the insights of realism and subjectivism while responding to their failures. Realism and subjectivism fail because they locate moral properties either in the world or in the valuer. Dispositionalists look to secondary qualities as a model for how a successful account of value might incorporate both elements. But perhaps dispositionalism does not go far enough in rejecting the binary model presupposed by both realists and subjectivists. Let us begin with the assumption that value arises in a transaction between valuers and the world, and is not solely attributable to one side of this divide or another. Once we look at matters in this way, we may find it more natural to think that what is central is valuing as an activity, rather than values as entities. Perhaps from this

[19] The simple fact that people see Mars as red rests on a great many not so simple facts about the structure of human visual systems, the properties of light in particular environments, the physical constitution of Mars, and so on. For present purposes we can note this and move on.

perspective, the various elements of an adequate account begin to come into focus.

Valuing implies both a subject and an object.[20] The idea that valuing occurs without a subject doesn't make any sense. Nor does it make any sense to think of a subject engaging in an act of valuing that has no object. To value is to value something. Once we see valuing as central, and subjects and objects as essential to this activity, then the fact that both the subject and the object constrain episodes of valuing comes into view. It is easiest to see this at the margins.

Consider first the subject. Every animal has a set of perceptual capacities and limitations. For example, humans are visually oriented animals, but even so are sensitive only to wavelengths from 400 to 700 nanometers, a small part of the electro-magnetic spectrum. Bees can detect light in the ultraviolet part of the spectrum to which we are insensitive, and the visual acuity of birds of prey far exceeds our own. When it comes to sensing sounds and smells, we are much more limited than many other creatures. Humans can hear only sounds up to 20,000 Herz (Hz), while dogs can hear up to 50,000 Hz. Cows and gerbils have much wider auditory ranges than humans. When it comes to smell, dogs are even more superior to humans than they are when it comes to hearing. Dogs can sense odors at concentrations nearly 100 million times lower than humans can. Remarkably, when it comes to smell, rabbits are as superior to dogs as dogs are to humans.

While we can value things that we do not directly experience, our sensory capacities deeply affect what things we value, how we value them, and the extent to which we value them. We can value the songs of the humpback whales even though we cannot hear them, but the character of the valuing is clearly affected by this failure. And while most of us will defer to the judgments of a "foodie" or a wine connoisseur whose capacity to experience smells and tastes exceeds our own, few of us are willing to privilege the experiences of dogs in the same way, even though their capacities in this regard leave Robert Parker and Julia Childs in the dust. (Think about this the next time that you see a dog going through the trash. He might really

---

[20] But must it be an actual object? What about non-existent objects such as my lovely springer spaniel named Marilyn? What about fictional objects such as James Bond? These are good questions for another day.

be right about what smells good. At any rate, you are not in a position to second-guess him.)

There is a lot of room for argument about exactly what the limits are and how they affect our experiences of value, but it is clear that there are subjective constraints and conditions on what we value. Some of this has to do with our nature as human beings and some relates to us as individuals. What structures our capacities as individuals is partly due to biological variation and partly due to culture and experience. The incredible divergence in food preferences (noted in 2.5) brings this out very clearly. Most Americans are repulsed by the idea of eating snails, whales, sheep lungs, or monkey brains. Yet these are the foods of choice for many people who are biologically indistinguishable from Americans. Thus, the explanation of these differences in attitude must be almost entirely cultural or due to individual experience.

Valuing can also be strongly affected by context. Just as it is difficult to appreciate a sixteenth-century fresco in a dark, cold, musty church, so it can be almost impossible to appreciate the Arctic wilderness when one is under attack from black flies and mosquitoes.

Even so, many people claim to value the Arctic wilderness, most without ever having been there, and this brings out the importance of the object in the activity of valuing. It is this insight that realism grasps and is captured in our moral language. It is also why the reasons we give for valuing typically make reference to the object.

What the views in the sensible center have in common is the attempt to reconcile the object-relatedness of realism with the motivational insight of subjectivism. To succeed, such views must hold that valuing is contextual, object-directed, and constrained by biology, psychology, and history. It is easy to say what a successful theory must do, but difficult to spell one out in convincing detail. The fact that the discussion is still very much alive shows that these efforts have not been altogether successful.

3.5 Intrinsic value

The concept of intrinsic value is the most important and contested notion in ethical theory. Almost every moral theory has some role for intrinsic value, and in some theories it has pride of place. This concept has been especially important in environmental ethics.

From its beginnings in the early 1970s, the galvanizing question for environmental ethics has been whether a new ethic is needed to regulate our behavior in the face of widespread environmental destruction.[21] Most environmental ethicists have at least been attracted to an affirmative answer to this question, and so the search for a new environmental ethic has been central to the development of the field. For many philosophers this involved developing a theory of intrinsic value that encompasses not just humanity and other sentient animals, but nature itself. There has also been a strong tendency to see nature's value, not just as one value among others, but as a value that takes precedence over other values. They wanted this new environmental ethic to be one that is grounded in the nature of things, and not just an expression of the current, perhaps passing, concern for the environment. It is thus not surprising (as I noted in 3.2) that realism has been the preferred meta-ethic for many environmental philosophers. In recent years there has been a reaction against this project, with some environmental philosophers arguing that the focus on intrinsic value has moved the field away from thinking about practical environmental problems.[22] Ironically, the ubiquity of these criticisms is yet more evidence for the centrality of the concept of intrinsic value.

What is intrinsic value? Intrinsic value is the "gold standard" of morality. Just as gold is what is of ultimate monetary value, so what is of intrinsic value is what is of ultimate moral value. In the case of both money and morality, other things obtain their value by their relations to what is of ultimate value.

While this is a good first approximation, digging deeper we discover that the term 'intrinsic value' is used in different ways. Indeed, we can distinguish at least four distinct senses of the expression 'intrinsic value'.

The first sense closely tracks our metaphor. In this sense, intrinsic value can be contrasted with instrumental value. What is of intrinsic value is what is of ultimate value; what is of instrumental value is valuable only because it is conducive to the realization of what is of intrinsic value. For example, suppose that pleasure is of intrinsic value. On this view, we might

---

[21] Richard Routley (1973) explicitly asked this question in a paper presented to the Fifteenth World Congress of Philosophy in Sofia, Bulgaria, later published in its proceedings, and subsequently multiply anthologized.

[22] E.g. Norton 1991. Generally on concepts of intrinsic value in environmental ethics see O'Neill in Jamieson 2001.

think that skiing is valuable, not for its own sake, but because it produces pleasure, which is of intrinsic value. (We will have more to say about this sense of 'intrinsic value' in 6.3.)

In a second sense, intrinsic value is seen as the ticket that admits something to the moral community. More precisely, having intrinsic value is both necessary and sufficient for being an object of primary moral concern (what philosophers call having "moral standing" or being "morally considerable"). Suppose that sentience – the capacity for pleasure and pain – has intrinsic value in this sense. It follows that anything that is sentient is a member of the moral community and its interests must figure in our decision-making. Different accounts can be given as to whether and how the interests of members of the moral community might be traded off against each other, but attributing intrinsic value to them in this sense marks an important distinction between them and "mere things" that do not matter in themselves. We might care about some of these "mere things" (e.g. artworks, deserts, ecosystems), but their value is derivative from their relationships to those things (for present purposes we are assuming sentient beings) which are the objects of primary moral concern.[23] Notice that it is consistent to hold that sentience has intrinsic value in this sense, but not in the first sense. For someone could consistently hold that the capacity for experiencing pleasure and pain is the ticket for admission to the moral community, but that having or exercising this capacity is not the sole or ultimate good.

The third sense of intrinsic value is sometimes called "inherent value" because in this sense the value of something depends entirely on what inheres in the thing itself. The Cambridge philosopher, G. E. Moore, characterized this notion of intrinsic value in the following way:

> "To say that a kind of value is intrinsic means merely that the question whether a thing possesses it, and in what degree it possesses it, depends solely on the intrinsic nature of the thing in question."[24]

---

[23] For further discussion see Jamieson 2002: chs. 14 and 16.

[24] Moore 1922: 260. Moore's use of the expression 'intrinsic nature' is ambiguous in ways that have played out in the subsequent discussion. Some philosophers take Moore to be saying that the intrinsic value of something is the value that it has in virtue of its intrinsic properties. Yet in other places it is clear that Moore is concerned with the intrinsic value of things themselves without reference to their properties. I ignore this complication in what follows.

It is often thought that this conception of intrinsic value rules out anything relational as being of intrinsic value. Thus it might be thought that experiences cannot be of intrinsic value because they require both a subject and an object. For example, although my experience of the Grand Canyon may be valuable, it might be denied that it is of intrinsic value since it involves a relation between me and the Grand Canyon. However, someone could disagree, arguing that the value is intrinsic to the experience, even though the experience itself is a relation. This objection brings out how difficult it is to draw the intrinsic/non-intrinsic distinction that is central to this sense of intrinsic value.

A further problem is that environmentalists often appeal to relational properties in explaining the value of various aspects of nature. For example, they often refer to the uniqueness or rarity of particular animals or ecosystems in making the case for their value. Yet uniqueness and rarity are obviously relational properties. What makes a particular Mountain Gorilla (call her "Helen") rare is the fact that there are very few other Mountain Gorillas in existence. Were many additional Mountain Gorillas suddenly to come into existence, then Helen would no longer have the property of being rare, thus whatever value she might have would not be in virtue of her rarity.[25]

However exactly the details are supposed to go regarding this conception of intrinsic value, it seems clear that something can be of intrinsic value in the first sense without being of intrinsic value in this sense. For there is no inconsistency in supposing that what is of ultimate value "depends solely on the nature of the thing in question."

Finally, a fourth sense of intrinsic value is one in which what is of intrinsic value is independent of valuers. The idea here is that there are certain things that are of value, even if no one were ever to value them. This sense is closely related to the previous one, but it is not identical. In this fourth sense of intrinsic value, relationships or things that stand in relationships can be intrinsically valuable, so long as the relationship is not one of "being valued by." For example, an ecological system that does not involve any valuers could be intrinsically valuable in this fourth sense, although it may

---

[25] A further complication is that it appears that some properties can be both relational and intrinsic. As Brian Weatherson points out (at <http://plato.stanford.edu/entries/intrinsic-extrinsic>), my left leg's being longer than my left arm is a relational property, yet it is one that is intrinsic to me.

not be of intrinsic value in the third sense since it is necessarily relational. Intrinsic value in this sense is value that is independent of valuers.

Fussing over these distinctions may seem pedantic, but it is important because these four senses of 'intrinsic value' are often conflated. For example, the "regress argument" for intrinsic value is widely accepted. Yet at most it establishes the existence of intrinsic value in the first sense even though it is often used as a license for assuming the existence of intrinsic value in all four senses. Here is the argument.

(1) Assume that there is something in the world – call it "x"– that is valuable.
(2) Either x has intrinsic value, or x is valuable instrumentally.
(3) If x has intrinsic value, then intrinsic value exists.
(4) If x has instrumental value, then x is valuable because it conduces to what is of intrinsic value.
(5) Thus, if x has instrumental value, then intrinsic value exists.
(6) So, if something in the world exists that is of value, then intrinsic value exists.
(7) Since something exists in the world that is of value, intrinsic value exists.

Premise (2) is suspect, in my opinion, because there are valuable things that don't fall neatly into the category either of intrinsic or of instrumental value. For example, I value the photograph of my mother because it represents my mother. I value the tail-wagging of the dog next door because it reminds me of the cheerful exuberance of my childhood dog, Frisky. I value my lover's smile because it embodies her kindness and generosity. I value each step of the ascent of Mount Whitney because it is part of the valuable experience of climbing the mountain. While there is much to say about these examples, the important point for present purposes is that none of them seems simply to be a case of instrumental or intrinsic value.

Premise (4) is also questionable since it is not clear why, in principle, there could not be a closed circle of items such that each is instrumentally valuable in that it contributes to the value of another, but no item is intrinsically valuable. On this picture, A is instrumentally valuable because it conduces to B; B is instrumentally valuable because it conduces to C; and C is instrumentally valuable because it conduces to A. If the world were like this, someone might want to say that the entire complex A–B–C is of intrinsic value, but this would invite the further question of how an item could be both of instrumental value and a constituent part of what is of intrinsic value.[26]

But never mind. The most important point that I want to make is that even if this argument succeeds, it only shows that intrinsic value exists in the first sense. Yet having gotten this much, there is a terrible temptation to suppose that this argument proves the existence of intrinsic value in all four senses.

While it is important to distinguish these four senses of 'intrinsic value', it is true that there are interesting relationships among them. The first two senses seem to be getting at a similar idea, and the other two senses seem to be getting at another idea.

What seems to be at work in the first two senses, though in different ways, is the idea of an "end in itself." In the first sense, what is of ultimate value is an end in itself, for its value is not contingent on its conducing to anything further. In the second sense, what has moral standing is an end in itself because it is the direct object of moral concern.

The third and fourth senses of intrinsic value, although distinct, are also getting at similar ideas. The idea seems to be that what is of intrinsic value is in some sense self-sufficient; it does not depend on anything else for its value or existence. In the third sense, this idea is developed in terms of intrinsic value as inherent in the thing itself. In the fourth sense the thought is developed in terms of the independence of intrinsic value from valuers.

This fourth sense is important to environmental ethicists because it is what connects intrinsic value to realism. For if what is of intrinsic value is valuable independent of valuers, then it follows that realism is true.

But what is the argument for intrinsic value in this sense? We have already considered one argument that, even if successful, does not establish the existence of intrinsic value in this fourth sense. However, another style of argument has been employed that, if successful, would prove the existence of intrinsic value in this fourth sense. This strategy employs "isolation tests" and was used by the early twentieth-century philosopher, G. E. Moore. It has been very influential in the literature of environmental ethics under the rubric "last man" arguments since it was introduced by

[26] For an overview of such concerns, see <http://plato.stanford.edu/entries/value-intrinsic-extrinsic>.

the Australian philosophers, Richard and Val Routley (1980). A version of the argument goes like this.

Suppose that Fred is the last sentient creature on the planet and he knows that, for whatever reason, sentient life will never again appear on this planet. Just before exiting the scene, Fred destroys all of the planet's geology and biology. What he destroys is of great beauty and majesty, but he defends his action by saying that it doesn't matter, since it will never again be appreciated or valued by anyone. Do we accept Fred's justification, or do we think that what he did was wrong?

Most of us would say that what Fred did was wrong, and this seems to commit us to the idea that non-sentient nature has intrinsic value in one or both of the latter two senses. For the belief that what Fred did was wrong seems to rest on the assumption that intrinsic value can exist even if there are no valuers or appreciators. The background picture seems to be something like this. A complete list of the features of the world that would be lost due to Fred's action would include a long list of features that are not intrinsically valuable, but would also include some intrinsically valuable features as well. For if there were no such features of the world, then Fred's action would involve a change in the state of the world but it would not be wrong. So, just as the scientific facts about the world don't depend for their existence on anyone appreciating them, so it appears that the same is true of intrinsic value.

Many people find this argument persuasive but I do not (and for the record, neither, I think, did the Routleys). Clearly we think that there is something wrong or bad about Fred destroying the world; the question is why. I think that there are more plausible explanations for why Fred's destruction of the world is wrong or bad than one that commits us to the idea that there is intrinsic value independent of all valuers or appreciators.

While the thought-experiment stipulates all valuers out of existence, there are still some left hanging around. For we who are contemplating the world without valuers are ourselves valuers, and indeed we are contemplating the loss of something that we find very valuable. Even if it is stipulated that we will never experience this world in either its preserved or its destroyed state, we are already experiencing these states in our imagination, and it seems plausible that this is what governs our response to this thought-experiment.[27] Moreover, our sense that something is wrong in this

---

[27] Elliot (1985) gives a similar account of how this thought-experiment goes wrong.

case may also reflect a judgment about Fred's character. Fred would have to be a really arrogant and self-important jerk to destroy an entire world for no reason whatsoever. What an amazing act of cosmic vandalism!

Where does this leave us with concepts of intrinsic value? We have reviewed two arguments for different conceptions of intrinsic value and found them both wanting. The regress argument is not persuasive in establishing intrinsic value in the first sense, and the "last man" argument fails to prove the existence of intrinsic value in the third or fourth sense. Despite these failures, I believe that most plausible theories will employ some conception of intrinsic value in the first or second sense. Ethical theory requires concepts of value, and in my view these concepts are constructed from acts of evaluation. As I hinted when discussing the regress argument, our patterns of evaluation are enormously complex and surprisingly uncharted. Some notion of intrinsic value is likely to loom as a significant landmark on any adequate map of our evaluative practices.

As I mentioned earlier, some philosophers have wanted us to move beyond discussions of intrinsic value and get on with saving the world. However, deep questions about the nature of value do not disappear upon command. It is the job of moral philosophers to address such questions. While moral philosophy can contribute to clear-headed activism, it is not the same thing, and should not be confused with it. Discussions of intrinsic value are not going to go away. However, sensitivity to the distinctions drawn in this section will help us to approach them with the care and suspicion they deserve.

4 Normative ethics

4.1 Moral theories

As we pointed out in the previous chapter, normative ethics is typically divided into two subfields: moral theory and practical ethics. Moral theory is concerned with what sorts of things are good, which acts are right, and what the relations are between the right and the good. Practical ethics is concerned with the evaluation of particular things as good and bad, and various acts or practices as right or wrong. Moral theory and practical ethics have the same subject-matter, though their perspective is different. Moral theory takes the broad view; it is the telescope through which we view the phenomena. Practical ethics views a narrow band of the same terrain in greater detail; it is the microscope through which we examine our moral lives. Don't worry if you can't keep track of the differences. It is difficult to distinguish cleanly between these fields. In this chapter, however, we will focus on moral theory, and in the rest of the book we will primarily be concerned with questions of practical ethics.

Moral theories often have different starting points, and this leads them to ask different questions. Imagine a typical case that might provoke moral reflection. Suppose that John is changing the oil in his car, and pours the used motor oil down the storm drain on the street. One kind of moral theorist will begin her reflection by focusing on the consequences of John's action: we will call her a "consequentialist." Her first thought is about the damage that this act will cause to the environment, and what alternatives were available to John. Another kind of moral theorist, a "virtue ethicist," will begin by wondering about John's character. What sort of person would act in this way? Finally, a "Kantian" will begin by trying to understand John's act. What did he think he was doing? What were his motives? Although different theorists will take different features as central, each theorist will have to provide some account of all the apparently morally relevant features of the case, even if only to explain some away as being of little importance, or derivable from other features.

Students often spend a lot of time refuting some theories and championing others. While this is not wholly out of bounds, it is important to recognize that the three families of theories that we will discuss all represent important strands in our moral traditions; they are part of the natural history of our species. If you really understand a theory, you will almost certainly feel some attraction to it. All these theories have strengths and weaknesses, and at some point all of them exact a price that some people are not willing to pay. Rather than viewing them as finished objects that should be either worshiped or condemned, these families of theories should be seen as ongoing research projects.

4.2 Consequentialism

Consequentialism is the family of theories that holds that acts are morally right, wrong, or indifferent solely in virtue of their consequences. Less formally and more intuitively, according to consequentialism, right acts are those that produce good consequences.

While the term 'consequentialism' may be recent, the idea is ancient. Scarre (1996) finds consequentialists in the fifth century BCE in China and in the fourth century BCE in Greece. Whatever its origins, consequentialism came of age in the eighteenth and nineteenth centuries, and was the dominant philosophy of the mature Enlightenment. Historically, consequentialism has been associated with social and political movements aimed at broadening political participation, abolishing slavery, securing the rights of women, and improving the treatment of nonhuman animals.

Consequentialism is a universalistic doctrine: all of the consequences matter in assessing acts, not just those that affect the actor. Suppose that I am deciding between taking my mother to lunch and going kayaking with my friends. Thinking about what would make me the happiest is not enough. I must also take the consequences into account for my mother and for my friends. According to consequentialism, when I am deciding what to do, I must take into account the consequences of my action for all those who are affected.

One thorny nest of issues that consequentialists must face concerns the nature of action and the relations between actions and consequences. On the face of it, it would appear that agents cause actions which cause consequences by bringing about states of affairs or events. For example, we might say that Kelly's black eye was caused by Sean's punching her. While this may seem obvious, some philosophers would deny that the relationship between agents and actions is in fact causal.

More troubling is the question of whether actions can constitute consequences as well as causing them. If bringing a lie into the world is one of the consequences of lying, then it would seem that consequentialists can assign value (or disvalue) to acts themselves (e.g. lies), as well as to the events or states of affairs that they causally bring about. This would allow the development of versions of consequentialism (often called ideal-consequentialism) that can occupy much of the terrain that anti-consequentialists claim for themselves.

This would matter in a case like this. Imagine that Sean has done everything he can to look good and that he will be happier if he believes he looks good than he will be if he does not have this belief. Suppose that he asks me how he looks, and I know that no one but he will be affected by what I say. I can tell him the truth, which will make him unhappy, or I can lift his spirits by lying to him. Normally we would expect a consequentialist to say that I should lie, since that is the act that would bring about the best consequences. But if we say that the fact that a lie has occurred counts as a bad consequence of lying, then we have to weigh this evil against the benefit of causing Sean to be happy.

In addition to these issues, there are various other features that serve to distinguish among consequentialist theories. One concerns the distinction between actual versus probable, foreseeable, or intended consequences. This distinction matters in the following sort of case. Suppose that Kelly picks up a hitch-hiker, believing that she is a well-meaning, decent person who needs a lift. In fact she is a serial killer on the way to do her work. The actual consequences of Kelly's act are bad, while the probable, foreseeable, or intended consequences may have been good. Whether we classify Kelly's act as right or wrong depends on whether we think that it is actual (as opposed to probable, foreseeable, or intended) consequences that matter in the assessment of action.

A consequentialist theory includes at least the following elements: an account of the properties in virtue of which consequences make actions right, wrong, or indifferent (i.e. a theory of value); a principle which specifies how or to what extent the properties must obtain in order for an action to be right, wrong, or indifferent; and an account of the levels at which actions are evaluated. While this is abstract, an example will help to clarify these elements.[1]

Consider hedonistic act utilitarianism. Hedonism is the theory of value that holds that pleasure is the sole good (as we mentioned in 3.2). Utilitarianism is the version of consequentialism which holds that something is right if and only if it produces the maximum amount of value. On the theory under consideration, it is individual acts that are being evaluated (as opposed to motives, practices, or rules, for example). So, hedonistic act utilitarianism is that version of consequentialism that holds that acts are right, wrong, or indifferent in virtue of the pleasure they produce.

By modifying these three elements, a wide range of alternative doctrines can be generated. Consider some examples.

Perfectionist act utilitarianism is identical to hedonistic act utilitarianism except that it holds that the properties in virtue of which consequences are right-making are various perfections to which humans can aspire. Exactly what these perfections are will depend on particular views about what counts as the most important human achievements. For me they might include being as spiritually evolved as the Dalai Lama, surfing like Duke Kahanamoku, and playing the guitar like Jimi Hendrix. For a perfectionist, what makes acts right is realizing these perfections even if the struggle produces more suffering than happiness.

Modifying the maximization principle allows us to generate hedonistic act minimalism, which holds that any act which produces any pleasure at all is right. Kelly can do the right thing either by volunteering at the homeless shelter or by playing his favorite Britney Spears record, since both acts produce pleasure, and the quantity or quality does not matter.

---

[1] Please be aware that not everyone defines these terms in the same way. In particular, my understanding of both consequentialism and utilitarianism is broader than that of some critics of these theories.

Finally, by changing the story about the level at which acts are evaluated we can arrive at hedonistic lifetime utilitarianism, which holds that acts are right if they are part of a life which produces more pleasure than any other life that the agent could have led.

It should be obvious that these four variants of consequentialism generate quite different judgments about the same act. Suppose that the following acts are open to Kelly: a night of passion with Sean, an evening at a self-improvement workshop, or a crime spree with Robin. If the right set of facts obtains, then the four versions of consequentialism that have been sketched would deliver the following judgments. Hedonistic act utilitarianism would declare that Kelly should choose the night of passion, since that would be the pleasure-maximizing act. Perfectionist utilitarianism would endorse the character-building workshop, since Kelly's attendance would do more to contribute to the realization of perfection than any other act. Hedonistic lifetime utilitarianism would judge the crime spree to be morally right, if we suppose that the crime spree happens to be (a perhaps deviant but necessary) part of the possible life history that produces more pleasure overall than any other life open to Kelly. Finally, hedonistic act minimalism claims that all of the acts open to Kelly would be right, on the assumption that Kelly would take pleasure in any of them (and the effect on others is neutral in aggregate).

This brief discussion of these four versions of consequentialism brings out the following important features. First, the conceptual space which consequentialism describes is vast. Second, versions of consequentialism vary radically in their plausibility. Finally, very few considerations will count against all versions of consequentialism.

On the last point consider an example. One of the objections most frequently deployed against consequentialism is the "demandingness objection." Consequentialism is too demanding to be a plausible moral theory, it is claimed, since it makes us responsible for all the consequences of our actions, however indirect, and thus requires too much of us. True, consequentialism does hold us responsible for all the consequences of our actions, and this may count against those versions of consequentialism that set the standard of rightness very high. But the standard of rightness can also be set very low, and thus consequentialism may demand very little. Even the most committed slacker may turn out to be a moral saint when judged by the standard of hedonistic act minimalism, which requires us only to produce some amount of pleasure, however small.

It is easy, of course, to invent unmotivated, implausible variants of consequentialist theories. These are cheap thrills, however. The real action is in identifying and evaluating views that are both motivated and plausible.

In many people's minds consequentialism is identified with hedonistic act utilitarianism. Indeed, this view is often called "classical utilitarianism" and associated with the eighteenth-century British philosopher, Jeremy Bentham, and the nineteenth-century British philosopher, John Stuart Mill. This association is rather dubious, however. Bentham was much more interested in laws and policies than in individual actions; it is implausible to think of him as an "act anything." Mill claimed to be a hedonist, but his hedonism is so sophisticated as to be all but unrecognizable. Bentham and Mill both claimed to be utilitarians, but they were often satisfied with something less than the best. Indeed, it is something of a scholar's playground to try to reconcile Mill's account of rights and virtues with utilitarian morality.[2]

Still, if one is committed to consequentialism, then utilitarianism seems to be a natural version of the doctrine to embrace. While there is a lot of space for disagreeing about exactly which properties of consequences are right-making (e.g. pleasure, happiness, ideals, desire-satisfaction, etc.), it is difficult to resist the thought that morality demands the maximization of this property, whatever it may be. For if it is the value of consequences that is right-making, then it seems plausible to suppose that right acts are those with the best consequences, and that merely good consequences are not good enough.

Enough has been said about the varieties of consequentialism to suggest that a great deal more could be said. But it is time to shift our focus to some objections to consequentialist theories. The demandingness objection has already been mentioned and I will say no more about it here (though some of what I say later will have implications for how a consequentialist might respond to it). The two objections that I will discuss are the "special relations objection," and the "rights and justice objection."

---

[2] There is a large and excellent literature on Mill, and a growing one on Bentham. See e.g. West 2003 and Harrison 1983.

The special relations objection is the charge that consequentialism can provide no account of "role morality." The argument begins by noting that consequentialism is not just a universalist doctrine but is also committed to impartiality. As Bentham put it, "Every individual in the country tells for one; no individual for more than one."[3] Yet it seems obvious that much of morality is constituted by duties and obligations that are by their very nature partial, counting some for more than one and others for less. Parents have duties to their children that they do not have towards other children, lawyers have duties to clients that are quite different from those that they have to judges or juries, and the very possibility of friendship, it is claimed, presupposes special relationships. The list could go on.

In 1793 William Godwin, a utilitarian philosopher and father of Mary Shelley (the author of *Frankenstein*), introduced a classic case that is supposed to divide consequentialists and their opponents on the importance of special relations. According to Godwin, if the illustrious and philanthropic Fénelon, Archbishop of Cambrai, and his chambermaid are both trapped in a burning building and only one can be rescued, then I should rescue the one who "will be most conducive to the general good." Since it is the archbishop who will be most conducive to the general good, he is the one I should rescue, even if the chambermaid is my mother, for "what magic is in the pronoun 'my' that should justify us in overturning the decisions of impartial truth?"[4]

The rights and justice objection arises in two forms. One form claims that in various circumstances consequentialists are committed to violating people's fundamental rights, while the second form charges consequentialists with indifference to distributive justice.

The classic example illustrating the first version of this objection was introduced by the Australian philosopher H. J. McCloskey, writing in the 1950s, when cases like this were not mere "thought-experiments."

> Suppose that a sheriff were faced with the choice either of framing a Negro for a rape that had aroused hostility to the Negroes (a particular Negro generally being believed to be guilty but whom the sheriff knows not to be

---

[3] Bentham 1827: IV: 475. I owe this citation to Philip Schofield (via Peter Singer). This passage is often misquoted as "Each to count for one and none for more than one" (as we will see in section 5.2.1).

[4] Godwin 1985: 169–70.

guilty) – and thus preventing serious anti-Negro riots which would probably lead to some loss of life and increased hatred of each other by whites and Negroes – or of hunting for the guilty person and thereby allowing the anti-Negro riots to occur, while doing the best he can to combat them. In such a case the sheriff, if he were an extreme utilitarian, would appear to be committed to framing the Negro.[5]

The second form of this objection can be stated in the following way. Imagine a world in which there is a fixed quantity of resources, two people, and two possible outcomes. In the first outcome Kelly and Sean share equally the resources. In the second outcome Kelly has a monopoly over the resources. If Kelly would enjoy the resources more than Sean (and if goodness is defined as enjoyment), then consequentialism would direct us to produce the second, radically inegalitarian, outcome. The core of the problem is that, from a consequentialist perspective, an act is right so long as the outcome it produces instantiates the right stuff to the right degree, regardless of how the stuff is distributed. So, oddly enough, it appears that impartiality can countenance extreme inequality in distribution.

As noted earlier, few considerations count against all versions of consequentialism, and it should be obvious that many versions of consequentialism are not vulnerable to either the special relations or the rights and justice objections. Indeed, these objections are not really aimed at consequentialism, broadly construed, but at (certain versions of) utilitarianism. Therefore the important question is how a utilitarian would respond to these objections.

One utilitarian response would be to "bite the bullet" and agree that utilitarianism finds no place for special relationships, that the sheriff should frame the Negro, and that we should not be concerned about the distribution of resources. Instead of taking these conclusions to be objections to utilitarianism, we should simply view them as consequences of the theory. What justifies this attitude is the thought that we should not reject a well-grounded theory simply because it fails to sanction the moral beliefs with which we happen to find ourselves. It is the moral beliefs that should be revised in the light of our best theory, not the other way around. This is also a common utilitarian response to the demandingness objection.

---

[5] McCloskey 1957: 468–9.

A second response would be to deny that utilitarianism sanctions these judgments. It might be argued that the best world is one in which parents take care of their children and people develop close friendships. Moreover, the evil and disorder that would result from the police framing innocent people whenever they thought that it would be best to do so would be much worse in the long run than what might occur in the present case as a result of the sheriff respecting the rights of an innocent man. As for distributive justice, it might be claimed that generally people are happier if resources are distributed in a broadly egalitarian way than if they are not.

While this response denies that utilitarianism has the untoward consequences claimed by its critics, it moves in the direction of modifying utilitarianism by appealing to prevailing social practices and institutional settings which particular acts help to shape and in which they are embedded. Reflection on these kinds of cases and on the contexts in which moral judgments occur have led some philosophers to embrace "indirect," rather than "direct," forms of consequentialism.

The core idea behind indirect consequentialism involves distinguishing consequentialism as a theory of justification from consequentialism as a theory of motivation. Even if consequentialism is true it may still be the case that, from a consequentialist perspective, it would be bad for people to try to live as consequentialists. We may be wired up in such a way that when we try to do what is best we actually do worse than if we simply were to conform to widely shared moral norms.

Many versions of indirect consequentialism have been developed, of which the best-known is the two-level theory of the twentieth-century British philosopher, R. M. Hare (1981). According to Hare, most of us most of the time do best operating at the "intuitive" level. We should only ascend to the "critical" level at which the consequentialist principle is explicitly invoked when we are faced with dilemmas or conflicts at the intuitive level.

Other forms of indirect consequentialism are rule and motive consequentialism. Rule consequentialism is (roughly) the view that an action is right if it is in accord with the set of rules which, if generally or universally accepted, would satisfy the consequentialist principle, while motive consequentialism is (roughly) the view that an act is right if it issues from the set of motives that would satisfy the consequentialist principle. While versions of indirect consequentialism have quite a lot to recommend them, they are open to Bernard Williams' charge against utilitarianism that

> it is reasonable to suppose that maximal total utility actually requires that few, if any, accept utilitarianism. If that is right, and utilitarianism has to vanish from making any distinctive mark in the world, being left only with the total assessment from the transcendental standpoint – then I leave it for discussion whether that shows that utilitarianism is unacceptable, or merely that no one ought to accept it.[6]

Environmental ethicists have typically regarded consequentialism with suspicion. This may have to do with the fact that the most prominent version of consequentialism is utilitarianism, and utilitarianism inspires a great deal of hostility among philosophers generally. Utilitarianism is often thought of as a crude view that prizes "usefulness" over other more important values and holds that "the end justifies the means." Exploitative policies by developers and government agencies are often called "utilitarian," and contrasted with "preservationist" or environmentalist policies.

However, as we have seen, this simple-minded idea of consequentialism is at best a caricature. Consequentialism, like other families of moral theories, comes in a variety of forms, some more sophisticated than others. Historically, consequentialists have a strong claim to being on the side of moral progress rather than being on the side of sexists, racists, and those who would despoil the environment. Furthermore, when it comes to concerns about the moral status of animals, consequentialists – even utilitarians – have been in the forefront, as we will see in detail in chapter 5.

4.3 Virtue ethics

Let us return to John pouring his discarded motor oil down a storm drain. The first question that occurs to a consequentialist is about the damage this will cause. The first question that occurs to a virtue theorist is about what sort of person would do such a thing. As I have suggested, whatever its starting point, any plausible moral theory must give some account of the value of consequences, the rightness of actions, and the goodness of

---

[6] Williams 1973: 135.

character. We can begin to understand virtue ethics by contrasting it with what a consequentialist would say about character.

Consequentialists would say that we can understand people's characters by the consequences they bring about. The way to find out about John's character is by looking at the pollution caused by his dumping. Of course, we should not be too hasty in inferring character from consequences. Maybe the spill was accidental, or this was John's one bad behavior in a lifetime of virtue. Character isn't about a single act; it's about habits and dispositions.

This is not good enough for virtue ethicists. They distinguish between "virtue theory" and "virtue ethics." A consequentialist who finds a role for the virtues has the former but not the latter. What is distinctive about a virtue ethic is that it puts the virtues at the center of morality. They are not derived from consequences or anything else; everything else is derived from them. Unsurprisingly, virtue ethicists also have a much richer conception of virtues than consequentialists.

The kinds of virtues that might figure in a consequentialist theory are good habits or dispositions to behave in ways that produce the best consequences. For a virtue ethicist, a virtue is more than a device for producing action. Having a virtue involves not just the disposition to act in a particular way but also the ability to identify cases to which the virtue is applicable, having the appropriate emotions and attitudes, acting for the right reasons and so on. While a consequentialist might say that someone whose behavioral dispositions lead her to behave moderately has the virtue of moderation, a virtue ethicist would agree only if the person in question acts for the right reasons, deplores extreme behavior, has appropriate emotional reactions, and is acute in identifying cases in which moderation is the appropriate response.

The origins of virtue ethics are in ancient Greek philosophy and in the Christian tradition. For the Greeks, the central question of ethics was "How should one live?" The task, as they saw it, was to show that living virtuously benefited the agent himself through its connection to human flourishing. For Socrates and Plato, the benefit is living in accord with reason. For Aristotle, the benefit is living an objectively desirable life by fulfilling one's proper function. Aquinas, the greatest Christian theorist of the virtues, supplemented the Greek catalogue of the virtues with the "theological virtues" of faith, hope, and charity. For him, human flourishing is necessarily connected to the contemplation of God.

The contemporary resurgence of virtue ethics is often dated from the 1958 publication of "Modern Moral Philosophy" by the British philosopher, G. E. M. Anscombe. Anscombe claimed that virtue ethics is not a rival to other theories such as consequentialism and Kantianism, but a wholly different way of looking at ethical theory. In her view, modern moral philosophy is incoherent. It is governed by a conception of morality as a kind of law, but there can be no law without a lawgiver, and this it does not allow. Anscombe advocated abandoning such juridical notions as duty, rights, and obligations, and reconstructing moral philosophy on the basis of such concepts as character, virtue, and flourishing.

Few virtue ethicists have followed Anscombe down this road. Indeed, one can question whether Anscombe herself really jettisoned the conceptual framework of modern moral philosophy. She endorsed absolute moral rules against killing the innocent, homosexual behavior and more besides. Her version of morality certainly sounded law-like, but then, as a Roman Catholic, she believed in a divine lawgiver.

Contemporary virtue ethicists, such as Rosalind Hursthouse, have presented virtue ethics as a competitor to the other families of moral theories. Indeed, she provides a virtue ethics account of what it is for an action to be right: "an action is right iff[7] it is what a virtuous agent would characteristically . . . do in the circumstances."

The first challenge in understanding this account is to get a grip on the idea of a virtuous agent. While it is not difficult to think of single virtues that it would be good for a person to have, such as the virtue of moderation discussed earlier, a virtuous person is one whose life expresses the virtues taken as a whole. Ordinarily, we would not say that this is the same as having one or two or three virtues. We commonly talk, for example, as if someone might be virtuous with respect to courage but not virtuous with respect to modesty.

Contrary to this, Socrates and Plato seem to have held that there was only one virtue: wisdom or knowledge. The distinctions that we normally draw between self-control and courage, for example, are, according to them, really distinctions in the subject matter to which the virtue of wisdom or knowledge applies. Aristotle thought that the virtues were distinct, but that

---

[7] Hursthouse 1999: 28. 'Iff' is short for 'if and only if.' 'X if and only if Y' means that X and Y are true and false together.

we could not have any virtues without the virtue of "practical wisdom," and if we have that virtue, then we have them all. So, for different reasons, both Plato and Aristotle thought of the virtues as inseparable.

Let's suppose that we can shape an account of what a good or virtuous person is. What, then, about Hursthouse's account of right action?

The first problem may be trivial, but is worth noticing. That something is what a virtuous person would do is surely not alone sufficient for an act to be right. A virtuous person may avoid stepping on cracks in the sidewalk (to return to an example from 3.3), but that would not make it a morally right action. Sometimes an action is only an action, without any particular moral valence, neither right nor wrong. Clearly, some further qualifications are needed for the account to be successful.

A more serious problem is that it appears that in some circumstances a virtuous agent may do what is wrong precisely because she is virtuous. Suppose that Adolph is in a sealed room where he is preparing to set off a device that will kill millions of people on the other side of the world. The room is in a building in which hundreds of innocent people live and work. The only way to stop Adolph is to blow up the building, killing the innocent people in addition to the guilty Adolph. In this case we should hope that the secret agent who has been sent to stop Adolph is not a virtuous person, but rather someone who is callous enough to kill hundreds of innocent people in order to kill the one person who is a guilty threat. A virtuous person would not do such a thing, even in extreme circumstances.

But hold on. As I have presented this case, it is a counter-example to a virtue ethics account of rightness. However, if I am correct about what a virtuous person would do in this case, what the virtue ethicist should say is that rather than being a counter-example to virtue ethics, this case is an argument against consequentialism. For if a virtuous person would not blow up the building killing hundreds of innocent people in order to save the millions that Adolph will kill, then it would be wrong to do so, and it counts against any moral theory that implies otherwise. Indeed, it is a consequence of virtue ethics that the secret agent who saves millions of people acts wrongly. Since rightness is defined by what the virtuous person would do, by definition cases cannot arise in which the virtuous person would act wrongly.

This is difficult to swallow, even for someone who is not a dedicated consequentialist. At the very least we would hope that our leaders do not reason in this way (especially if we are among the threatened millions). If we think that there is any question about this case, then this suggests that there are features that bear on the rightness of actions in addition to, or even instead of, the character of the agent who performs the action. This thought challenges the basic idea of virtue ethics.

Virtue ethics claims that right actions should be understood in terms of virtuous agents rather than the other way around. Suppose that I ask what's wrong with killing innocent people and I'm told that a virtuous person would not do such a thing. It seems natural to ask why a virtuous person wouldn't do such a thing. Either the virtue ethicist says, "Just because," or she adverts to some story about human flourishing. People who kill innocent people fail to flourish or to benefit themselves in some way. But this seems implausible: just think of your favorite tyrant who lived a long and happy life (e.g. Mao, Lorenzo the Magnificent, or whoever). But even worse, this seems to be the wrong kind of answer. It is strange to say that the wrongness of an action ultimately rests on some idea of what benefits the agent, and has nothing directly to do with the act itself or its consequences. It is wrong to kill innocent people, one would have thought, because of what it does to the victims or because of the nature of the act itself. The explanation of why certain acts are wrong that is available to a virtue ethicist sounds at best like a step on the way to an explanation rather than the explanation itself.

Another challenge to virtue ethics is presented by the fact that different cultures and theorists have endorsed different catalogues of the virtues. I have already mentioned that Christians supplemented the Greek virtues with the theological virtues. However, it is striking that two traits that we today would think of as being central to the virtues – truth-telling, and compassion or charity – do not figure in the Greek catalogue at all, at least in our sense of the terms. The reason for cultural differences in the catalogue of the virtues may be because each catalogue is tied to a conception of human flourishing that is itself culturally relative. This seems plausible. The idea of human flourishing characteristic of the Spanish conquistadors seems quite different from that of the Native Americans they encountered. If this is correct, then we must reject the Aristotelian notion, endorsed by some contemporary virtue ethicists, that the virtues are what they are in virtue of what is essential to our humanity, not in virtue of being ancient Greeks, medieval Christians, contemporary Americans, or whatever. But if we go down this road of relativizing the virtues, where does it end? The Dalai Lama's notion of flourishing is quite different from that of Donald Trump. Does this mean that there is a different set of virtues, and therefore right actions, to which each is subject? Or is one right and the other wrong? If the latter, how can we determine who is right and who is wrong?

It is also difficult to see exactly how virtue ethics helps in actual decision-making, especially in difficult cases. Consider the case discussed by the twentieth-century French philosopher, Jean-Paul Sartre, of the young man who is torn between joining the resistance against the Nazis and staying at home to care for his aged mother.[8] All kinds of helpful advice could be offered the young man, but "act as a virtuous person would act" does not come immediately to mind as an example.[9]

Matters are even more difficult in cases in which traits associated with different virtues seem to conflict. Consider the case of the "innocent lie," discussed earlier, in which I may be able to benefit someone by lying to him. Both someone who believes in a morality of rules and a consequential-ist would have clear, though contradictory, advice. But what does a virtue ethicist say when lying would seem to express the virtue of compassion but not lying would express the virtue of truth-telling?

In recent years virtue theory (if not exactly virtue ethics) has become influential in environmental ethics. In 1983 Thomas Hill Jr. published an influential article in which he asked us to consider the case of a wealthy eccentric who buys a beautiful house surrounded by ancient trees and splen-dorous plantings. This natural beauty means nothing to the eccentric, how-ever. What he cares about is security. He cuts down the trees, uproots the plants, paves the yard, and installs security lights and video monitors. Most of us are repelled by what he does, but our initial inclination is not to talk in terms of rights that have been violated or benefits that have been forgone. On the contrary, we may even be inclined to admit that the eccentric had the right to do what he did. We may grudgingly agree that he has bene-fited himself and not really harmed anyone else. The repugnance we feel is most naturally expressed in the form of a rhetorical question, voiced in a

---

[8] In his essay, "Existentialism is a Humanism," available on the web at <www2.cddc.vt. edu/marxists/cd/cd2/Library/reference/archive/sartre/ works/exist/sartre.htm>.

[9] Of course, the virtue ethicist might (not unreasonably) reply that the utilitarian's advice to bring about the best possible world is hardly any better.

particular way: What sort of person would do such a thing? Our primary objection is to the character of the eccentric, not that he has violated the rights of trees, animals, or even his neighbors. We see his behavior as express-ing arrogance and a lack of humility. What is wrong with him in a small way is the same thing that is wrong with Fred in a big way (remember Fred, from 3.5, who destroys an entire planet when he sees no further use for it).

In the wake of Hill's paper, other philosophers noticed that many of the most influential environmental thinkers, including Henry David Thoreau, John Muir, Aldo Leopold, and Rachel Carson, often expressed themselves in the language of virtue. Thoreau tells us that he went to Walden Pond in order to "flourish" and to "live well." John Muir speaks of nature as giving "strength to body and soul alike." Rachel Carson tells us to "turn again to the earth and in the contemplation of her beauties to know of wonder and humility." Aldo Leopold tells us that if we do not love nature we will not protect it.[10]

Environmentalists are just as articulate in denouncing vice as in prais-ing virtue. They often see greed, selfishness, lack of sensitivity and other failings as the heart of our indifference to nature. As we saw in chapter 1, many influential writers see such failings as the ultimate cause of our envi-ronmental problems.

There is no doubt that these writers have a point. Much of our disappoint-ment about the way animals and nature are treated is centered on our fellow humans who act in ways that are sometimes scarcely believable. Indeed, it is because of this reaction that environmentalists sometimes have the rep-utation of being misanthropic. Consider, for example, the first of several autobiographies written by the nineteenth-century British thinker, Henry Salt, who may have been the most important animal rights philosopher in history: his title, *Seventy Years Among Savages*, tells you everything you might want to know about what he thought of his contemporaries.

However, we should remind ourselves that while a great deal of environ-mentally destructive human behavior can rightly be denounced as greedy

---

[10] The quotations from Thoreau and Muir are from Sandler and Cafaro (2005: 32–3); the Carson quotation can be found by visiting <http://en.wikiquote.org/wiki/Rachel_Carson>; and Leopold's remarks about the importance of loving nature if we are to protect it are on the web at <http://home.btconnect.com/tipiglen/landethic.html>.

or vicious, much is humdrum and ordinary. As we also saw in chapter 1, many of our environmental problems have the structure of collective action problems. They involve many people making small contributions to very large problems. They do not intend to cause these problems, and in many cases feel quite powerless to prevent them. The "soccer mom" driving her kids to school, sporting events, and music lessons does not intend to change the climate. Yet, in a small way, that is exactly what she is doing.

It remains an open question whether virtue ethics, as opposed to virtue theory, is required to account adequately for these attitudes. It is worth noting that Hill himself is not a virtue ethicist, but a Kantian who takes character quite seriously. This leads us naturally to an investigation of the strengths and weaknesses of Kantian moral theory.

4.4 Kantianism

One of the deepest strands in our moral consciousness focuses not on the consequences of an action, or directly on the character of the agent, but rather on the act itself and the purity of its motivation. This strand was systematically developed by the eighteenth-century German philosopher, Immanuel Kant. Kant's writings are both difficult and rich, and this has led to voluminous literatures both interpreting and developing his insights. In recent years there has been a revival of Kantian philosophy and an attempt to apply its insights to questions of contemporary importance. Though inspired by Kant, much of this work is not presented as direct applications of his philosophy. The place to begin, however, is with an overview of some of his central doctrines.

According to Kant, we are rational agents living in a world populated by other rational agents. The fundamental questions of ethics concern how rational agents ought to relate to themselves and each other. The right answers to these questions, in Kant's view, have implications both for how we ought to reason about what to do, and for what is permissible for us to do.

Rational agency, both in ourselves and in others, makes categorical demands on us that are felt in the form of imperatives. A categorical imperative applies to us unconditionally, without reference to any ends or purposes that we may have. Such imperatives apply to all rational agents whatever their desires, interests, projects, roles, or relationships. Categorical imperatives can be distinguished from hypothetical imperatives or conditional commands such as:

(1) If you intend to go to medical school, then take organic chemistry;

(2) If you want a good coffee, then go to Joe's.

These hypothetical imperatives or conditional commands apply to us only in virtue of our desires or because we happen to will some particular end. A categorical imperative, on the other hand, applies to us simply because we are rational agents. There is only one categorical imperative, according to Kant, though he gives several formulations of this single imperative, thus giving rise to generations of scholarship devoted to exploring the relationships between the various formulations.

The version of the categorical imperative most discussed by philosophers is the "universal law" formulation: "act only according to that maxim through which you can at the same time will that it should become a universal law."[11] The idea is that if you want to know whether some act is permissible, you should formulate the maxim on which you propose to act and see whether you could will this maxim to be universal law. If you cannot, then the act is impermissible.

It is important to understand that Kant's test for maxims concerns what can be willed, not what you would like, prefer, or want. This point is illustrated by the following rather silly, non-moral example. Consider the maxim, "Give your friends chocolate on their birthdays." Since I don't like chocolate I would be very unhappy if this maxim were made universal law. However, this does not rule out my giving my friends chocolate on their birthdays. For I can consistently will that this maxim become universal law, even while preferring that it did not.

Kant gives several examples of how the categorical imperative works in moral cases. Taking some liberties with the text, this is more or less what he says about two cases.

---

[11] Kant (IV: 421; 1996: 73). All my citations of Kant follow the convention of referring both to the volume number and pagination in the standard German edition of his works (the "Academy" edition), and to the year of publication and page number in the English translation that I quote. Thus 'IV: 421' refers to volume IV, page 421 in the standard German edition of Kant's works, while 1996 is the publication year of the translation and page 73 is where the quoted passage appears.

Suppose that I am tempted to ask you for money, promising to pay you back next Friday, but really intending to skip town as soon as I get my hands on your dough. The maxim that I propose to act on is (something like):

(3) Make promises without intending to keep them whenever it serves my interests.

Adopting this maxim commits me to willing a world in which everyone makes promises without intending to keep them whenever it serves their interests. But such a world is not possible, since the institution of promising would wither away without a commitment to keep promises even when it is contrary to an agent's interests. Since the maxim on which I propose to act cannot consistently be willed to be universal law, it is not permissible to act on this maxim.

A second example concerns truth-telling. Suppose that I am tempted to lie in order to bring about good consequences. This maxim too, according to Kant, fails the universal law formulation. For the very possibility of lying requires a presumption of truth-telling, and this presumption would not survive in a world in which everyone acted on the maxim of lying in order to bring about good consequences.

Kant was adamant that it is wrong to lie even to a murderer in search of his innocent victim. Many commentators, including some of Kant's contemporaries, pointed out that his philosophy need not be as absolutist as he himself understands it. For the categorical imperative is fundamentally a test of maxims, not of actions or rules. What it forbids is actions that flow from particular maxims, not entire classes of actions. Lying to protect an innocent victim from a murderer may issue from a very narrowly framed maxim, one that would not allow us generally to lie in order to produce good consequences. For example, it may flow from the maxim,

(4) Lie to those who would murder innocent people when this is the only way to prevent them from doing so.

Since such circumstances rarely arise, it is difficult to see how acting on such a maxim would threaten the presumption in favor of truth-telling. Thus it would appear that acting on such a maxim would not fail the universal law formulation.

However, this raises the difficult question of what exactly a maxim is for Kant, and how we can tell which particular maxims are the bases of specific actions. We may not be able to tell, for example, whether an honest shop-keeper is acting on the categorical imperative, or only strategically waiting for an opportunity to get away with something. Kant was skeptical about whether we could be certain even about our own maxims: "The depths of the human heart are unfathomable," he wrote.[12]

There are many difficulties in identifying maxims, figuring out what it would mean for a particular maxim to be a universal law, and in determining whether a failure in this regard involves a contradiction in the will or some other malfunction. We will not worry about these details here, but instead turn to the second formulation of the categorical imperative, the one that is the most intuitive expression of Kant's moral outlook.

This second formulation is called the "formula of humanity": "Act so that you treat humanity, whether in your own person or in that of another, as always an end and never as a means only." It is this thought (or something like it) that is at work when we object to people failing to respect other people, to manipulating them, or to using them for their own purposes. However, here too, we must be careful. Treating the postman as a means of receiving one's mail does not run foul of the formula of humanity unless we treat him as a "mere" means: that is, as if he has no value apart from being an efficient mail delivery device. It is permissible to treat the postman as a means, but not as a mere means, for this is what violates the formula of humanity.

However, animals and the rest of nature can be treated as mere means because they are mere things. What makes them mere things is that they are not rational agents, which Kant closely connects to the idea of self-consciousness. He writes:

> The fact that the human being can have the 'I' in his representations raises him infinitely above all other living beings on earth. Because of this he is a *person* . . . i.e., through rank and dignity an entirely different being from *things*, such as irrational animals, with which one can do as one likes.[13]

Since animals are mere things, they cannot be wronged. Kant writes: "we have no immediate duties to animals; our duties towards them are indirect duties to humanity."[14]

---

[12] Kant VI: 447; 1996: 567.   [13] Kant VII: 127; 2006: 15.   [14] Kant XXVII: 459; 1997: 212.

Despite this dim view of the moral status of animals, Kant did not think that they could be treated with impunity. Indeed, we can collect from his writings a long list of duties that Kant thought that we owed regarding animals, though not directly to them.[15] Animals should never be killed for sport; vivisection should not be carried out "for the sake of mere speculation" or if the "end can be achieved in other ways"; when animals are killed, it should be quick and painless; animals should not be overworked; faithful animals who have served well should be allowed to live out their days in comfort "as if they were members of the household." Charmingly, Kant praised his predecessor, the seventeenth-century philosopher and mathematician Gottfried Leibniz, for returning a worm to its leaf, after examining it under a microscope. The claim has even been made that Kant was as influential in the development of animal protection law in Germany as Bentham was in Great Britain.[16]

The question, of course, is how Kant can ground these duties and how strong they can be, given his view that animals are mere things. Most commentators find Kant's ground in such passages as "Tenderness [shown towards animals] is subsequently transferred to man." He writes that "in England, no butcher, surgeon or doctor serves on the twelve-man jury because they are already inured to death."[17] The idea is that there is a causal connection between how we treat animals and how we treat people. This idea goes back at least to the seventeenth-century British philosopher John Locke, and is immortalized in Hogarth's *Four States of Cruelty*, a cycle of engravings from 1751, specifically referred to by Kant.

There is some evidence, though hardly definitive, that supports the claim that there is some connection between animal abuse and some forms of violence against people.[18] However, as a general ground for the panoply of duties regarding animals that Kant endorses, the claimed connection between human and animal abuse is not very persuasive. Even if there is some connection, surely there are other more salient causes of human abuse than animal abuse.

Suppose that it turns out that rather than increasing the likelihood that one will abuse people, abusing animals reduces the likelihood by purging

---

[15] For citations, see Wood 1998.   [16] Baranzke 2004.
[17] Kant XXVII: 459–60; 1997: 213.
[18] <www.animaltherapy.net/Bibliography-Link.html>.

aggressive impulses that would otherwise be aimed towards people. Or, more modestly, suppose that there is no more connection between abusing animals and abusing humans than between hitting baseballs and hitting heads. If either of these were true, then it would seem that there would be no empirical foundation for duties regarding animals in Kant's system.

Recently some philosophers have argued that Kant's ground for duties regarding animals is much stronger than this account would suggest. They rely on passages such as this: "Any action whereby we may torment animals, or let them suffer distress, or otherwise treat them without love, is demeaning to ourselves."[19] Kant's real ground for our duties concerning animals, according to the contemporary philosopher Allen Wood, is in the duties that we owe to ourselves, and these duties are at the foundation of Kant's moral philosophy. Wood writes:

> By grounding duties regarding nonrational nature in our duty to promote our own moral perfection, Kant is saying that whatever our other aims or our happiness may consist in, we do not have a good will unless we show concern for the welfare of nonrational beings and value natural beauty for its own sake.[20]

However, as Wood recognizes, this is not a fully satisfactory account of our duties to animals and the rest of nature, though it may be the best that one can do working within the confines of Kant's system. No matter how we try to spin it, Kant's view of the wrongness of abusing animals and nature seems to miss the point. If someone tortures an animal the primary wrong is not to himself or to other people, but to the animal he is torturing. Abuses to nature are more complicated, but at least part of why it's wrong to destroy Grizzly habitat is that it harms the Grizzlies. These are the sorts of simple truths that Kant cannot utter.

The fundamental problem for a Kantian environmental ethic is that, on Kant's account, only rational agents are the direct objects of moral concern, and indirect arguments for the wrongness of abusing animals and nature are at best only partially successful. The question, then, is whether a Kantian theory (as opposed to Kant's own theory) can provide an account in which at least some elements of non-human nature are the direct objects of moral

---

[19] Kant XXVII: 710; 1997: 434.   [20] Wood 1998: 195.

concern. Is there a plausible Kantian theory that views animals and nature as ends in themselves, rather than mere means?

One approach would be to claim that many animals are rational agents and are owed the same respect as other rational agents. While this is plausible on some understandings of 'rational', there is a distinctive idea of rationality at the heart of Kant's philosophy that rules this out. A rational agent, according to Kant, must be capable of grasping the categorical imperative. Even many creatures who in some way might be said to have a sense of right and wrong are not rational in this sense. If you give up this idea of what it is to be a rational agent, then you give up any claim to being Kantian.[21]

Another approach is to distinguish between the source and the content of values. From this perspective we might say that while rational agents are the source of value, they do not exhaust the content of value. The contemporary philosopher, Christine Korsgaard (2005), gives a Kantian version of such an argument.

Korsgaard begins by echoing Kant's claim that rational agency is the source of value. Rational agents themselves are valuable because they so regard themselves. Their ends are valuable because, when reasoning about what to do, rational agents imbue them with value. These values are universalized in response to the demands of the categorical imperative. One way of putting this point is to say that rational agents legislate value, and value arises because rational agents are self-valuing legislators.

The main question in environmental ethics, from this perspective, centers on whether we are rationally required to legislate protection for other animals or nature. Korsgaard answers "yes," and gives two reasons.

The first reason begins with the observation that we are not only rational agents but also animals, and in virtue of this we have an animal nature. Our animal nature includes "our love of eating and drinking and sex and playing; curiosity, our capacity for simple physical pleasure; our objection to injury and our terror of physical mutilation, pain and loss of control."[22] Our animal nature can be thought as forming part of our "natural good" because it enables us to function, and to function well. For this reason, we

---

[21] In his defense of animal rights, Tom Regan accepts much of the Kantian picture, substituting 'subject of a life' for 'rational agent' as determining the class over which duties are owed. We will discuss Regan's views in section 5.2.

[22] Korsgaard 2005: 105.

value not only our rational nature but also our animal nature. When we legislate the value of our own animal nature, we legislate the value of these same features wherever they arise, even when it is in creatures who are not rational agents.

Korsgaard has a second reason for the claim that we are rationally required to legislate protection for animals or nature. Even when we are legislating the value of distinctively human goods, we are legislating a principle that confers value on other animals. For what we are legislating is the value of the natural goods of all those creatures who experience and pursue their own goods. As Korsgaard (2005: 105–6) puts the point:

> The strange fate of being an organic system that matters to itself is one that we share with other animals. In taking ourselves to be ends-in-ourselves we *legislate* that the natural good of a creature who matters to itself is the source of normative claims. Animal nature is an end-in-itself, because our own legislation makes it so. And that is why we have duties to the other animals.

Drawing these two lines of argument together, we can say that Korsgaard's basic idea is that since we value the goods that flow from our animal nature, we are committed to valuing these goods when they are instantiated in other creatures as well; moreover, we are committed to valuing goods that are valued by creatures who pursue goods, even if we don't value those particular goods ourselves. Thus, if we value our tendencies towards enjoying food and sex, then we are committed to valuing an elephant's tendencies towards enjoying food and sex as well. If we value our own appreciation of art, then we are also committed to valuing a dog's appreciation of (what are to him) interesting smells, and a monkey's valuing of swinging from trees.

If we accept this much, then a path comes into view that might enable us to move beyond animals to plants and even to artifacts. Individual trees and even entire forests can be seen as teleological systems that have goods of their own. One can even say that it is good for a snowmobile for its engine to be clean. Of course, this may be shorthand for saying that a clean engine is good for the owner or user of the snowmobile. But as artificial life advances and cyborgs become more ubiquitous, the distinction between artifacts and organisms may break down. Whatever the case with artifacts, if we accept the basic idea that the natural goods of those entities that have a good of their own are valuable, and that natural goods can be understood in terms of their contributions to how entities function, then it seems clear how someone might argue that we are rationally compelled to value plants, animals, and ecosystems.

This trail has been blazed by other contributors to environmental ethics. There has long been a temptation to begin from such premises as

(5) X is good for creature Y

and conclude that

(6) X is good.[23]

There are treacherous shoals here, however. Eating veal may be good for humans, and disemboweling wildebeest may be good for lions, but we feel little inclination to say that these things are good *simpliciter*. Sometimes this point is made by saying that the notion of something being good for a creature is descriptive, while the idea of goodness *simpliciter* is prescriptive.

A further question about Korsgaard's approach concerns exactly how Korsgaard's views are different from consequentialism. One difference is this. For consequentialists, wrongness is at least to a great extent a function of harm production, and it is typically thought that non-sentient nature cannot be harmed. Thus, it is difficult for consequentialists to defend the idea that it is wrong to destroy plants and ecosystems, except insofar as this harms sentient beings. Korsgaard, on the other hand, separates wrongness from harming. Thus it is open to her to say that it is wrong to clear a forest (for example), even if doing so entails no harms. However, what we don't have from Korsgaard is an account of how to make trade-offs when choosing between actions, each of which would cause some environmental destruction. This brings out an important difference between consequentialism and Kantianism. Since consequences are the currency of morality for consequentialists, they are quite concerned about how different courses of action play out in the world. For Kantians, morality is fundamentally about the acceptability of the maxims on which we act, and questions of trade-offs do not directly touch this concern.[24]

---

[23] For discussion see Regan 1982: chs. 6, 8, 9; and Attfield 1987.

[24] But see the work of Paul Taylor (1986), who has a Kant-inspired theory (if not exactly a Kantian theory), which does pay close attention to priority rules and trade-offs.

Korsgaard's account can successfully be distinguished from consequentialism, but some of her fellow Kantians may still balk at her story. For example, they may deny that we are rationally compelled to legislate the value of our animal nature wherever we find it. They may say instead that valuing animal nature is optional rather than required. The thought is this. Rational agency is essential to us, and so we are rationally compelled to value it; but our animal nature is not essential to us, so valuing it is not rationally required. It is true that our rational agency manifests itself in a particular species of primate, but there is no necessity in this. In principle, it could manifest itself in other sorts of organisms or even artifacts. Suppose, for example, that the Tin Man is a rational agent. Firmly welded rivets are part of his "natural good," since they enable him to function and to function well. The Tin Man reasons that because he legislates the value of having his rivets firmly welded, firmly welded rivets are valuable wherever they may occur. Some may think that supposing that we are rationally compelled to value our animal nature wherever it manifests is no more plausible than the Tin Man valuing firmly welded rivets wherever they occur.

4.5 Practical ethics

The primary focus of this chapter has been moral theory. But since it is difficult to disentangle moral theory from practical ethics, we have discussed various matters of practical concern ranging from dumping used motor oil into storm drains, to lying to a murderer in search of his victim. In the next two chapters we will discuss a range of questions concerning our duties with respect to animals and nature. This will involve not just abstract moral considerations, but also facts about various practices. Since the main focus of practical ethics is on what we ought to do, it is important to understand the practices we are assessing and the acts we are contemplating.

5   Humans and other animals

5.1 Speciesism

What makes humans different from other animals? This question has been at the center of philosophical discussion since at least the time of Socrates and classical Greek civilization.[1] Indeed, anxiety about our relations to other animals figures in the Bible, as well as in the stories and myths of other ancient cultures. In some societies, animals were viewed as agents with whom one made agreements and in some cases even entered into conjugal relationships. They were worshiped and respected, but also hunted. They were a source of inspiration, but also of protein. Clearly, complex stories are required in order to make such a multiplicity of uses morally and psychologically palatable.

This question of what makes humans different from other animals is more than merely "academic." We would never do to humans much of what we do to animals. Not only do we eat them, but we cause them unspeakable suffering before slaughtering them. They are no longer sacrificed for religious purposes in most societies, but they are still routinely killed and made to suffer in scientific and medical research, as well as in the cause of producing new cosmetics and household products. As for wild animals, we like having them in our parks and sometimes even in our neighborhoods, but our patience quickly wears thin when there are "too many" of them or they do not behave "properly."[2]

---

[1] Passmore 1974.

[2] Despite the fact that the 2004 German constitution specifically protects the rights of animals, in 2006 German officials killed Bruno, the only wild bear seen in Germany since 1835. An official in Bavaria's environment ministry explained: "It's not that we don't welcome bears in Bavaria. It's just that this one wasn't behaving properly" (<www.guardian.co.uk/germany/article/0,,1806304,00.html>).

One way of explaining why we treat humans and animals in such different ways is to say that humans are members of the moral community while other animals are not. In the language of philosophers, members of the moral community have "moral standing"; they are "morally considerable," while non-human animals are not.[3] They have intrinsic value in the second sense which we distinguished in 3.5.

However, as we saw in our discussion of Kant (in 4.4), it would be a mistake to suppose that it follows from the view that we owe duties only to humans that we have no duties regarding animals. For example, you may have a duty in regard to my dog (e.g. not to harm her) that is owed to me (e.g. she's my property). In such cases Kant speaks of the duty as owed directly to a human and indirectly to an animal.[4] Because some animals are within the scope of our indirect duties, they are treated to some extent as if they were members of the moral community. It is important to remember, however, that on this view, they are not.

The President's annual ritual of "pardoning" a Thanksgiving turkey illustrates how contingent the fate is of one who is not a member of the moral community.[5] Out of the billions of turkeys slaughtered each year as part of the holiday celebration, the President spares one who would otherwise have ended up on his plate. He eats a different turkey instead, and the lucky survivor goes to a refuge to live out her life in peace. If someone were to kill the turkey whom the President has spared, they would be doing something wrong. But it is the President (or whoever now is the turkey's legal owner) who would be directly wronged; the turkey would be wronged only indirectly (if at all).

This view under consideration can be stated in a more formal way as holding that all and only humans are members of the moral community.

---

[3] For an overview see Kuflik 1998.

[4] There is an unresolved ambiguity in Kant as to whether the terms 'direct' and 'indirect' modify the source of the duty or its object. If I owe an indirect duty to an animal, does this mean that I owe the animal a duty in virtue of duties that I owe a human? Or does it mean that my duties are only to the human but concern the animal? While the latter seems more in the spirit of Kant's official view, it would seem to imply that I have indirect duties regarding all sorts of things over which you have rights, including all of your property. It seems strange to suppose that I have indirect duties regarding your accordion in exactly the same sense in which I have indirect duties regarding your dog.

[5] For discussion of this bizarre ritual see Fiskesjo 2003. It is especially odd that the turkey in question is "pardoned," since she has committed no crime.

This raises the following question: In virtue of what are all humans and no non-humans member of this community?

An important strand in the western philosophical tradition views linguistic competence or self-consciousness as the crucial criterion.[6] While these criteria are distinguishable, many philosophers have closely associated them (e.g. the seventeenth-century French philosopher, René Descartes, and the twentieth-century American philosopher, Donald Davidson).

These criteria, on reflection, would appear both too demanding and not demanding enough to support the claim that all and only humans are members of the moral community. They are too demanding because not all humans are self-conscious: not newborns, the comatose, or those suffering from advanced dementia. Nor are newborns linguistically competent. These criteria are not demanding enough, since some non-human animals appear to be self-conscious: for example, our fellow Great Apes and perhaps some cetaceans (e.g. dolphins).[7] Moreover, the idea that having language is an "all or nothing" capacity that sharply distinguishes humans from other animals is increasingly being called into question by experiments with other animals and work in historical linguistics. The classical scholar, Richard Sorabji (1993: 2), suggests a more sweeping criticism when he caricatures the linguistic criterion as holding that "they [animals] don't have syntax, so we can eat them." What Sorabji seems to be asking is why on earth we would think that linguistic competence should have anything to do with moral status?

Other philosophers, rather than finding the criterion of moral considerability in linguistic competence or sophisticated cognitive or reflective states, have instead looked to sentience: the capacity for pleasure and pain. Such a criterion may succeed in catching all humans in its net: newborn babies and many other humans who are not self-conscious or linguistically competent can experience pain and pleasure, and therefore would count as members of the moral community on this criterion. However, this criterion would be

---

[6] For Kant (as we saw in section 4.4), self-consciousness is what separates humans from other animals. For much of the Greek philosophical tradition, it was the ability to speak that mattered (Heath 2005, Sorabji 1993).

[7] It may sound odd to speak of "our fellow Great Apes," but as a sober matter of biological classification, *Homo sapiens* is a member of the subfamily, *Hominae*, which also includes chimpanzees, bonobos, gorillas, and orangutans. For a good start on self-consciousness in non-humans visit <http://plato.stanford.edu/entries/consciousness-animal>.

satisfied by many non-human animals as well. Indeed, most of the animals that we commonly use for food and research are clearly sentient: cows, pigs, chickens, dogs, fish, cats, rats, monkeys, and so on. The eighteenth-century English philosopher Jeremy Bentham saw this point clearly, and drew some startling implications, when he wrote:

> The day *may* come when the rest of animal creation may acquire those rights which never could have been witholden from them but by the hands of tyranny. The French have already discovered that the blackness of the skin is no reason why a human being should be abandoned without redress to the caprice of a tormentor. It may one day come to be recognized that the number of the legs, the villosity of the skin, or the termination of the *os sacrum* are reasons equally insufficient for abandoning a sensitive being to the same fate.[8]

One way of stating what is at issue between these two families of criteria is whether being a moral agent is a necessary condition for being a moral "patient." A moral agent is someone who has moral obligations; a moral patient is someone to whom obligations are owed.[9] We do not normally attend to this distinction because reciprocal duties are so much at the heart of our everyday morality. For example, the wrongness of my lying to you is related to the wrongness of your lying to me. This has led some to suppose that there is a necessary connection between being a moral agent and being a moral patient. On this view, only creatures who themselves have moral obligations can be owed moral obligations. But this goes too far. Newborn infants and severely brain-damaged humans are moral patients (we owe them obligations), but they are not moral agents (they do not owe obligations to others because they are not capable of fulfilling them). If we accept the idea that there are human patients who are not moral agents, then why should we not accept the idea that there are non-human patients who are not moral agents?

While much more can be (and has been) said about these matters, it would appear that there is no morally significant criterion for membership in the moral community that is satisfied by all and only humans.[10] If the criterion is demanding enough (e.g. language), it is likely to exclude some

---

[8] As quoted in Singer 1990: 7.

[9] This distinction was introduced into the contemporary discussion by Warnock 1971.

[10] For further discussion, see Singer 1990 and Dombrowsky 1997.

humans. If it is permissive enough to include all humans (e.g. sentience), it is likely to include many non-humans.

In response, some philosophers would say that the correct criterion has been under our noses all along. Think about the idea of universal human rights. We believe in this idea, not because we think that there is some further, morally relevant property shared by all and only humans, but rather because we believe that simply in virtue of being human there are rights that all humans have. As the late English philosopher, Bernard Williams, wrote, "we afford special consideration to human beings because they are human beings."[11] When it comes to clashes between fundamental human and non-human interests, there is, according to Williams, "only one question left to ask: Which side are you on?"[12]

Much of what Williams says is probably true by way of explaining our attitudes. But explaining our attitudes is not the same as justifying them. There is still a question about whether an appeal to our common humanity is sufficient justification for dividing the moral world along the lines of species membership. What we want to know is not only whether the following view is widely accepted, but whether it can be defended: that all and only members of the species, *Homo sapiens*, are members of the moral community.[13]

This view is not exactly new, and it has been subjected to grueling criticism. In 1970 the British psychologist, Richard Ryder, coined the term 'speciesism' to refer to the prejudice that allows us to treat animals in ways in which we would never treat humans.[14] In his 1975 book, *Animal Liberation*, Peter Singer popularized this term, defining it as "a prejudice or attitude of bias in favor of the interests of members of one's own species and against those of members of other species."[15]

[11] Williams 2006: 150.   [12] Williams 2006: 152.

[13] However, it is important to note that our question is not exactly that of Williams. For he explicitly denies that being human is equivalent to being a member of the species *Homo sapiens* (he says that a human embryo "belongs to the species," but that it is not a human being in the sense in which human beings have a right to life (Williams 2006: 143). This invites the question: In virtue of what (if not species membership) is something a human being in the sense in which humans have a right to life? The search for an answer to this question seems to return us to the hunt for some "other set of criteria" for membership in the moral community. On another point, it is not entirely clear that Williams excludes all non-human animals from the moral community.

[14] See Ryder 1975 for discussion.

[15] Singer 1990: 6. The term 'speciesism' has now entered the *Oxford English Dictionary*. For more on the concept, see Pluhar 1995.

The basic idea is that speciesism, like sexism and racism, is a prejudice involving a preference for one's own kind, based on a shared characteristic that in itself has no moral relevance. Speciesism serves various interests and beliefs, but, according to Singer, in large part it is the vestigial remains of traditional theological dogma about the importance and dignity of human beings. According to the middle-eastern religions most influential in shaping western culture, humans are the crown of creation. They have a special role in God's plan, and their value far exceeds that of the rest of the created world. These views are echoed in the philosophical tradition in such writers as Descartes and Kant.[16] But if we reject the religious dogma which lurks in the background and instead embrace the naturalistic worldview of modern science, it is difficult to see how we can continue to defend this prejudice in favor of our own kind. Indeed, what we learn from Darwin and contemporary biology is that rather than being the crown of creation, we are one branch (of a branch) of evolution's tree, a small part of the story of life on earth. From this perspective what is striking is how much we share with other animals, not what distinguishes us from them. Our claim of moral superiority is nothing more than a transparent case of special pleading.

In my opinion, a series of thought-experiments counts decisively against the view that membership in a favored species is alone necessary and sufficient for membership in the moral community.

Imagine that the space program gets going again, and we succeed in visiting the outer reaches of the galaxy. On one planet (call it "Trafalmadore" in homage to the writer, Kurt Vonnegut), we encounter a highly sensitive and intelligent form of life. By any normal standards, Trafalmadoreans are superior to us in every way. They are more intelligent, knowledgeable, compassionate, sensitive, and so forth. However, they suffer from one "defect": evolution has followed its own course on Trafalmadore, and they are not members of our species. Would we think that we were therefore justified in gratuitously destroying their civilization (which is in every way superior to ours) and causing them great suffering (more intense than we can imagine), simply because they are not human?

Consider another example closer to home. As a matter of fact, anthropologists have recently claimed to have discovered a hominid species that

---

[16] The denigration of non-human consciousness has historically been one important strategy in the defense of speciesism. For discussion, see Jamieson 2002.

lived as recently as 18,000 years ago on the Indonesian island of Flores.[17] Like *Homo sapiens* of the same period, *Homo floresiensis* used tools and fire for cooking. Although they were quite small compared to *Homo sapiens* (they stood a little over 3 feet [1 metre] tall and have been nicknamed "hobbits"), the brain region which is associated with self-awareness is about the same size in *Homo floresiensis* as in modern humans.[18] Suppose that a remnant population of *Homo floresiensis* were discovered today, living on this large, rugged island. (There are anecdotal reports of *Homo floresiensis* surviving into the nineteenth century.) What would be the appropriate attitude for us to take towards them? Should we regard this as another rare hunting opportunity for Texas oil millionaires and Arab sheiks, or should we regard them as creatures to whom we owe moral respect?

Even closer to home, suppose that some remnant Neanderthals (*Homo neanderthalensis*) survived in remote regions of the world, slowly assimilating themselves to human culture and society. Despite the fact that they mingle with humans, they remain a reproductively isolated, distinct species.[19] They can recognize each other (perhaps by a secret handshake), but we cannot normally distinguish them from ourselves. Now suppose that somehow you discover that your roommate or the person whom you are dating is a member of this species. Do their moral claims on you suddenly vanish? Instead of taking your date to the movies, can you now take her to the local medical school to be used for vivisection?

I take it that most of us will agree in our answers to these questions. Trafalmadoreans, *Homo floresiensis*, and Neanderthals, as I have described them, all matter morally. The fact that they are not human is not sufficient for excluding them from from moral protection.

However, if this is not enough to persuade you, consider the fact that there are at least two distinct forms of speciesism. The version that we have been discussing, call it "*Homo sapiens*-centric speciesism," holds that

---

[17] This discovery was first reported by Brown *et al.* (2004) and Morwood *et al.* (2004). The claim that this constitutes a new species was challenged by Martin *et al.* (2006). The controversy continues, but it is unimportant for the purposes of our thought-experiment.

[18] Region 10 of the dorsomedial prefrontal cortex, for those who like to keep track of such things.

[19] Recent research suggests that Neanderthals may actually have hybridized with *Homo sapiens* (Evans *et al.* 2006). Whether or not this is true, it is clear that the differences between *Homo sapiens* and *Homo neanderthalensis* have often been exaggerated.

all and only members of the species, *Homo sapiens*, are members of the moral community. A second version, call it "indexical speciesism," holds that members of each species should hold that all and only members of their species are members of the moral community. The former principle would imply that Trafalmadoreans (for example) have a duty to sacrifice even their most fundamental interests for the trivial interests of human beings, while the latter principle would hold that Trafalmadoreans should hold that all and only Trafalmadoreans are members of the moral community. The former view seems preposterous. Why should Trafalmadoreans, who are superior to us in every way, hold that only members of some inferior species (*Homo sapiens*) matter morally? Surely the latter view, indexical speciesism, is more plausible. But on this view if Trafalmadoreans, *Homo floresiensis*, or Neanderthals were to cause utterly gratuitous, horrific suffering to humans, this would not be morally objectionable. We would be within our rights to resist them, but there would be no place for moral denunciation.[20]

Some philosophers would respond that while these thought-experiments may show that being human is not a necessary condition for membership in the moral community, nevertheless it still has some moral relevance.[21] They would distinguish "absolute speciesism," the view that holds that in virtue of being human, all and only humans are members of the moral community, from "moderate speciesism," which holds that in virtue of being human, humans are morally more important than non-humans. Moderate speciesism, it would be said, is consistent with our common responses to the thought-experiments. The main evidence for moderate speciesism (as opposed to anti-speciesism) is that as a matter of fact most of us feel that we owe more to humans than to non-humans.

The challenge for the opponent of moderate speciesism is to show either that our everyday convictions are in error, or that they are consistent with rejection of speciesism.

There are at least three reasons why someone who rejects speciesism might often prefer the interests of humans over those of other animals. First, they might hold (as does Peter Singer, as we will see in 5.3.2) that some forms of conscious life are more valuable than others, and these forms are

[20] In order to get a feel for what this might be like, rent the episode of the old television series, *Twilight Zone*, entitled "To Serve Man."
[21] Cf. Williams 2006 and Holland 1984.

typically manifested in humans but not in most other animals. John Stuart Mill, the nineteenth-century British philosopher, espoused just such a view when he claimed that it was better to be Socrates dissatisfied than a pig satisfied. He asserted this because he thought that any being (whether human, pig, God, or bacterium) who was capable of understanding what it was like to be both Socrates and the pig would come to the same conclusion. This claim, Mill thought, expressed a preference, not for humans over other animals, but for one kind of conscious life over another. A second reason why one might think that we owe more to humans than other animals is that many of our obligations arise from special relationships: through professional or familial obligations, promises, contracts, agreements, particular forms of dependency, and so on. While special relationships can exist between humans and other animals, such relationships between humans are at the very center of human society. Finally (and especially in light of these first two reasons) someone might think that we should follow the general practice of giving preference to humans over other animals because the stakes are high and we are likely to get it wrong by trying to work out the balance in particular cases. Failing to give our conspecifics their due might lead to an erosion of trust and a general unraveling of human society with all of its attendant advantages.

These arguments may not be all that persuasive. I myself have trouble taking the third one very seriously. I can't quite imagine a human society collapsing because, for example, Germans are giving way too much preference to bears and neglecting the interests of their fellow humans. Nevertheless, these arguments on behalf of systematically preferring humans to other animals are all consistent with the rejection of speciesism. The moderate speciesist must claim more. In addition to whatever preferences for humanity might be obtained on the basis of these considerations, there is a further preference as well, based simply on species membership. We should prefer Socrates dissatisfied to the pig satisfied not only because Socrates' psychological state is more valuable than that of the pig, but also because Socrates is human. I don't see an argument for this view. Moreover, it seems to me to be vulnerable to another thought-experiment as well as a further objection. First the thought-experiment.

Imagine two creatures (Dylan and Casey) whose psychologies are indistinguishable, as are the networks of relationships and the patterns of special obligations that obtain in their lives. Indeed, both of them may be friends of yours. In the case that we are imagining only two features distinguish Dylan and Casey. The first is that Dylan is suffering significantly more than Casey. The second is that only one of them is human but you do not know which. Suppose further that you can relieve the suffering of only one.

Do you know enough to decide whose suffering to relieve? Of course you do! You know that Dylan is suffering significantly more than Casey and that they are the same in all other respects that might be regarded as relevant (except, perhaps, species membership). The idea that you should be caught in indecision until you know where they fit in some biological taxonomy seems absurd. You know what you need to know to decide what to do: you should relieve Dylan's suffering. To suppose that you don't have enough information to decide until you know which of these otherwise indistinguishable creatures happens to be human would be to suppose that species membership alone is sufficient for making the suffering of one more morally significant than the suffering of the other, independent of all other factors including the intensity of the suffering.

However, the world (and philosophy) being as it is, I know that not everyone will agree. For those who do not, I have a further question for you.

Suppose that Dylan is suffering the torments of the fiery furnace while Casey has a hangnail. Do we know enough now to decide to relieve Dylan's suffering? Some will be unmoved by this example, and I suspect a little more pressure will show that they are not moderate speciesists, but absolute speciesists, and so subject to the arguments given earlier. But some will come over to my side in response to this example. They will say that species membership matters morally but not that much. But this invites a further question: How much exactly does species membership matter? Quite a lot hangs on the answer, since a moderate speciesist could have a view that is virtually indistinguishable from someone who rejects speciesism altogether, for she may think that species matters only when it comes to breaking ties (e.g. in the case in which the suffering of Dylan and of Casey is exactly the same). On the other hand a moderate speciesist might think that species differences do almost all the work in informing moral decision-making. It is clear that any answer to the question about exactly what moral difference species membership makes will face a difficult burden in saying why it matters exactly this much and not a little more or a little less. Rejecting this question, on the other hand, suggests an arbitrary, rather than principled, embrace of moderate speciesism.

To summarize, speciesism comes in (at least) two forms: absolute, and moderate. Absolute speciesism holds that species membership makes all the difference for mattering morally. Various thought experiments show that this view is implausible. Moderate speciesism holds that species membership makes some, but not all, the difference morally. It suffers from the inability to give a convincing account of what exactly this difference is, how much it matters, and why this is the case.

The rejection of speciesism in the writings of animal liberationist philosophers has two important features. First, what is of primary moral relevance is individuals and the properties they instantiate, not the fact that they may be members of various collectives or kinds.[22] Thus, for the purposes of morality, properties such as being a member of the Lions Club or a citizen of the United States are not in themselves of central moral relevance. Second, the individual characteristics that are morally relevant are not properties such as species, race and gender, but rather characteristics such as sentience, the capacity for desire, or self-consciousness. If we were to reduce the principal insight of anti-speciesism to a slogan it would be this: facts about biological classification do not determine moral status; to suppose otherwise is to commit the same fallacy as racists and sexists. It is wrong to kick me, not because I'm white, male, and human, but because it hurts.[23]

Even if we reject speciesism, as I think we should, the field is still quite open regarding the moral views that we should accept. In the next section we will discuss some of the most prominent views that have emerged in the wake of the rejection of speciesism.

5.2 Animals and moral theory

As I have already indicated, questions about moral relationships between humans and animals are ancient. However, since the 1970s our treatment of non-human animals has been subjected to a withering critique. The case is all the more compelling because it has been mounted from a broad range of moral perspectives. Kantians, consequentialists, and virtue ethicists have

---

[22] This feature is emphasized by James Rachels (1990), who argues persuasively that the roots of this insight are in the work of Charles Darwin.

[23] Of course, there may be other reasons why it's wrong to kick me, but this one is good for starters.

argued that many non-human animals have rights, that they should be respected as ends in themselves, or that the interests of humans and non-humans should be given equal consideration.[24]

In this section I will consider the two most influential versions of such theories: the utilitarianism of Peter Singer, and the rights-based theory of Tom Regan. While they agree about many (but not all) practical issues, there are important theoretical differences between them. Three are particularly important. The first has already been mentioned: Singer is a utilitarian in the tradition of Bentham and Mill, while Regan is a rights theorist in the tradition of Kant. Second, for Singer, the criterion for moral considerability is sentience; for Regan it is being "the subject of a life." Finally, Regan is an absolutist about some moral rules while Singer is not. These differences will become clear as we go on to examine these two philosophies.

5.2.1   Singer's animal liberation

Peter Singer's 1975 *Animal Liberation* is the single most influential book on the moral relations between humans and other animals. Inspired by the social movements of the 1960s and 1970s, Singer observed that the movements for black, women's, and gay liberation had at their heart a common demand for equality. To a great extent the book is an attempt to understand what kind of equality is at the heart of these liberation movements, and to extend this notion to animals.

What kind of equality do these movements demand? Certainly not equality of treatment, since equality does not require that if women have a right to abortion then so must men. Nor are these movements simply asserting the factual claim that everyone is equal. Such a claim would be false, since people are manifestly unequal in many respects, from their ability to sink a putt to their facility in cooking a tasty soufflé. It might be said in reply that everyone has equal potential to do anything that anyone can do. But this too is false. We are not all potential Einsteins. To take a more homely example, my potential to learn French really is not equal to that of some of my classmates. Yet, despite the fact that I am inferior to many people in this and many other ways, there is still some important respect in which we are all equal. What is that respect?

---

[24] For an overview of the broad range of anti-speciesist philosophies, visit <http://plato.stanford.edu/entries/moral-animal>.

The kind of equality that is central to liberation movements, according to Singer, is not factual equality, but moral equality; and the kind of moral equality that matters is the "equal consideration of interests."[25] Singer finds this principle in the utilitarian tradition. It is implicit, he thinks, in Bentham's slogan, "Each to count for one and none for more than one." It is what the nineteenth-century English philosopher Henry Sidgwick had in mind when he wrote that "the good of any one individual is of no more importance from the point of view . . . of the Universe than the good of any other."[26]

The principle of equal consideration of interests is often confused with other principles of equality. This principle does not say that all people – black or white, male or female – ought to be considered equally or equally considered. What the principle says is that the significance of an interest should not be discounted on the basis of whose interest it is. The interests of an octopus (for example) cannot be discounted relative to those of humans because of the sort of creature it is whose interests they are. The proper objects of equal consideration, according to this principle, are interests, not beings.

This raises the question of what interests are and how we can identify them. An interest can (roughly) be thought of as something such that its satisfaction makes its bearer better off and its frustration makes them worse off. Sentient beings generally have an interest in pleasure and the avoidance of pain.[27] For example, Vladimir Putin, an elephant, a fish, and I are all sentient beings; thus we have a common interest in pleasure and the avoidance of pain.

The principle of equal consideration of interests requires that our interests must be equally considered, regardless of who we are and what else may

---

[25] Singer takes utilitarianism's universalism (which we discussed in section 4.2) as implying the equal consideration of interests. There are other notions of moral equality that some philosophers would endorse instead of Singer's principle of equal consideration of interests. For an overview, visit <http://plato.stanford.edu/entries/equality>. Note also that Singer (1990: 5) misquotes Bentham. As we saw in section 4.2, the actual text is "Every individual in the country tells for one; no individual for more than one" (Bentham 1827: IV: 475).

[26] As quoted in Singer 1990: 5.

[27] Of course pleasure and the avoidance of pain may not be in a sentient being's interests on a particular occasion. For example, the pleasure of shooting heroin may not be in my interests, while suffering the pain of a life-saving operation may be.

be true of us. My interests cannot be discounted because I'm bad at French, Putin's interests cannot be discounted because he's Russian, the elephant's interest cannot be discounted because she's an animal, and the fish's interest cannot be discounted because he's a "mere" fish. However, it does not follow from this that the same sorts of things cause us pleasure and pain, or that the same pleasures and pains are of equal value.[28]

Consider some examples. Listening to Russian military music gives pleasure to Vladimir Putin but leaves the elephant cold. On the other hand, wallowing in a mudflat gives the elephant pleasure but doesn't do much for the fish. Being taken out of the water and left on dry land is horrific for the fish, but perfectly fine for me. I dig listening to Dick Dale, but surf music is not much to Putin's taste. Clearly different things cause us pleasure ("different strokes for different folks"). But even when we all experience what seem to be the same pleasures and pains, they may have different values. I believe that the pain of losing a mother is much greater for me than for the fish, but that the pain caused by noise pollution may be greater for the whale than for Putin.

As a utilitarian, Singer is committed to assessing acts by calculating the value of their consequences. He grants that it can be difficult to compare pleasures and pains across species, but points out that it can also be difficult to make such comparisons across humans. Would it be best, all things considered, for me to spend the evening with my family or to play my guitar in an amateur show at the senior citizens' center? It's not easy to tell what effect my guitar-playing would have on the happiness of these folks whom I've never met. Nevertheless, insofar as I am a utilitarian, I must make some rough and ready calculation that includes this consideration in order to decide what to do.

When it comes to our treatment of non-human animals, our moral mathematics does not have to be very sophisticated to see that much of what we do harms them much more than it benefits us. Can anyone really think that the pleasure that a human takes in eating *foie gras* (as opposed to eating, for example, *caviar d'aubergine*) really outweighs the misery caused to ducks and geese by force-feeding them until their livers swell and become

[28] How do we know when two beings share the same pain or the same kind of pain? What is it for them to do so? These are more good questions that have to be put aside for now.

dysfunctional, and they can no longer move? Whatever the theoretical difficulties involved in interspecies comparisons of pleasures and pains, this question, once asked, answers itself. Indeed, once we ask the questions and are willing to apply the principle of the equal consideration of interests, it is obvious that much of our treatment of animals in laboratories, factory farms, and zoos stands condemned.

At this point it may be difficult for us to understand how one and the same action can be seen from such radically different points of view. It would not occur to most people that McDonald's or the local zoo may well be the site of a major moral outrage. Yet this is how it looks to Singer.

Speciesism provides the explanation for the pervasiveness of our moral blindness with respect to the treatment of animals. Many of our practices persist only because we do not give the interests of animals equal consideration. We discount their suffering or ignore it all together. Indeed, in many cases, animals are almost entirely invisible from our moral deliberations. But once the prejudice of speciesism is overcome, we see that what we do to non-human animals is justified only if we are willing to do the same thing in the same circumstances to human beings as well. Most of us would rightly recoil in horror at such a thought. What this shows is not that we should get over it and start doing horrific things to humans, but rather that many of our practices with respect to animals cannot be justified from a non-speciesist point of view. And that is to say, they cannot be justified at all.

5.2.2   Regan's rights theory

Tom Regan defends the sanctity of human life, contrary to Singer. Contrary to most of the rest of us, he also defends the sanctity of a great deal of animal life as well. In his 1983 book, *The Case for Animal Rights*, Regan generalizes and extends some core notions of Kantian moral philosophy.[29] Regan's theory is ambitious and his book is densely argued. His story beings with the rejection of utilitarianism.

---

[29] As we saw in section 4.4, Christine Korsgaard also defends from a Kantian perspective the idea that humans have strong duties to other animals. A full comparison of the views of Regan and Korsgaard would be quite interesting, but cannot be pursued here.

The fundamental problem with utilitarianism, according to Regan, is that it sees individuals only as means rather than as ends. Individuals are valuable, from a utilitarian perspective, only insofar as they contribute to making the world better. They are "receptacles" of value rather than valuable in themselves. One only has to examine Singer's core principle, the principle of equal consideration of interests, to see that this is true. This principle takes interests as morally significant, rather than the individuals whose interests they are. According to Regan, this gets things exactly the wrong way round. The reason a being's interests matter is that the being matters. On Regan's view, value fundamentally inheres in individuals. In opposition to utilitarianism, Regan asserts the "Postulate of Inherent Value": individuals have value independently of their experiences and their value to others.

Regan goes on to claim that everything that has inherent value has it equally. The main argument for this is that the alternative view – that inherent value comes in degrees – is unacceptable. Such a view is unacceptable because it is "perfectionist." A perfectionist view is one in which a creatures' value varies according to the degree to which she exemplifies some favored qualities ("perfections"). Those with various "imperfections" (perhaps disabilities of various sorts) would be regarded as having less inherent value than those who are "more perfect." Presumably those with less inherent value could be sacrificed in order to benefit those with greater inherent value. Not only is such a view morally pernicious, according to Regan, but it simply recapitulates the mistakes of utilitarianism. So, according to Regan, everything that has inherent value has equal inherent value.

But what has inherent value? Everyone who is the "subject of a life" has inherent value, according to Regan. He characterizes a subject of a life in the following way:

> Individuals are subjects of a life if they have beliefs and desires; perception, memory, and a sense of the future, including their own future; an emotional life together with feelings of pleasure and pain; preference- and welfare-interests; the ability to initiate action in pursuit of their desires and goals; a psychophysical identity over time; and an individual welfare in the sense that their experiential life fares well or ill for them, logically independently of their utility to others.[30]

[30] Regan 1983: 243.

Regan wants to focus on the clear cases and not to get hung up on questions about exactly which creatures are subjects of a life and which are not. He intends this as a sufficient, but not a necessary, condition. Any being who satisfies this condition is the subject of a life, but there may be other creatures who are subjects of a life who do not satisfy this condition. He thinks that it is clear that all mammals over the age of one satisfy this condition. They are subjects of a life and thus have inherent value. Since everything that has inherent value has equal inherent value, all mammals over the age of one, human or non-human, have equal inherent value.

The Respect Principle is the bridge from value to duty (from an "is" to an "ought"). It implies that we have a duty to treat those individuals who have inherent value in a way that respects their inherent value. The Respect Principle implies the Harm Principle, which tells us that we must not harm those creatures who have inherent value, and that we must come to their defense when they are threatened by moral agents. This, in turn, implies a familiar set of basic moral rights, including rights to life, liberty, and freedom from torture.

These rights are not absolute, however. They may be overridden in cases of self-defense by the innocent, punishment of the guilty, "innocent shields," innocent threats, and what Regan calls "prevention cases." In cases of punishment and self-defense, those whose rights are overridden are not innocent: they have acted on the intention to harm others. Innocent shields and threats do not intend to harm us but we are permitted to do what is necessary to save our own lives. An example of an innocent shield case is one in which a guilty aggressor has taken an innocent hostage (e.g. he has strapped her to the front of his tank), and we can save our life only by killing the hostage. An innocent threat case is one in which we are threatened by an aggressor who is not functioning as an agent. This may be because of a breakdown in her capacity for agency (e.g. she suffers from a particular kind of mental illness), because she was never a functioning agent (e.g. she is a lion who seeks to have you for lunch), or because her agency is over- whelmed by an external force (e.g. a tornado is hurling her in your direction and will crush you if you don't blast her with your ray gun). In prevention cases we act, not to save ourselves, but to save others who would otherwise be harmed. When we act to save some we are allowed to harm only those who would be harmed even if we were to do nothing.

Serious questions have been asked about Regan's principles for overriding rights. I will briefly discuss prevention cases in order to convey some sense of the issues that are at stake.[31]

As an example of a prevention case, Regan asks us to consider fifty-one miners who are trapped in a cave-in. All will die if we do nothing. We can save fifty by killing one, or save one by killing fifty. What should we do? Regan invokes what he calls "the miniride principle":

> Special considerations aside, when we must choose between overriding the rights of many who are innocent or the rights of few who are innocent, and when each affected individual will be harmed in a prima facie comparable way, then we ought to choose to override the rights of the few in preference to overriding the rights of the many.[32]

What we should do, according to Regan, is to kill the one so that the fifty may live.

It is not difficult to agree with Regan's conclusion, but one may be suspicious of how he has arrived at it. The most plausible reason for believing that we should kill one so that fifty may live rests on an appeal to consequences. All fifty-one will die unless we act. The outcome would be better were we to kill one (or even fifty). This is certainly true, but it cannot be Regan's reason for telling us to kill an innocent miner. For he specifically rejects such consequentialist reasoning, telling us instead that the reason for overriding the rights of "the few is that this is what we must do if we are to show equal respect for the equal inherent value, *and* equal prima facie rights of the individuals involved."[33] What is puzzling is why killing any innocent miners at all is consistent with respecting their inherent value. Of course, the consequences would be worse if we were to kill no miners, but Regan and other anti-consequentialists often grant that the price of respecting rights comes at the price of allowing worse outcomes to come about.

A second kind of prevention case is one in which the harms that would be suffered are not comparable. Here, Regan asks us to imagine a case in which there are four normal humans and a dog on a lifeboat, and all will

---

[31] For further discussion see Jamieson 1990.   [32] Regan 1983: 305.
[33] Regan 1983: 307.

die unless one is thrown overboard. In this case, Regan thinks, the harms that would be suffered are not comparable, since "death for the dog though a harm is not comparable to the death of a human. This is because the magnitude of harm that death is is a function of the number and variety of opportunities for satisfaction it forecloses for a given individual."[34]

The principle that holds sway in cases such as this is the "worse-off principle." This principle states: "Special considerations aside, when we must decide to override the rights of the many or the rights of the few who are innocent, and when the harm faced by the few would make them worse-off than any of the many would be if any other option were chosen, then we ought to override the rights of the many."[35]

Because death for the dog would not be as great a harm as death for a human, it is the dog that must go. Indeed, it follows from this principle that any number of dogs must go in order to save the life of a human in such cases.

In a case like this, one feels as though the principle of equal inherent value is sliding from our grasp. Like the animals in George Orwell's book, *Animal Farm*, all animals are equal, but some animals are more equal than others.

We have already learned that moral philosophy is a difficult subject, and no single theory seems immediately satisfying in every respect. Every theory has its problems. Regan's theory also has great strengths. Indeed, one could reject everything he says about overriding rights and still be left with a theory that is quite sweeping in its scope. In its ambition, Regan's project is second to none. He gives us a chain of inference that moves from the rejection of utilitarianism to very strong claims about the rights of animals. If what he says is correct, then it is just as wrong to kill a cow as a human being. It is not surprising that there are places in this theory where one might balk.

5.3 Using animals

Humans use other animals for many different purposes. We use them in scientific experiments, in product testing, for amusement and entertainment. We care for them when they live in our homes as our companions, we

[34] Regan 1983: 351.   [35] Regan 1983: 308.

manage them when they live in nature, and we view them as commodities on farms and ranches. We bet on them at the track, laugh at them at the circus, fear them at the rodeo, and sometimes even act as their "stage mothers" in trying to get them on television.

These diverse, seemingly contradictory uses are endlessly fascinating. Of all the ways we use animals however, surely our most profound use, and the one with the greatest impact on all of us, is our use of them for food. Each year, globally, about 45 billion animals are killed for food. The United States kills about 10 billion of them, including 9 billion chickens and another billion cattle, pigs, sheep, and turkeys.[36] In the remainder of this chapter it is on this use of animals that I will focus.

5.3.1   Factory farming

The dominant system of animal agriculture in the United States, the European Union, and increasingly the rest of the world is usually called "factory farming."[37] This system is designed to produce the greatest amount of meat at the lowest possible cost. Factory farms are typically very large scale, with each element of the system tightly controlled. Animals are closely confined, fed highly processed food, and routinely dosed with hormones, antibiotics, and other drugs. They are viewed as no more than one factor of production, alongside other factors such as energy, water, and labor. The grain which animals are fed is produced in the same way. Vast monocultures are planted, fertilizers, pesticides, and moisture applied, labor is minimized, and little attention is paid to the ecological system in which these operations are embedded.

Factory farming is the most successful system in the history of the world in maximizing food production while minimizing labor. At the beginning of the twentieth century, 40% of the American workforce was involved in

---

[36] These figures are based on data from the United Nations Food and Agriculture Organization and the United States Department of Agriculture, and are widely available on the web (e.g. at <www.armedia.org/farmstats.htm>). They exclude aquatic animals, since their deaths are typically expressed in weight rather than number.

[37] Other terms are used, including 'industrial agriculture' and 'intensive agriculture'. The US Department of Agriculture uses the expression, 'concentrated animal feeding operation'. It should also be noted that the European Union is moving away from the most extreme practices involved in factory farming, especially as they affect animal welfare. For more on this visit <www.ari-online.org>; for discussion, see Singer and Mason 2006.

agriculture. By the end of the century the number had shrunk to 2%. Yet, since 1930, agricultural output has quadrupled.[38] Consumers have benefited from this productivity in lower food prices. As late as 1950 Americans spent about 22% of their disposable income on food, while today they spend about 7%. In 1928 President Herbert Hoover promised to put a "chicken in every pot." Today the average American eats 190 pounds of meat per year, more than anyone else in the world.[39]

There is a large, dark side to this increase in productivity, one aspect of which is the disappearance of the family farm and the resulting economic and social disruptions. The extinction of the traditional farm economy has led to depopulating large areas of the American Midwest. The new agricultural economy is highly concentrated. Today, only 3% of hog farms are responsible for 50% of production. Two percent of the nation's feedlots "finish" 40% of all cattle.[40] The top four companies in each industry control approximately 79% of beef-packing, 57% of pork-packers, and 42% of turkey slaughter. Just one company, Tyson foods, slaughtered more than two billion chickens in 2001 alone. Slaughterhouse jobs, which were once well compensated, are increasingly dangerous and low paid. The migrant workers who now dominate them are seen, like animals, as nothing more than another factor of production.[41]

The environmental costs of factory farming are also very high. In 1996 the US cattle, pork, and poultry industries produced 1.4 billion tons of animal waste, 130 times more than was produced by the entire human population. While some of the manure is used to fertilize crops, most is stored in large pits or "lagoons" where it poses serious threats to land, air, and water quality. The US Environmental Protection Agency has designated 60% of US rivers and streams as "impaired," and cited agriculture runoff as the major factor.[42] In just one three-year period (1995-8), pollution from the hog and chicken industries was responsible for killing more than one billion fish.[43]

Cattle production also contributes heavily to air pollution. Cows produce, as a byproduct of digestion, volatile organic compounds (VOCs) that are chemically active in producing smog. California's San Joaquin Valley,

---

[38] <http://eh.net/encyclopedia/article/gardner.agriculture.us>.

[39] <www.ers.usda.gov/publications/sb965/sb965f.pdf>. Fifty-seven pounds of an American's average annual consumption of meat consists of chicken.

[40] "Finishing cattle" refers to fattening them on high-calorie foods just prior to slaughter.

[41] On slaughterhouse working conditions, see Eisnitz 1997 and Schlosser 2001.

[42] <www.hfa.org/factory>.   [43] <www.factoryfarm.org/resources/factsheets>.

America's richest agricultural heartland, has some of America's worst air quality, with its 2.5 million cows being the largest contributors. According to the San Joaquin Valley United Air Pollution Control District, each cow in the valley annually contributes more VOCs than an automobile or light truck.[44] In addition to contributing to smog, cows also contribute to climate change by producing 50% of the world's methane, a greenhouse gas that is twenty times more powerful than carbon dioxide.

Antibiotics are another major pollutant produced by factory farms. Of the fifty million pounds of antibiotics used in the US each year, twenty million are given to animals, most of it (80%) being used to promote rapid growth. The remaining 20% is used to help control diseases that occur when animals are closely confined, including anemia, influenza, intestinal diseases, mastitis, metritis, orthostasis, and pneumonia. Many of these antibiotics find their way into waterways, where they contribute to creating strains of drug-resistant bacteria, an increasingly serious health problem for human beings.[45]

Food is energy, and what an agricultural system does is to cycle energy from one trophic level to another, producing food calories from inputs such as water, nitrogen, and fossil fuels.[46] When assessing the environmental consequences of an agricultural system, in addition to the pollution it produces, the broader impacts on global cycles must be taken into account. How does our current system of factory farming fare when viewed from this perspective?

The most important feature of our current system, from this point of view, is that most of the food that is produced is not directly consumed by humans but fed to other animals who are then consumed by humans. Since the rule of thumb in ecology is that about 90% of energy is lost in moving up a trophic level (e.g. from plants to animals), it is obvious that this system is massively inefficient. In order to function, it requires overproduction of both grain and animals, involving huge inputs of fossil fuels, water, and nitrogen fertilizer.

On average, animal protein production in the US requires 28 calories of energy input for every calorie of protein produced for human consumption.

[44] <http://news.nationalgeographic.com/news/2005/08/0816_050816_ cowpollution.html>.

[45] <www.sciencenews.org/articles/20020629/bob7.asp>.

[46] Trophic levels are locations in a hierarchical food chain. For example, green plants are primary producers, herbivores form the second trophic level, while carnivores form the third and fourth trophic levels.

Beef and lamb are the most costly, in terms of fossil fuel energy input to protein output at 54:1 and 50:1, respectively. Turkey and chicken production require 13:1 and 4:1, respectively. The result is that 80% of the grain produced in the United States each year is fed to animals, resulting in the loss of about 34 million tons of protein. David Pimentel calculates that it takes nearly twice as much fossil energy to produce a typical American diet than a pure vegetarian diet. This works out to about an extra 150 gallons of fossil fuels per year for a meat-eater. When we look at how much extra fuel it takes to feed them, meat-eaters are effectively "driving" an extra eleven miles every day whether they really drive or not.[47] A recent study shows that the average American family would more effectively reduce their greenhouse gas emissions by adopting a vegan diet (one that uses no animal products), than by switching to a hybrid car.[48]

Factory farming is even more wasteful of water than fossil fuels. Agriculture accounts for 87% of all the fresh water consumed each year in the United States. It takes 25 gallons of water to produce one pound of grain, and 2,500 gallons to produce one pound of meat. When water shortages occur, citizens are often requested to not wash cars or water lawns, and to use low-flow shower heads. However, cutting back on meat consumption would save much more water than these sacrifices. Ten pounds of steak equals the water consumption of the average household for a year.

As a consequence of using huge amounts of fertilizer to produce the grain required to feed animals, humans are now the most important influence on the global nitrogen cycle.[49] Much of the nitrogen that is dumped on crops runs into the water and soil, where it reacts chemically to form nitrogen oxides, or flows off to fertilize something else. Nitrous oxide is a greenhouse gas that is 310 times more powerful than carbon dioxide, and is also involved in creating acid rain. Much of the fertilizer runs into streams and creeks, eventually into rivers, and then into the sea, creating large algae blooms that suck all the oxygen from the water, killing most forms of marine life. There is a "dead zone" the size of New Jersey at the mouth of the Mississippi River in the Gulf of Mexico that was created by this process.

[47] Much of the information in this and the following paragraph is taken from Pimental and Pimental 2003, but similar material is widely available in recent books by Singer and Mason (2006) and Polland (2006), and on websites such as <http://bicycleuniverse.info/transpo/beef.html>.

[48] Eshel *et al.* 2006.   [49] <www.esa.org/science/Issues/FileEnglish/issue1.pdf>.

One wonders how it will end, since it is almost unimaginable that the Earth could support even its current population of more than 6.6 billion with these agricultural practices. Yet factory farming is spreading to the developing world, along with increasing meat consumption. Mexico now feeds 45% of its grain to livestock, up from 5% in 1960. Egypt went from 3% to 31% in the same period, and China, with a fifth of the world's population, has gone from 8% to 26%.[50] According to the United Nations Food and Agriculture Organization, global meat production will more than double by 2050, with dairy production increasing by almost as much.[51] Livestock currently use 30% of Earth's land surface and is a major driver of deforestation, especially in Latin America, where some 70% of forests in the Amazon have been cleared and the land used for grazing. When it comes to global greenhouse gas emissions, livestock production accounts for a larger fraction than transport.

Thus far we have mainly been discussing the broad ecological effects of factory farming, but the impacts on animals' welfare and suffering are both huge and visceral. Animals in factory farms live terrible lives, and nothing I can say adequately reflects the realities involved. I encourage you to visit factory farms or slaughterhouses. Failing that, there are numerous videos on the web that will allow you a peek (for example, at <www.meat.org>). Sometimes people think that we should not view such images because they appeal to the emotions rather than reason. I think that avoiding these images is a way of trying to deceive ourselves about what actually goes on in such places.[52] Rather than trying to conjure up what cannot adequately be represented, I will simply describe a little of what it is like for chickens who are raised for food in contemporary America. I tell a little about their story rather than that of other animals only because they are the ones who are are most commonly slaughtered for food. Is factory farming worse for chickens, cows, or pigs? I don't know, but I do know that it is plenty bad for all of them.[53]

---

[50] <www.harpers.org/TheOilWeEat.html>.

[51] This report is available on the web at <www.virtualcentre.org/en/library/key_pub/ longshad/A0701E00.htm>.

[52] For discussion of this point see Jenni 2005.

[53] For what factory farming is like for other animals raised for food, see Eisnitz 1997 or visit various websites such as <www.hfa.org/hot_topic/slaughterhouse.html>.

"Broilers" (the name for chickens who are raised primarily for their meat) live little more than six weeks. (Their natural life-span is 6–12 years.) Their lives begin in a hatchery, where they are "sexed," vaccinated and "debeaked." Debeaking involves using a white-hot blade to slice off a large portion of the beak. This is done without pain relief. The beak is a highly sensitive organ with which chickens explore the world, but it is also used in pecking and even cannibalizing other chickens when they are stressed. The chicks are then sent from the hatchery to contract farms where they are kept in "growing-houses," which contain up to 20,000 chickens, each with about a sheet of computer paper for space. This is not enough room for a chicken to flap or even stretch her wings, preen, or turn around. Growing-houses are usually windowless and barren, except for litter material on the floor and rows of feeders and drinkers. Everything is automatic. Lights are on 22 hours per day to facilitate eating. After about 45 days, the chickens have reached market weight, and most suffer from chronic and acute structural problems due to the enormous, rapid weight gain.[54] "Catching teams" arrive and stuff about 1,000–1,500 birds per hour into crates for transport to the slaughterhouse. During the journey, the chickens are not given food, water, or protection from extreme temperatures. Once they arrive, they are herded into a dim room where they are hung by their feet from metal shackles on a moving rail. Their heads are dunked in an electrified water bath in order to immobilize them and expedite assembly-line killing (the US government does not require that chickens be rendered unconscious before they are slaughtered). An automated, rotary blade cuts their throats at a rate of more than one bird per second. The chickens that survive are killed by hand. They are bled in a blood tunnel, defeathered in a scalding tank, and disassembled. They are bagged and cooled to inhibit bacterial growth, and within 50 minutes of arrival at the slaughterhouse, they are in a box on the way to a supermarket or restaurant.[55]

---

[54] To put the growth rate of today's chickens into perspective, consider this statement from a report from the University of Arkansas Division of Agriculture: "If you grew as fast as a chicken, you'd weigh 349 pounds at age 2" (available on the web at <www.kidsarus.org/kids_go4it/growit/raiseit/chickens.htm>, visited February 19, 2007).

[55] This account is based on the following sources: <http://query.nytimes.com/gst/fullpage. html?res=9405E7D71538F93AA35751C1A962948260&sec=health&pagewanted=print>; Singer and Mason 2006; <www.hsus.org/farm/resources/research/welfare/broiler_industry. html>.

This is the best that a chicken can hope for. However, a system that slaughters 9 billion chickens per year has a predictable error rate. Many chickens do not survive the growing-houses or transport to the slaughterhouse. Since stunning procedures in the slaughterhouse are not monitored, they are often inadequate. Because of concerns that too much electricity would damage the carcasses and diminish their value, the electrical current is commonly set lower than what is required to render the birds unconscious. The result is that while birds are immobilized after stunning, they are still capable of feeling pain, and many emerge from the stunning tank still conscious. Since slaughter lines run at speeds of up to 8,400 chickens per hour, workers or machines sometimes fail to cut both carotid arteries, which can add two minutes to the time required for birds to bleed to death. As a result, birds may be conscious when they enter the tanks of scalding water that are used to loosen their feathers. One study found that up to 23% of broilers were still alive when they entered scalding tanks.[56]

When matters are clearly laid out in this way, it is difficult to see how anyone could defend such practices. Indeed, in my experience, few will defend them. Nevertheless, most of the meat that we eat continues to be produced in the way that I have described. Whatever reservations one may have about factory farming in an environmental ethics class tend to fade by dinnertime. The fact is, these practices continue because they have widespread political and consumer support (or at least acceptance).

5.3.2   Killing versus causing pain

It is natural to ask, at this point, whether there is a moral distinction between killing animals, and causing them pain. Would it be permissible for us to use animals for food if we make sure that they have happy lives and are painlessly killed?

Different moral theories answer this question in different ways. Tom Regan, as we have seen, thinks that animals (at least adult mammals) have a right to life that is every bit as stringent as the one that you or I enjoy. No one would think that if we were treated well, then it would be permissible to painlessly kill us. Our right to life is distinct from, and additional to, our right not to be harmed. Both rights must be respected, not traded

[56] Gregory and Wotton 1986.

off against each other. The implications of this view for factory farming are clear. According to Regan:

> The fundamental moral wrong here is not that animals are kept in stressful close confinement . . . or that they have their pain and suffering, their needs and preferences ignored or discounted . . . They are symptoms . . . of the deeper, systematic wrong that allows these animals to be viewed and treated as lacking independent value, as resources for us. . . . Nothing less than the total dissolution of commercial animal agriculture will do.[57]

Regan's view is demanding: no matter how well we treat animals, it is wrong to kill them for food. Some will want to reject Regan's philosophy because they don't like this conclusion, just as some would like to reject utilitarianism because they find it too demanding. But the first law of philosophy is this: it cannot be the case that the only mistake in an argument is that the conclusion is false. If you reject an argument's conclusion, then you have an obligation to find a flaw in the reasoning or a falsehood in the premises. When it comes to doing philosophy, there is no substitute for engaging with the arguments.

Singer's utilitarianism is more receptive to the possibility that killing animals for food may be morally permissible. In principle, what matters to a utilitarian such as Singer is the total value of the world rather than the identity or welfare of the particular individuals who happen to inhabit it.[58] Thus it would seem that it might be permissible to painlessly kill animals for food, so long as we replace them with other animals who are just as happy and would otherwise not have lived. While something like this view may follow from some versions of utilitarianism, characterizing it precisely and defending it persuasively are not easy.

For Singer, as we have seen, sentience is both necessary and sufficient for moral considerability. All and only sentient beings' interests, and all of their interests, must be equally considered. However, it does not follow from this that all sentient beings or all interests are equally valuable.

Some sentient beings are self-conscious; in Singer's vocabulary, they are "persons." Other sentient beings are not self-conscious; they are non-persons,

---

[57] Regan 1985: 24–5.

[58] Some consequentialists (including some utilitarians) say that what matters is the average welfare of individuals rather than the total welfare in the world. See Hurka 1992 for an overview that shows that each view faces serious objections.

what I will call "simple" creatures. This distinction between persons and simple creatures marks an important psychological and moral difference, according to Singer.

Persons experience the world, and some of these experiences are pleasurable (or more broadly, pleasant) and others are painful (or more broadly, unpleasant). Moreover, persons experience themselves as having such experiences. Since they see themselves as subjects that persist through time, persons can have attitudes towards their past, and desires about their future. Simple creatures also experience the world, and some of these experiences are pleasurable and others are painful. What simple creatures do not experience is themselves as experiencing the world, or themselves as having pleasurable or painful experiences. Simple creatures do not see themselves as beings with a past and future, whose experiences are knitted together in virtue of having themselves as a common subject. These differences in the psychological capacities of persons and simple creatures give rise to differences regarding how their lives can go better and worse.

The lives of simple creatures go better when they experience pleasure, and go worse when they experience pain. There is no more to it than that. Persons, on the other hand, have an additional source of both value and disvalue. Because they see themselves as persisting through time, they can have desires about the future (as opposed to, say, attractions and aversions). When their desires are satisfied, their lives go better; when their desires are frustrated, their lives go worse.

Among the desires that persons normally have is the desire to continue living. Thus, it is normally bad for a person to be killed, even painlessly, because this frustrates one of her desires. Simple creatures, on the other hand, have no desires for continued life because they have no awareness of having a life in the first place. Thus, painlessly killing a simple creature does not frustrate a desire that she has, so her life does not go worse as a consequence. This would seem to open up the possibility that such creatures can be painlessly slaughtered and used for food.

However, many are troubled by the fact that the distinction between persons and simple creatures is not the same as the distinction between humans and other animals. All of the Great Apes, not just humans, are good candidates for personhood on this view, as are some cetaceans, including dolphins. Among the animals normally eaten for food, pigs are the most likely to qualify as persons (although Singer suggests that all normal, adult mammals may be persons).[59] On the other hand, newborn infants and severely brain-damaged humans of all ages would not count as persons, for they do not see themselves as persisting through time. If what we are contemplating is killing simple creatures for food, it would appear that there are some humans who could wind up in the slaughterhouse while some animals who are currently used for food would escape.

Some are skeptical about whether this account can provide even persons with anything like a right to life. First, there is the charge that for a utilitarian like Singer, no right to life can be very strong, since whether or not it is permissible to kill someone always depends on the consequences of doing so, and consequences are highly sensitive to contexts and circumstances that may change. But second, it is hard to see why being self-conscious makes some creature irreplaceable rather than simply raising the price of replacing her. Remember that happy simple creatures cannot be killed willy-nilly. Such killing can only be justified if they are replaced by creatures who are just as happy and who would otherwise not have existed. But what if a person who prefers to live is painlessly killed and replaced by a person who would otherwise not have lived, but who prefers to live once she comes into existence? From "the point of view of the universe," it is hard to see why one should object.

At this point it is important to remember another feature of utilitarianism. Our duty is not merely to avoid reducing value, but actually to maximize it. It is a necessary condition for the permissibility of painlessly killing simple creatures that they are replaced by creatures who are at least as happy but who would otherwise not have lived. But this is not a sufficient condition. If there is another action or practice that is open to us that produces more value, then we are obligated to embrace it. So even if painlessly killing and then replacing simple creatures would not make the world worse, becoming vegetarian might actually make the world better. If this is the case, then killing and replacing simple animals would be wrong from a utilitarian perspective.

Moreover, as we learned from Kant, there are reasons for protecting the lives of beings beyond what is owed to them directly as individuals. Most of us would be horrified at the idea of the family dog being used by someone for food. Similarly, most of us have strong sentimental attachments to our

[59] Singer 1993: 87, 132.

conspecifics, whatever the exact structure of their consciousness. We also worry about "slippery slopes": today it is humans who are simple creatures in the slaughterhouse, but who knows whether it will be persons tomorrow? But perhaps our unwillingness to kill humans who are simple creatures is not really a matter of these "indirect" effects, but rather indicates that in some way we believe that they have a "right to life," even though they are not persons. But what would be the basis of such a belief? If humans who are simple beings have a right to life, should not the same be true of other animals who are simple beings? At this point Regan's argument begins to look more plausible.

5.3.3   The conscientious omnivore

Despite the questions and objections that one can raise, Singer's perspective does seem to leave open a possibility that is closed by Regan and that many people find attractive: the idea of the "conscientious omnivore."[60] A conscientious omnivore eats meat, but only if the ecological consequences of doing so are acceptable, and the animals have had good lives and painless deaths. Each consideration raises its own questions.

When it comes to ecological consequences, certain kinds of hunting are vastly superior to eating factory-farmed meat. Indeed, some would say that from an ecological point of view it is better to eat a wild animal whose kind is not endangered, such as an elk or a deer, than a veggie burger or some other vegetarian alternative.[61] Growing soybeans for tofu is to some extent ecologically destructive, while obtaining meat from (the right kind of) hunting simply involves exploiting nature's processes of self-renewal. Of course, if the vegetarian alternative involves food-gathering rather than agriculture, then this kind of hunting would have no ecological advantage over vegetarianism. Moreover, the ecological advantage of hunting can be lost if the prey animals are to any extent grain-fed (e.g. through winter feeding), or if the landscape is modified in order to affect herd size or to make hunting easier or more attractive. These practices introduce elements of (what

---

[60] The expression is from Singer and Mason 2006, but the most prominent advocate is Pollan (2006).

[61] Better still, some would say, would be hunting an animal which is itself ecologically destructive, such as feral pigs in much of the world. See section 6.5.2 for discussion of some ethical issues in relation to exotic animals.

is, in effect) agriculture into what otherwise would purely be a matter of hunting.

In addition to its ecological acceptability, hunting wild animals whose kind is not endangered seems to score well with respect to animals' quality of life prior to being killed. Either animals who are killed have had good lives, or hunting them would be an act of mercy. Moreover, since we are assuming that the hunted animals are part of a naturally sustainable population, it is reasonable to suppose that the ecological space cleared by hunting would be filled by new animals coming into existence who would otherwise not have lived. There is no reason to believe that the lives of these new animals will be any less good than those of the animals they replace.

What about the character of the animals' deaths? There are various conflicting stereotypes about deaths caused by hunters. Many hunters would have you believe that they are the noblest and most ethical of humans: every kill is a clean kill; otherwise they wouldn't have taken the shot. On the other hand, those who oppose hunting often portray hunters as drunken louts, indifferent to animal suffering. The fact of the matter is that it is very difficult to obtain reliable, quantitative information about how much animals suffer when killed by hunters for food. Some, no doubt, suffer a great deal, while others are killed painlessly.

Whatever the case with how hunted animals die, there are other ethical concerns that one might have about this kind of hunting. Even if you reject Regan's view that (at least) all adult mammals have a strong right to life, you might still worry that many of the animals killed in hunting are persons in Singer's sense, with a desire to continue living. You might also have concerns that have their source in virtue ethics (discussed in 4.3). Even if there are no other objections to be made, do we really want to encourage widespread participation in killing?

However we answer such questions, it is clear that this way of being a conscientious omnivore does not play a significant role in how meat is generally obtained in industrial societies. Even if they believe that it would be ethical to do so, many people shrink from hunting for their own food. Moreover, opportunities for this kind of hunting are rare, and will become increasingly so in the future as human populations continue to grow and wildlife populations become even more intensely managed.

What being a conscientious omnivore means to most people is buying organic food, purchasing "happy" eggs from free-range chickens, and obtaining meat from animals who have had good lives and are humanely slaughtered before presenting themselves at the meat counter. However appealing and even romantic this vision may be, it is morally much riskier than the kind of hunting that I have described.

Generally, in the United States, it is quite uncertain exactly what one is buying when one buys organic meat, milk, or free-range eggs. In many cases there are no government standards, or they are only now being developed, often in a vortex of political controversy and negotiation. The actual labels that appear on products are often placed by manufacturers, or are certified by voluntary associations or trade groups. There is no assurance that what they mean by terms such as 'natural' or 'humane' is what a conscientious consumer might expect. Even where government standards exist, they are often vague and compliance is not monitored.[62]

Since 2002 when the United States Department of Agriculture adopted organic standards there have been no fines or prosecutions for violations, and the Department is unable to say how many violations have occurred, although many have been documented by journalists, agricultural experts, and others. Much of the production for the American organic market occurs in China or Latin America, where there is almost no effective oversight.

Many examples can be given of the vagueness of the standards but here is one that is particularly important for conscientious omnivores. The standards require that livestock have "access to pasture," but they are silent about how much pasture, for how long, or what fraction of an animal's diet must come from grazing. As a result there is a great deal of variation in actual practices. There are producers selling organic products from cows who live with as many as 6,000 other animals and seldom see pasture, and there are farms where non-organic cows are brought in as replacements and where antibiotics and hormones are used.

Moreover, many of the animals slaughtered for food (e.g. virtually all chickens and pigs) will have been fed grain as part of their diet at some point in their life cycle. Thus, to some extent, the ecological impacts of factory farming will be implicated in this way as well.

At the very least, we say this: much of the industry that appeals to compassionate omnivores is quite different from what many people imagine. To a great extent it recapitulates the structure of factory farming. Most organic

---

[62] "Is Organic Food the Real Deal?," *The Dallas Morning News*, July 17, 2006, available at <www.dallasnews.com/sharedcontent/dws/dn/latestnews/stories/071606dnccoorganics. 19c550e.html>.

goods are produced on large farms, shipped long distances, prepackaged, and distributed through large, centralized networks. Indeed, some of the largest organic producers are subsidiaries of the food-processing giants.

Still, it seems clear that from an ecological perspective that consuming these products is better than consuming products from factory farms, though it is difficult to say how much better. Quality of life for farm animals is probably better too, though again it is difficult to say how much better, especially given the wide range of variation.

Finally, there is the question of painless slaughter. Most of the standards that have been established, either by government or by voluntary associations, pay relatively little attention to slaughter. Yet we know that painlessly killing a conscious being is extremely difficult. One of the controversies surrounding the death penalty in the United States concerns whether it is possible to administer it in a painless way. These are cases in which a large amount of state resources are mobilized in killing a single human being under precisely controlled scientifically monitored conditions. Chickens and pigs are not normal humans in terms of their psychological sophistication, but they are certainly aware and sensitive; and the task of creating a system of mass commercial slaughter is orders of magnitude more difficult than attempting a single painless killing. Whatever else may be true, we cannot assume that the animals we eat have been painlessly slaughtered, even if they have enjoyed relatively good lives up to that point.

More surprising, given the great amount of attention that the conscientious omnivore enjoys, is what a small fraction of the population she represents. Both globally and in the United States, only 1–2% of all the food that is marketed even purports to be organic. The amount of meat produced from animals who have led happy lives and been painlessly slaughtered is certainly much lower than that. Despite the hype, not many people could really be following the diet of a conscientious omnivore: there is just not that much food available that even claims to pass any ethical test. Perhaps this will change in the future, but given the increasing concentration in the food industry and the resistance to regulation, it is certainly not obvious that this is so, at least in the United States.

The lack of effective options for many people who might want to follow the life of the conscientious omnivore gives rise to another problem: the possibility of moral corruption. The line between eating meat and not eating meat is very bright; the distinction between eating meat from humanely raised and slaughtered animals, and the products of factory farms, is not so distinct. A conscientious omnivore might easily slip into becoming a normal consumer by something like the following route. The conscientious omnivore prefers to eat meat to being vegetarian. She prefers meat from animals who have been humanely raised and slaughtered, and when it is available this is what she eats. However, on particular occasions when it is not available she might think of eating factory farmed animals as a "second-best" choice, better than not eating meat at all. She might even think something like this: "Since it is permissible on some occasions to eat some meat, it couldn't be that bad for me to eat this meat now." However, if the choice that is regularly presented to her is between factory-farmed meat and no meat at all, she may slide into the life of a normal consumer while thinking of herself as a conscientious omnivore.

One version of being a conscientious omnivore observes a bright line between the kinds of animals who can be consumed. This kind of conscientious omnivore refuses to eat land animals, but will eat some seafood. The argument for this is that marine creatures are psychologically simpler than the land animals we use for food, that they live freely before they are caught and killed, and that eating seafood is more ecologically responsible than eating land animals. I will discuss these claims in turn.

First, it is quite difficult to assess consciousness in creatures who are as different from us and as diverse among themselves as marine animals. Since the lineages of mammals and marine creatures separated so long ago, many anatomical structures, including brain structures, are quite different. However, we know that evolution often produces different structures with similar functions through different evolutionary processes (this is known as "convergent evolution"). Thus, from a purely biological point of view, there is no reason why psychological states characteristic of mammals and other land animals should not occur in marine creatures as well.

Indeed, it is almost certain that they do. Octopuses, cuttlefish, and squid are mollusks whose ancestors separated from our vertebrate ancestors (which include fish) between 600 million and one billion years ago.[63] Yet they are widely regarded as cognitive creatures, displaying foresight,

[63] Although it is extremely difficult to date points of separation in evolutionary lineages precisely, it appears that our last common ancestor with pigs was about 95 million years ago, and with chickens about 200 million years ago.

planning, play, and perhaps even tool use. They learn to solve mazes, learn cues, and remember solutions. A leading scientist has stated that octopuses "very likely have the capacity for pain and suffering and, perhaps, mental suffering."[64] Captive cuttlefish have been shown to respond positively to environmental enrichment. However, clams and oysters, their fellow mollusks, appear to be at the other end of the spectrum. Almost no one regards them as sentient or cognitive, though these passive filter feeders have simple nervous systems.

The ancestors of today's fish and mammals divided about 400 million years ago. Fish are also extremely diverse, but generally they have well-developed nervous systems organized around a central brain that is divided into different parts. Much of the brain appears to be devoted to processing sensory input and coordinating body movement. Most fish possess highly developed sense organs, and many have extraordinary senses of taste and smell. Many fish also have receptors that allow them to detect currents and vibrations, as well as to sense the motion of other nearby fish and prey. Some fish, such as catfish and sharks, have organs that detect low-level electric current. Other fish, like the electric eel, can produce their own electricity. In experimental settings, fish have displayed substantial memory, the ability to learn by observing other fish, and the ability to cooperate. Fish often behave in ways that are consistent with supposing that they are in pain, and most scientists agree that fish are sentient.[65]

Does this add up to evidence for the claim that marine animals are psychologically simpler than the land animals we use for food? This is a difficult question to answer. The answer is probably no for octopuses, cuttlefish, and squid, and certainly yes for oysters and clams. When it comes to fish, the answer might depend on which land animal we are comparing them to. In any case, the answer would not be very clear.

When it comes to quality of life, the wild-caught marine creatures who currently make up two-thirds of the global seafood supply clearly do much better than land animals raised for food. However, their deaths are often

---

[64] Mather 2001: 155. For more on cephalopods see <www.cephbase.utmb.edu>, accessed February 20, 2007; for an overview, visit <www.discover.com/issues/oct-03/features/feateye>.

[65] For popular accounts visit <www.awionline.org/pubs/Quarterly/05_54_04/05_54_4p19.htm> and <www.commondreams.org/views06/1008-26.htm>. See also Chandroo *et al.* 2004.

much worse, since they are usually left to suffocate slowly after being pulled from the water, or they are crushed to death by the weight of other creatures who have been caught in the same net.

In any case, the wild-caught fraction of the global seafood supply is dropping rapidly (it was 97% in 1970), and will continue to drop as a consequence of overfishing. What is occurring in the oceans is what previously occurred on land. Just as human action radically transformed grasslands, forests, and other terrestrial ecosystems, so we are now in the process of systematically altering marine ecosystems. From 1950 to 1994, global fish production increased by 400% and has been stable or dropping since then. Sixty percent of the earth's marine fish stocks are now considered fully or overexploited, and one influential study claims that commercial fishing has wiped out 90% of the ocean's large fish.[66]

Fish farming (also known as "aquaculture") is the future of seafood production. Fish farming should be thought of as a kind of factory farming. The methods, goals, and principles are the same, and so are many of the consequences.

Like land animals in factory farms, fish on fish farms live very short lives in high-density environments, and are fed and medicated with a view to maximizing production and minimizing costs. Uninhibited by government regulations, fish are often starved before slaughter, and no attempt is made to stun them before killing them. Slaughtering methods including clubbing, gill-cutting, and suffocation.

Pollution from fish farms is a serious problem. The World Wide Fund for Nature has shown that Scottish salmon farms produce twice as much waste as the human population of that country.[67] There is also evidence of fish farms introducing disease and parasites into wild fish stocks. Especially worrisome is the possibility that fish who escape from farms will affect the genetics of wild populations.

As we saw in chapter 1, environmental problems often involve negative feedbacks. In response to a problem, we often act in a way that exacerbates it. For example, in response to global warming we increase our use of air

---

[66] Myers and Worm 2003. A less bleak study is Sibert *et al.* 2006. There are many sources available on overfishing, but a good place to start is with the factsheet based on United Nations Food and Agricultural Organization statistics, available on the web at <www.greenfacts.org/fisheries/index.htm#3>.

[67] Cited in Singer and Mason 2006: 123.

conditioners, which contributes further to global warming, and so on. Similarly, fish farming is partly a response to collapsing fisheries, but in turn it contributes to their further collapse.

Fish farming, like other forms of factory farming, is extremely inefficient; indeed, especially so, since the creatures most commonly raised on fish farms are carnivores.[68] They must be fed fishmeal rather than vegetable matter. Thus, eating farm-raised tuna, salmon, trout, or shrimp involves eating even higher on the food chain than eating pigs or chickens.

In practice, it takes about five pounds of wild fish to produce one pound of farmed fish.[69] One of the fish most commonly used as fishmeal is krill, a keystone species near the bottom of the ocean food chain. Krill are also a major food source for whales, seals, penguins, squid and wild fish. Harvesting krill for fishmeal is already having serious ecological impacts. Experts say that the krill catch would have to be reduced by more than 95% in order to avoid impacting the wild predators that feed on krill. A similar problem is occurring with herring, who are the backbone of the North Atlantic food chain. Herring is used to make salmon feed, and increased pressure on their numbers is a serious threat to all other fish species which depend on them for food.

A conscientious omnivore who eats seafood but not land animals faces the same challenges as any other conscientious omnivore. The choices are not always clear, and there is often not a lot of help in making them. Environmental Defense makes available on the web a list of seafood choices that are better and worse both for health and for the environment.[70] However, they do not take animal welfare into account. Making matters even more difficult is the fact that seafood labeling, at least in the United States, is often quite unreliable. In 2005, The *New York Times* published an article in which they showed that most of the fish being sold in New York City as wild salmon were, in fact, farmed salmon.[71]

---

[68] China's carp industry is an exception, since carp either are filter feeders or eat living plants.

[69] For more on aquaculture and its ecological impacts, see Goldburg and Naylor 2005, Naylor and Burke 2005, and Naylor's presentation available on the web at <http://chge.med.harvard.edu/education/course_2006/topics/04_06/documents/naylor_06.pdf>. For a good survey of the problems of global fisheries, see Pauly *et al.* 2002.

[70] <www.oceansalive.org/eat.cfm>.

[71] "Stores Say Wild Salmon, but Tests Say Farm Bred," *New York Times*, April 10, 2005, available at <www.nytimes.com/2005/04/10/dining/10salmon.html?ex=1270785600&en=e7a754a302504017&ei=5088&partner=rssnyt>.

Despite the difficulties and uncertainties, there is little doubt that the diet of a conscientious omnivore is easier on animals than the diet of someone who dines regularly on the products of factory farms. The question is how much better it is, and whether it goes far enough in respecting our duties to animals. The implicit baseline against which to compare this diet is that of the vegetarian. It is now time to discuss that option explicitly.

5.3.4   Vegetarians and vegans

The vegetarian takes no moral risks about whether the animals she eats have had happy lives and been painlessly slaughtered. By abstaining completely from eating animals, she evades these questions; or so at least it seems. However, questions do arise about a vegetarian diet.

The first concern is an ecological one. Mass vegetarianism would entail large-scale agriculture. Although its ecological consequences would not be as severe as factory farming animals, they might well be very serious, depending on the size of the population, the level of its consumption, and the nature of the agricultural practices employed.

Moreover, the land-use changes required for such agriculture harms animals through habitat destruction, treating some animals as pests, and so on. Many of these harms may be thought of as indirect and unintended, but such harms are every bit as real as those that are intended and caused directly. While Kantians and virtue ethicists have other resources for responding, utilitarians (at least as a first approximation) are committed to treating these harms as the same when it comes to assigning moral responsibility. Still, in a Darwinian world, there is no such thing as a (morally) free lunch, and everyone to some extent is involved in harming animals in some way or another in order to survive. The moral questions about our treatment of animals are not "all or nothing," but rather concern the nature, extent, and character of the harms and actions involved. What seems clear is that, on the whole, vegetarians cause less harm to animals than do omnivores.

Some have denied this, however.[72] They claim that as far as the lives and welfare of animals go, it doesn't matter whether or not I eat them because there is no causal connection between eating animals who have miserable lives and the existence of such animals. More precisely, the claim is that an individual decision to eat or refrain from eating meat has no consequences

---

[72] E.g. Zamir 2007.

for whether any animals live or die. If this claim is true, then it would appear that a consequentialist should not condemn an individual's meat-eating, since the consequences would be the same whatever the individual eats. If successful, this argument counts against both vegetarians and conscientious omnivores whose diets are founded on a sense of moral obligation.

If this argument were sound, it would prove too much. Since each individual could make such a claim, it would lead to the conclusion that there is no causal connection between whether we collectively choose to eat meat and whether animals live or die. But this is obviously false. If no one ate meat, no animals would be killed for meat.

The same fallacious reasoning is at work in our thinking about other environmental problems as well. Some claim that whether or not I drive has no consequences for climate change, so it doesn't matter what I do. But each person can reason in this way, so we arrive at the conclusion that, collectively, it doesn't matter whether we drive because this will have no consequences for climate change. This too is false. Many environmental problems involve large numbers of people acting in such a way that the consequences of each action are imperceptible, and so we think that the action has no consequences. What this overlooks is that imperceptible consequences are real consequences.[73]

There are outcomes that require thresholds to achieve, and so long as my action does not contribute to reaching the threshold then it doesn't matter what I do (some think voting is like this). But I see little reason for supposing that the connection between eating meat and the raising and slaughter of animals for meat is like that. The relation between the amount of meat that I eat and the number of animals killed may be sticky and lumpy rather than simple and smooth, but surely there is some mapping. Similarly, there may be no computationally tractable answer to the question of how much climate change can be attributed to a single act of my driving, but it doesn't follow from this that there is no increment that is caused by this behavior. If no one emitted greenhouse gases, climate change would not be occurring. Similarly, if no one ate the products of factory farms, they would not exist.

However, even if we suppose that there is no causal relation between my individual action and the harm being produced by a practice, there may still be other reasons why it is wrong to participate in such a practice.

---

[73] This is one of the mistakes in moral mathematics discussed by Parfit 1984: ch. 3.

We may find one reason in virtue ethics. What would you think of a person who can tell you in vivid detail about the horrors of factory farming, while serving you a nice plate of veal parmigiana that he has prepared especially for you, all the time revealing no sense of shame, embarrassment, or untowardness? Isn't there something wrong with such a person? Isn't he the proper object of moral criticism? Or we might think that participating in a practice that is wrong is itself a further wrong, independent of the wrong involved in causally bringing the practice about. Knowingly participating in an evil might be considered wrong because it is a way of endorsing the evil, even if it is not a way of bringing it about.

There is much to think about here, but the main point is this. We have supposed that if factory farming is bad or wrong, then it is wrong to eat meat that is produced in this way. There are a number of independent grounds for thinking this, of which supposing that there is a causal connection between individual action and the existence of the practice is only one. Having said this, I must confess that I find it astonishing that anyone would deny that eating animals causally affects the number of animals who are slaughtered and the quality of their lives.

Thus far vegetarians may look pretty good, but not in the eyes of vegans, who eat no products at all that derive from animals: no meat, cheese, eggs, or honey. Vegans point out that the dairy industry typically treats animals as badly as the meat industry, and "layers" (chickens who produce eggs) arguably have worse lives than "broilers," since they live longer and are often disposed of in even more horrific ways.[74] All animals that are used to provide food for humans are eventually slaughtered, some directly for food, and others when they are no longer productive. Even vegetarians are implicated in the killing of animals.

Of course any theory, however rigorous, must make accommodation for people with special needs. No one is morally required to sacrifice their own life so that another may live (much less are they required to sacrifice their life in order to avoid participating in an immoral practice). Vegans (and vegetarians) will surely exempt people with special nutritional requirements.

Still, the vegan challenge is serious. There are responses to these arguments, but much turns on the exact nature of our duties, what moral theory we accept, and how far we think the demands of morality extend.

[74] Singer and Mason 2006: ch. 3.

Consequentialists, Kantians and virtue ethicists may or may not come to the same conclusions, but what is certain is that their reasons will be different. As I have said, these questions about the foundations of morality are not to be answered simply by selecting the view with which you are most comfortable. They call for rational reflection and argument; they are not a matter of consumer choice. Much of your reflection, however, will have to go on off-stage, beyond the covers of this book.

5.4 Animals and other values

One intriguing possibility is that "*in vitro*" meat production could make some of the controversies about the use of animals for food moot. Experiments are currently under way in growing meat from tissue cultures using stem cell technology.[75] Such a process would provide people with meat, but would entail virtually no animal suffering or deleterious ecological consequences. Such meat could even be healthier than what is available today. People seem quite divided about the desirability of such technology. People for the Ethical Treatment of Animals, one of the most militant animal rights groups, actively supports its development. However, many people, even some who care deeply about animals and nature, reject the idea of eating (or perhaps even producing) such meat. To some extent this is probably due to the novelty of the technology, but it is also because there are other values involved in our reactions to food that we have not yet made explicit.

Gathering and sharing food are at the heart of many of our cultural forms and social practices. Indeed, special meals and styles of food preparation are at the center of some religions. Jains and Hindus are vegetarian, Orthodox Jews keep kosher, and Muslims avoid pork and alcohol and require halal slaughter. An act of cannibalism (variously understood as real or symbolic) is at the heart of Christian ritual. It is difficult to imagine the historical shape of these religions independent of their dietary demands. Even beyond religion, many societies associate specific meals with special days and particular occasions. The American tradition of the Thanksgiving turkey has already been mentioned.

Moreover, there is more to our relationships to animals than using them for food, perhaps abusing them along the way. Whatever value we place on

[75] Edelman *et al.* 2005.

animal life and suffering must in the end coexist with other values that we endorse. Some think that there are important values at stake in the very process of obtaining food. Hunting has often carried a special significance in this regard. In some societies the transition from boy to man is marked by participating in the hunt. The twentieth-century Spanish philosopher, José Ortega y Gassett (1972), celebrated the hunt as involving an authentic relationship between animals. It takes people out of the artificial and contingent conditions of their everyday lives, and puts them in touch with their animal nature. Holmes Rolston has also written that hunting can be a sacred way of participating in nature.[76]

Such sentiments often strike non-hunters as absurd. They say that whatever benefit can be gotten out of hunting can just as well be obtained by spending a day in the woods with a camera. But Ortega says that at least the possibility of a kill is essential to the experience that he finds valuable. A hunter does not hunt in order to kill, but he kills in order to hunt. It is the hunt that is valuable but, tragically, the kill is necessary.

Even some who find it easy to dismiss such philosophers' paeans may find it difficult to arrive at considered views about aboriginal hunting. A well-publicized case in recent years concerns the right to whale claimed by the Makah Indians in the Pacific Northwest of the United States under an 1855 treaty. Less well known is that aboriginal whalers kill hundreds of whales each year in Alaska, Russia, Canada, Greenland, Indonesia, Grenada, Dominica, Saint Lucia, and Bequia.

Most of us are inclined to respect traditional values, especially those of a people who have been oppressed by the culture of which we are a part. At the same time it is important to acknowledge that many of the whales who are being killed are persons, in Singer's sense of the term. Moreover, if traditional values were always observed, we would be living in theocratic, hierarchical societies. To some extent, moral progress and respect for traditional values are at odds with each other. How can we reconcile diverse and conflicting values?

The main point here is that our concerns about animals exist against the background of other things that we value and cherish. One domain of value that we have said little about is the value of nature. Thus far we have assumed fairly uncontroversial views: undisturbed ecosystems are good,

[76] Rolston III 1988: 90ff.

pollution is bad, and so on. However, many of the views characteristic of environmentalism hold that nature in itself is very valuable indeed. Nature's value, on some of these views, can come into conflict, not only with our ordinary patterns of production and consumption, but also with the interests of other animals. It is now time for the value of nature to take center stage.

6   The value of nature

6.1   Biocentrism

Many philosophers who endorse an environmental ethic are uneasy with the philosophies of Singer and Regan. They see the central focus on animals as not much better than traditional moralists' obsession with humans. These critics agree that an environmental ethic will require better treatment of animals, but this concern for animals follows from a larger concern for nature. The trouble with Singer and Regan is that they have it the other way around: whatever concern they have for nature comes from their concern about animals. The preeminent value of nature is still not at the center of the big screen where it belongs.

According to the critics, Singer and Regan make the following mistake. They suppose that either sentience or being the subject of a life is a necessary condition for moral considerability (i.e., having intrinsic value in the second sense that we distinguished in 3.5). For biocentrists, sentience and being the subject of a life are only part of the story. The rest of the story is the value of life itself.

The view that all life is morally considerable goes back to the extraordinary Nobel Prize-winning humanitarian, theologian, missionary, organist, and medical doctor, Albert Schweitzer. In his 1923 book, *Philosophy of Civilisation*, he wrote: "True philosophy must start from the most immediate and comprehensive fact of consciousness: 'I am life that wants to live, in the midst of life that wants to live.'"[1] The appropriate moral response to this insight, Schweitzer thought, is reverence for all life.

This view, that all life is morally considerable, was forcefully inserted into the contemporary discussion in 1978, when Kenneth Goodpaster

---

[1] This passage is from chapter 26, entitled "The Ethics of Reverence for Life." It is available on the web at <www1.chapman.edu/schweitzer/sch.reading1.html>.

challenged the view of Peter Singer and others that all and only sentient beings are morally considerable. According to Goodpaster, "nothing short of *being alive* seems to me to be a plausible and nonarbitrary criterion."[2] Goodpaster claimed that there are good reasons to be suspicious of the sentience criterion at the outset, and that the strongest argument for it is unconvincing. Moreover, understanding why the argument is unconvincing reveals the strength of the case for the life criterion, according to Goodpaster. Finally, Goodpaster provides an explanation for why the sentience criterion seems so plausible even though it is false (this is what philosophers call an "error theory").

Goodpaster thinks that we should be suspicious of sentientism because the capacity for pleasure and pain is simply a means that some organisms use to realize their ends. It provides a way of obtaining information about the environment. More precisely, sentience is a biological adaptation that occurs in some organisms that is conducive to fulfilling their biological functions. When seen in this way, Goodpaster thinks that we should find it implausible that some particular adaptation directed towards solving some particular biological problems faced by some organisms should be seen as the criterion of moral considerability.

According to Goodpaster, the most plausible argument for the view that sentience is the criterion of moral considerability is the following:

(1) All and only beings who have interests are morally considerable;

(2) Non-sentient beings do not have interests;

(3) Therefore, non-sentient beings are not morally considerable.

Goodpaster agrees that the argument is valid and that the first premise is true. It is the second premise, which rests on

(4) The capacity for experience is necessary for having interests,

which he denies. In his view, there are beings that have interests that do not have the capacity for experience.

Plants have interests, he thinks, that are based on their needs for such things as sun and water. Indeed, Gary Varner (1998: ch. 3) has claimed that some of our interests are based on needs and are independent of the fact that we are experiencing creatures. He cites the example of vitamin C, which

---

[2] Goodpaster 1978: 310.

it is in the interests of all humans to absorb whether they are in any way conscious of this fact. In this respect, we are like plants: we have certain biological needs and it is in our interests to satisfy them. Robin Attfield (1987) goes further, claiming that plants, like humans, can flourish, and it is in their interests to do so.

The sentience criterion seems so plausible, according to Goodpaster, because we are inordinately concerned with pleasure and with organisms who are like us in this respect. However, when seen in an impartial light, it is more plausible to suppose that all living things are morally considerable than that only living things who happen to be sentient are. According to Goodpaster, the life criterion is the only one which is not based on privileging some morally arbitrary feature.

The sentientist reply is quite simple: without sentience, there is nothing for morality to take into account, for nothing that happens to an organism that is incapable of pleasure or pain matters to it. For this reason, identifying sentience as the criterion for moral considerability is not arbitrary.

Compare a well-watered plant to a well-oiled car. In both cases we can say that each is a good of its kind, that they function at a very high level, and so on. It is also clear that the language of interests can be applied to both: we can say that it is in the interests of trees to have adequate hydration and nutrition; and we can say that it is in the interests of cars to have their oil changed regularly and to be kept in good repair. When it comes to cars, it is uncontroversial that this is a non-literal use of the word 'interest'. We can speak as if cars had interests, but we don't really believe that they do. What is at issue between sentientism and biocentrism is whether the sense in which plants have interests is the sense in which humans have interests, or whether the fact that we speak in this way regarding plants is a non-literal use as it is in the case of cars. Those who favor a life criterion say that plants have interests in the same sense as humans; those who support sentientism say that talking about the interests of plants is non-literal, as it is when we talk about the interests of cars. For the sentientist, the reason a person has interests and a car does not is that what happens to the person matters to her, while nothing matters to the car. In this respect, the car and the tree are similar and a person is different: it matters to the person that her interests are respected, but not to the tree or the car. We may prefer that the car or the tree be in tiptop condition, but that is our preference, not theirs.

In reply it might be pointed out that trees and other plants have various mechanisms for responding to threats and noxious stimuli. There is a sense in which they seek to flourish, or, it might be said, to satisfy their interests. But so, arguably, do many machines. The elevator in my building shuts down rather than putting itself at risk whenever its sensors tell it that it is under some stress (perhaps someone is dancing in the elevator, its cables need attention, or whatever). But the biocentrist might say in reply that these are not really responses to the interests of the machine, but responses to those of its designers. Living things, on the other hand, have interests of their own. But can this distinction really be maintained?

Imagine two organisms, duplicates in all respects. They have exactly the same requirements for nutrition, hydration, sleep, and so on. One was constructed by natural selection, the other by Haliburton Biotech Inc. While it might be reasonable to say that one is an artifact and the other is not, it seems weird to suppose that one has interests and the other does not. If this example does not convince you, imagine two children, one manufactured the good old-fashioned way, and the other by cloning or some other sexless method of reproduction. Is the second child an artifact? Does she fail to have interests because of the facts about her origins? Perhaps we had all better ask our parents some questions!

What the sentientist says is that nothing about a being's origins affects whether or not she has interests. What is essential for having interests is that it matters to the being what happens to her. This is what is true of humans and many other animals, and what is not true of plants. This is why the sentientist is unmoved by the observation that natural selection creates sentience as a means for solving certain biological problems in some organisms, rather than as an end in itself. Something is morally considerable in virtue of its features, not because of its history.

On this point the sentientist and Kant would agree. Features or entities may have come into existence in order to be used as means, or they may in fact be used as such; but this does not determine whether the feature or entity in question is morally considerable. Returning to an example from section 4.4, my postman is morally considerable, according to Kant, in virtue of being a rational being; the fact that he is also the means by which I receive my mail is irrelevant to his moral status.

Suppose, as some apparently think, that plants not only respond to threats and noxious stimuli, but that they actually care what happens to

them. To put the point positively, suppose that not only do plants grow better when you play Mozart to them, but they actually like it and want you to
do it. If this were the case, it would not prove biocentrism. Rather, it would
show that the domain of sentience is vastly larger than we had thought.[3]

Biocentrism has been worked out carefully, and in great detail.[4] It rests
on an intuition that many people find compelling. However, not everyone
who rejects sentientism thinks that the biocentrists have gone far enough.

6.2   Ecocentrism

Some philosophers and environmental theorists claim that neither sentientism nor biocentrism succeeds in capturing the moral lessons of ecology.
Rather than giving us a new outlook which respects the ecological insight
that "everything is related to everything else," they give us nothing more
than another episode in the long march of "moral extensionism."[5] Starting
from the traditional idea that humans are morally considerable and have
rights, sentientists and biocentrists have struggled to extend these concepts
to animals and the rest of the biosphere. The result is a lawyer's paradise
in which every living thing has rights against every other living thing. Can
a wildebeest sue a lion for violating his right to life? Do elephants have
rights to take acacia trees or do acacia trees have rights to be protected
from elephants? Should I worry about the welfare of the bacteria living in
my gut? What about all the trees in the southeastern United States that are
being strangled to death by kudzu?[6]

This is, of course, a parody that is quite unfair to both sentientists and
biocentrists. Nevertheless, it makes vivid the criticisms of the ecocentrists.
What is needed, they think, is a new way of looking at morality that recognizes the moral primacy of the ecological wholes of which we are a part.
Appreciating the lessons of nature should move us away from our traditional individualist paradigm of rights and interests, and lead us to see our
moral relations with nature in an entirely new light.

---

[3] Agar 2001.   [4] E.g. by Paul Taylor (1986).

[5] That "everything is related to everything else" is one of the "four laws of ecology"
according to Barry Commoner (1971); John Rodman (1977) was an influential critique of
moral extensionism.

[6] In an important early article, Christopher Stone (1972) gave a rough sketch of how such
a system might work.

The twentieth-century American forester, wildlife biologist, and naturalist, Aldo Leopold, is often regarded as the inspiration for such ideas. Leopold
was not a philosopher (some would say he wrote too well for that!), and his
writings are quite diverse. It is not easy to weld his life and language into
a single coherent view. His philosophy is generally referred to as "the land
ethic," and the dictum for which he is best known is this: "A thing is right
when it tends to preserve the integrity, stability, and beauty of the biotic
community. It is wrong when it tends otherwise."[7]

Leopold wrote movingly about the importance of extending our ethical
sensibility to encompass "man's relationship to the land and to the animals
and plants which grow upon it," of the need for us to change our role from
"conqueror of the land-community to plain member and citizen of it." He
spoke of the importance of "love, respect, and admiration for land," and the
need for harmony between "man and the land."

There are various interpretations of Leopold. Some view him as a consequentialist, others as a virtue ethicist. The most influential expositor of
Leopold's views has been J. Baird Callicott, and he is the one who has most
fully developed the ecocentric interpretation of Leopold. What follows may
or may not be a faithful rendition of Leopold's views. What matters, for our
purposes, is that it is a fair account of what ecocentrism holds, why many
have found it attractive, and why, on reflection, most philosophers reject it.

In his dictum, Leopold uses the phrase 'biotic community' to refer to what
should be the central object of moral concern. This seems both too broad
and unclear. It is too broad since it apparently includes all of the Earth's
biota; it is unclear in that it is far from obvious how this is supposed to
form a community. The peanut shells left on the floor of Yankee Stadium
after a baseball game are part of the Earth's biota. I, for one, go blank when
I think about what they might have to do with my moral obligations (pick
them up?). For these reasons and others, most ecocentrists have focused on
the ecosystem as the fundamental object of moral concern, rather than the
biotic community.

The concept of the ecosystem is recent, appearing first explicitly in the
work of the British botanist, Sir Arthur Tansley, in 1935. Not until the 1940s,

[7] Leopold 1949: 224. The quotations in this paragraph are from the essay in the book
called "The Land Ethic," which is available on the web at <www.luminary.us/leopold/
land_ethic.html>.

shortly before the time when Leopold was writing, did it begin to figure prominently in scientific thinking. Unfortunately, for the purposes of framing an environmental ethic, it is not clear that this concept fares much better than that of the biotic community.

In the broadest sense, an ecosystem can be thought of as an assemblage of organisms together with its environment. Exactly which organisms and what elements of the environment count as elements of a particular ecosystem are matters of dispute. There is no consensus when it comes to precisely defining ecosystems or telling us where one stops and another begins. This may not be a problem for doing science, but it is a problem for discerning our obligations from an ecocentric perspective.

Ecosystems are supposed to be the primary objects of moral concern, yet some would deny that they exist independently of the elements that constitute them. Skeptics say that talking about an ecosystem is simply a way of conceptualizing a collection of individual organisms and features of their environment. On this view, ecosystems are like constellations, while organisms and features of their environment are like stars. Talking about ecosystems (like talking about constellations) is a way of talking about other things. It may be useful to do so, but we shouldn't think that the world responds to every useful turn of phrase by manufacturing an entity. It might be useful to talk about the average Australian, but don't expect to meet him and his 2.5 children.

More problematic is how we can tell where one ecosystem begins and another ends. This problem arises on both temporal and spatial dimensions. Grasslands turn to shrubs and small trees, and then to forests. Presumably these are different ecosystems successively inhabiting the same space. What happens on the temporal borders of succession? Do we have a little of one and a little of another? When it comes to space, the problems become even more difficult. It makes sense to say that a little ecosystem has emerged on the north side of the large rock in my garden. But it also makes sense to say that my garden is an ecosystem, and so is the valley in which I live, and so on. What exactly is the relationship between these different ecosystems?

I want to be clear that I am not condemning the science of ecology as resting on a mass of confusions. Nor am I denying that we can use words in different senses and conceptualize things in different ways for different purposes. My point is that if we are going to understand what ecocentric morality demands of us, we need to know what is the nature of the community of which we are supposed to be "plain citizens."

In addition to these problems, there are two further reasons why philosophers have rejected ecocentrism. First, it is not clear what moral concepts we are allowed to have and how we are supposed to use them. Second, there is a suspicion that the moral implications of ecocentrism are radically unacceptable.

At the beginning of this section I pointed out that embracing ecocentrism is often a response to frustration with the plodding, moral extensionism of sentientists and biocentrists. But if we reject these views, what concepts are left to work with? Can we say that ecosystems have interests that ought to be respected? If so, how do we identify those interests? What do we say about ecological succession, for example? Does a succeeding ecosystem violate the interests of its predecessor? Worse, does the preceding ecosystem in effect commit suicide by creating the conditions that lead to succession? If an ecosystem does not protect its own interests, why should we? On the other hand, if we are not allowed the language of interests, how do we know what our obligations are as "plain citizens" of the land? Even more radically, if we are denied the use of such traditional notions as duty and obligation, what exactly are we supposed to do as a consequence of embracing ecocentrism?

Some philosophers are confident that they know what ecocentrism requires. Tom Regan (1983: 362) calls Leopold's view "environmental fascism" because it subordinates the rights of individuals to biotic concerns. He claims that Leopold's dictum suggests that it would be permissible to kill humans to save rare wildflowers. Callicott (1980: 326) certainly gives support to such readings of Leopold when he writes, for example, that "the preciousness of individual deer, as of any other specimen, is inversely proportional to the population of the species." This suggests that the value of each existing human being is diminished by each birth that takes place. It also seems to suggest that any individual member of any endangered species of plant or animal is worth vastly more than a human being. It's no wonder that this is not a view that many humans embrace.

For all of its self-proclaimed fidelity to nature, it is striking that there are natural features that many find valuable that are difficult to account for even on an ecocentric outlook. We find rainbows, canyons, rock formations, clouds, and caves valuable, even though they are abiotic. How are these values to be explained? It seems quite a stretch to say that somehow they are all ecosystems (or elements of ecosystems) because there are some bits of organic material in the vicinity. What we value about such things has little to do with anything biotic. At the same time going beyond ecocentrism and adopting a view in which even the abiotic environment is morally considerable seems somewhere between unacceptable and mad. The looming idea of rocks having rights is what drives many people to dismissing radical environmental thought altogether. How would we know what to do in such a world? The distinction between everything and nothing having value is a thin one. Rather than extending the domain of moral considerability even further, we need to return to the source by reconsidering valuing itself.

6.3   Valuing reconsidered

As I suggested in section 3.4, value arises from transactions between valuers and the world. When we speak of values we are in some way talking about what is, ought to be, or would be valued by valuers under some conditions or another. When seen in this light, it is not surprising that our evaluational structures exhibit remarkable depth and complexity, and are expressed in wide-ranging and diverse acts of valuing. Some of these acts can be characterized as valuing intrinsically, others as valuing instrumentally, and others do not fall neatly into either category.

In section 3.5 I gave some examples of valuing that do not fall neatly on one side or another of the intrinsic/instrumental distinction. They are worth repeating here. I value the photograph of my mother because it represents my mother. I value the tail-wagging of the dog next door because it reminds me of the cheerful exuberance of my childhood dog, Frisky. I value my lover's smile because it embodies her kindness and generosity. I value each step of the ascent of Mount Whitney because it is a constituent part of what it is to climb the mountain.

Environmental philosophers have tended to fixate on the distinction between intrinsic and instrumental value as if this distinction marked the only (or most) important feature of every evaluation. Much of what is said seems to presuppose that what I value intrinsically must always be more important than what I value instrumentally. But this is not true. Suppose that I am on a cliff, hanging by a thread above the boiling waters thousands of feet below. I value the thread by which I am hanging vastly more than my stamp collection, even though I value my stamp collection intrinsically and the string instrumentally.

Not only do other features of valuing matter, but the distinction between intrinsic and instrumental valuing can itself be unstable. Consider the following story.

Suppose that I buy a painting to cover a hole in the wall. Initially I value the painting instrumentally, but when it is hung on the wall I come to value it intrinsically (i.e., ultimately, the first sense of 'intrinsic value' distinguished in section 3.5) as well. Indeed, I come to value it so greatly that I move it to another wall where it can be seen to greater advantage. I no longer care about its role in covering the hole in the wall. I have come to value the painting only intrinsically, not instrumentally. But through time I become tired of the painting. A figure in the background begins to remind me of the wicked stepfather who made my childhood so painful. I find that I no longer value the painting intrinsically. I return it to its previous position. But the image of the wicked stepfather continues to haunt me. The house isn't big enough for the two of us. What happens next? Like any other soap opera, this saga could continue indefinitely. The point is that our evaluational outlooks are dynamic; they are not stable through time, life, and experience.

In section 3.5 I distinguished four senses of 'intrinsic value': (1) intrinsic value as ultimate value; (2) intrinsic value as moral considerability; (3) intrinsic value as inherent value; and (4) intrinsic value as independence from valuers. What we value intrinsically in the first sense may go far beyond what is of intrinsic value in the second sense. We can value mountains, caves, species, and trees intrinsically in the first sense, even though we do not regard them to be of intrinsic value in any of the other three senses. Moreover, one and the same thing can be valued intrinsically and non-intrinsically at the same time as well as at different times. Finally, we can value things urgently, intensely, and even desperately, yet not value them intrinsically. If we put all this together, then it is clear that we have very rich resources for valuing nature, whether we are anthropocentrists, sentientists, biocentrists, ecocentrists, or whatever.

Biocentrists and ecocentrists suppose that if individual plants or ecosystems do not have intrinsic value in the second sense of moral considerability, then they cannot have intrinsic value in the first sense of being of ultimate value. Thus the late political scientist John Rodman writes: "I need only to stand in the midst of a clear-cut forest, a strip-mined hillside, a defoliated jungle, or a dammed canyon to feel uneasy with assumptions that could yield the conclusion that no human action can make any difference to the welfare of anything but sentient animals."[8] But human action can make a difference, indeed a moral difference, even if such natural entities are not themselves morally considerable. As the contemporary British philosopher David Wiggins writes: "The human scale of value is by no means exclusively a scale of human values."[9] An anthropocentrist or sentientist can value forests, mountains, jungles, and wild rivers. They can also value justice, both for their contemporaries, and future generations (a theme to which we shall return in section 7.2).

The richness and complexity of an evaluational structure do not depend solely on whether one is an anthropocentrist, sentientist, biocentrist, eco-centrist, or whatever. They also depend enormously on one's experience of the world and what values one recognizes. When former President Ronald Reagan said, "A tree is a tree. How many more do you have to look at?" he was mainly displaying his insensitivity to nature rather than his philosophical ignorance.[10]

6.4 The plurality of values

For those whose evaluational systems are in good working order, there is an enormous amount to value in nature. One way of trying to understand this domain is to distinguish kinds, types, or varieties of value. But reader beware: philosophers load a lot on to such language. There is ongoing debate about the meaning and plausibility of value-pluralism. Some think that value-pluralism is the view that there are distinct values that cannot be reduced to a single master value such as pleasure. Others think that value-pluralism holds that distinct values cannot meaningfully be compared or ranked.[11] I aim to steer clear of those controversies. My purpose in distin-guishing a variety of values is simply to try to order some of the features of nature that we find valuable.

---

[8] Rodman 1977: 89.   [9] Wiggins 2000: 16.

[10] President Regan made this remark in 1966, when, as Governor of California, he opposed the expansion of the Redwood National Park. For this and similar quotations visit <www.dkosopedia.com/wiki/Quotes/Ronald_Reagan>.

[11] For an overview, visit <http://plato.stanford.edu/entries/value-pluralism>.

6.4.1   Prudential values

Prudential values, broadly speaking, are those that relate to an agent's own interests. Some question whether prudential values can count as moral values, while others think that our concern about others can be subsumed under our concern for our own interests. Whatever we may think about these controversies, there is little doubt that we value nature to a great extent for reasons relating to our present and long-term interests. It is therefore useful to begin an exploration of the value of nature by reminding ourselves of what nature does to support our survival and flourishing.

In the 1960s the visionary economist, Kenneth Boulding, contrasted what he called the "cowboy economy" of the past with the "closed economy of the future in which the earth has become a single spaceship, without unlimited reservoirs of anything, either for extraction or for pollution, and in which, therefore, man must find his place in a cyclical ecological system."[12] Just as the crew of a spaceship has very strong prudential reasons for valuing the spaceship, so we have very strong prudential reasons for valuing our planet.

What Boulding calls "reservoirs . . . of extraction [and] pollution" is what in 1.8 I called sources and sinks. Nature is the ultimate source of water, food, air, and the materials that we fashion into usable goods. It is also the sink in which we dispose of both personal wastes and those that result from the processes of production. A 1997 study that attempted to value these services arrived at the following conclusion: "For the entire biosphere, the value (most of which is outside the market) is estimated to be in the range of US\$16–54 trillion (10^{12}) per year with an average of US\$33 trillion per year."[13]

While there are ample reasons (both conceptual and empirical) to be skeptical about this study, it does provide some indication of the enormous benefits that we derive from nature. The estimated benefit is huge and it is ongoing, not like a one-time trip to the supermarket. Like any good mother, nature is always there for us. Sure, she can be moody, but we expect her to be basically stable and predictable. Some years will be wetter, others dryer, some more tumultuous and others calmer, but we expect these variations

---

[12] Boulding 1966; available on the web at <www.eoearth.org/article/The_Economics_of_the_Coming_Spaceship_Earth_(historical)#citation>.

[13] Costanza *et al.* 1997.

to occur against a background of relative stability. The assumption that the future will be like the past, at least on the timescales that we care about, is built into our investments in infrastructure, including agricultural and water systems. The way we think about our lives and how they unfold presuppose such a background assumption. However, as we will see in chapter 7, this assumption of stability appears increasingly implausible, both because we have misunderstood the Earth system, but also because we are systematically insulting it. But this gets ahead of our story.

In recent years many have tried to make the case for environmental preservation wholly on prudential grounds, often as expressed in the language of economics. Every species ought to be preserved, we sometimes hear, because for all we know the cure for cancer may be found in some plant whose powers have not yet been appreciated. Sure, and someday I may play in the World Cup.

This prudential argument for environmental preservation has two problems. First, it is an argument from ignorance. It assigns a positive value to preserving a particular species on the grounds that we do not know that there will not be positive benefits from preserving it. Think about what is being said: if we don't know that something is not the case, then we can assume that there is some chance that it is. This inference is fallacious. All that follows from ignorance is ignorance. To say more than this, we have to know something. The second problem with this argument is that it assigns no value to the activities that drive species to extinction. But people do not go around gratuitously causing extinction. What drives species to extinction are activities from which people benefit. Real money is being made from the farming and mining that are deforesting Amazonia. Great fortunes have been founded on drilling for oil and transporting it around the world. Consumers as well as producers benefit from these activities.

The failure of this argument does not mean that a strong case cannot be made for protecting species, even perhaps every species. What it does mean is that we need to look for some additional reasons. This is a good thing to do anyway. Most people who want to protect nature are not motivated solely (or even primarily) by sober cost-benefit analysis. They have other values that they also bring to bear on these questions. This is not a reason to be embarrassed, but a reason to come clean and to put these values forward for discussion and examination.

6.4.2   Aesthetic values

When we look at nature we find not only sources and sinks, but also beauty. Clearly, natural beauty is part of the reason why we protect some places rather than others. Think of Yosemite Valley in California, the Great Barrier Reef in Australia, the Mercantour in France; these are some of the most beautiful places in the world. Beauty moves us, whether we find it in art or in nature. Indeed, it is instructive to look at the following analogies between art and nature.[14]

In both cases, beauty's value is widely regarded as perhaps including but also transcending pleasure. Experiencing the baroque churches of Rome is the sort of activity that improves us. So is a six-day backpacking trip in the Sonoran Desert. Both can be life-changing experiences. If we were to revisit Routleys' "last man" thought-experiment (discussed in 3.5), I suspect that our intuitions would run about the same when it comes to destroying artworks as they do when it comes to destroying nature. In both cases it seems shockingly wrong to gratuitously destroy them, even if we stipulate that neither will figure in future experience.

In the case of both art and nature, authenticity matters. A quick trip to the Las Vegas mock-up of Rome is not an adequate substitute for the real thing, no matter how much pleasure it may give us. Nor can an IMAX movie substitute for actually being in nature, even if the IMAX film we are imagining is a futuristic one with all sorts of cool virtual-reality features.

In the case of both art and nature, context is very important to the character of our experience. It is one thing to see a statue of the reclining Buddha in a London museum and it is another thing to see it in a temple in Thailand. There is all the difference in the world between seeing a cheetah in the San Diego Zoo and seeing the same animal in the Serengeti. Generally, the beauty and significance of an artwork are greatest in the setting for which it was made.[15] Similarly, our experience of nature is most profound when it is on its own terms.

Finally, in the case of both art and nature we value rarity. Of course, we do not denigrate Picasso and Matisse because they were prolific, but the particular value we assign to Vermeer's paintings has something to do

---

[14] The next three paragraphs are indebted to Sober 1986.

[15] There are exceptions: my teacher, Paul Ziff, used to say that the lighting designers at New York's Museum of Modern Art could make dry dung look magnificent.

with the fact that only thirty-six are known to exist. Each is treated with the loving care that is often lavished on an only child. And while most of us would reject an ecocentrism that holds that rarity alone is sufficient for preferring the life of one being over another, we do tend to value rare animals or natural features more than common ones. Indeed, we often thoughtlessly drive species to near extinction, and then spend millions in the attempt to bring them back from the brink.

Of course there are differences between the beauty we find in nature and the beauty we find in art. We see art's beauty as intentional, designed, representational, and expressive. We see it through the lens of an artworld, and against the background of art history and criticism. Most of us do not see nature's beauty as an intentional product of a designer, so many of the features that go with this way of seeing are left behind. Still, it is not clear how deep these differences go. One could argue that there is little difference between artists and natural selection as engines of design, and that scientific disciplines such as geology and biology play the same role in appreciating natural beauty that art history and criticism do for appreciating the beauty of works of art.[16] Moreover, a theist who sees nature as God's handiwork may see little difference between natural beauty and the beauty of artworks; they are both the intentional products of a designer. Similarly, someone who, for whatever reason, fails to experience an artwork as an artifact and has no background in the conventional practices of art appreciation may see little difference between artworks and natural objects. He may appreciate both for their beauty, but as far as he is concerned both of them may be mute with respect to representational and expressive properties.

The appreciation of natural beauty was at least as as important as the appreciation of artworks in the development of aesthetics as a field of philosophical inquiry. The eighteenth-century British founders of the field (e.g. the Third Earl of Shaftesbury and Francis Hutcheson) developed their views of aesthetic appreciation primarily by considering the aesthetic appreciation of nature. Kant, who was as important to the development of aesthetics as to the development of ethics, treated the appreciation of nature as the paradigm of aesthetic experience.

Given the importance of beauty to our appreciation of nature, it may seem surprising that environmentalists have tended to deemphasize this

---

[16] Carlson 2000.

dimension of nature's value. There are two related reasons for this. The first is the apparent subjectivity of the experience of beauty, and the second is the apparent triviality of such experiences.

While this is not the place for a full survey of various theories of beauty, it is important to recognize that a range of accounts is on offer. To a great extent, but not entirely, they map on to the families of theories identified in chapter 3 (i.e. realism, subjectivism, and the sensible center).

For the ancients and medievals (e.g. Plotinus, Aquinas), beauty was seen as the manifestation of the divine; for many of us, beauty is something that exists only in the eye of the beholder. This looks like the familiar stand-off between those crusty old realists and we postmodern subjectivists. However, what the eighteenth-century philosophical tradition noticed was that an object's being beautiful and our having experiences of a certain sort are very closely coupled yet extremely difficult to explain on the basis of general principles. David Hume, for example, holds that although beauty and "deformity" are not properties of objects, "there are certain qualities in objects, which are fitted by nature to produce those particular feelings."[17]

Some of these eighteenth-century founders of the field can be considered more or less subjectivist and some more or less realist, but what they share is the insight that attributions of beauty seem to require both subjective experience and the commitment to claims that we regard as objectively true. It seems obvious to us today that beauty necessarily involves subjective experience, but we tend to overlook the fact that such claims as the following are obvious as well:

(5) Michelangelo's *David* is beautiful;

(6) Yosemite Valley is beautiful;

(7) Angelina Jolie is beautiful.

Someone who denies that Michelangelo's *David*, Yosemite Valley, and Angelina Jolie are beautiful isn't just someone with different taste; there are things about the world that this person just doesn't understand. As Hume claims, when our "organs" are operating properly, our responses to beauty are as reliable as our responses to color.

---

[17] Hume 1965; available on the web at <www.mnstate.edu/gracyk/courses/phil%20of %20art/hume%20on%20taste.htm>. The reference to Hume below is from the same text.

Developments in cognitive neuroscience are beginning to show how such tight coupling might occur between our individual experiences of beauty and a set of widely accepted claims about what is beautiful. Recent studies employing fMRI brain-imaging techniques have illuminated relationships between people's judgments of beauty and specialized areas in the brain.[18] It would be a mistake to attach too much significance to this work, but it does appear that there is increasing evidence for the tight correlations between features of the world and our experiences of beauty that were noticed by the eighteenth-century philosophers, as well as a growing understanding of how these correlations may be physically realized.

Nature's beauty is only one of its features to which we respond aesthetically. Other features of nature and forms of experience have been discussed in the literature (e.g. the picturesque), but none as extensively as the experience of the sublime. This kind of experience goes beyond what can be seen and incorporates sounds and smells as well as sights.

Like beauty, the idea of the sublime is an ancient notion that became a central concern in the eighteenth century. Edmund Burke's *A Philosophical Enquiry into the Origin of our Ideas of the Sublime and Beautiful* (1757) was especially influential. The sublime is often associated with experiences of mountains or oceans. Such experiences may occasion wonder, awe, astonishment, admiration, reverence, or respect. At its extreme, the experience of the sublime may cause total astonishment. According to Burke, the human experience of the sublime is a "delight," and one of the most powerful human emotions. Yet, perhaps paradoxically, the experience of the sublime involves such "negative" emotions as fear, dread, pain, and terror, and can occur when we experience deprivation, darkness, solitude, silence, or vacuity. The experience of the sublime arises when we feel we are in danger, but are not actually in danger. Immensity, infinity, magnitude, and grandeur can cause this experience of greatness, significance, and power.

Perhaps the best way of conveying the sense of the sublime is to quote at length John Muir's account of a tumultuous night he spent camping on the summit of Mount Shasta in California, probably in the 1870s:

> Next morning, having slept little the night before the ascent and being weary with climbing after the excitement was over, I slept late. Then,

---

[18] Zeki and Kawabata 2004.

awaking suddenly, my eyes opened on one of the most beautiful and sublime scenes I ever enjoyed. A boundless wilderness of storm clouds of different degrees of ripeness were congregated over all the lower landscape for thousands of square miles, colored gray, and purple, and pearl, and deep-glowing white, amid which I seemed to be floating; while the great white cone of the mountain above was all aglow in the free, blazing sunshine. It seemed not so much an ocean as a land of clouds – undulating hill and dale, smooth purple plains, and silvery mountains of cumuli, range over range, diversified with peak and dome and hollow fully brought out in light and shade . . .

Presently the storm broke forth into full snowy bloom, and the thronging crystals darkened the air. The wind swept past in hissing floods, grinding the snow into meal and sweeping down into the hollows in enormous drifts all the heavier particles, while the finer dust was sifted through the sky, increasing the icy gloom. But my fire glowed bravely as if in glad defiance of the drift to quench it, and, notwithstanding but little trace of my nest could be seen after the snow had leveled and buried it, I was snug and warm, and the passionate uproar produced a glad excitement.[19]

Aesthetic values, in their various forms, can play important roles in our lives, and we should not underestimate their power to motivate. That they are closely tied to experience is not a reason for supposing that these values are trivial, unimportant, or idiosyncratic. They constitute part, but only part, of the case for nature's value.

6.4.3   Natural values

When it comes to aesthetics, the dance between the subjective and the objective seems quite delicate. However, many people see nature as valuable in virtue of properties that are at least to some extent independent of our experience.

Indeed, the very idea that something is natural carries value for many people.[20] Of course, such terms as 'natural' and its cognates are multiply ambiguous. I will not try to sort out the senses here. Instead I will simply assert that the sense of naturalness that is important for many who value

---

[19] Muir 2006: ch. 4; available on the web at <www.sierraclub.org/john_muir_exhibit>.
[20] E.g. Elliot 1997 and Goodin 1992.

nature is this: something is natural to the extent that it is not a product of human influence.

One way to understand what I mean by this is to consider the claim that is sometimes made that we are living at "the end of nature" because human influence is so pervasive that no part of nature remains untouched.[21] Since every part of the Earth's surface is affected by climate, it is true that human interference with the climate system is affecting every part of the planet. However, it doesn't follow from this that we are at the "end of nature." There is an important distinction between X affecting Y, and Y being a product of X. I may affect your decision about what to study in many ways, for example by providing you with information or advice that you may or may not take into account. This, however, is quite different from the case in which your decision about what to study is a product of my influence.

Consider the following example. Human action affects the length of the growing season in the Great Lakes region of North America, but the fact that there are zebra mussels in the Great Lakes is a product of human influence. They were transported there by ships, and deposited along with ballast water. The distinction between these two cases (the human impact on the length of the growing season and human impact on the presence of zebra mussels in the Great Lakes) has intuitive force (or so I hope), but all sorts of complications remain. In addition to appealing to human influences, a fuller account of why zebra mussels exist in the Great Lakes would have to appeal to various other factors including biological facts about zebra mussels themselves. If natural selection had not produced zebra mussels in the first place, they could not have been introduced to the Great Lakes; and had they not found a conducive environment when they arrived, they would not have survived. Moreover, quite different things can be said to be products of human influence (e.g. Texas Longhorn cattle and plastic tablecloths). And the philosophers among us will rightly worry about whether it is events, facts, states of affairs, or something else that is being produced in these cases. They will also ask pesky questions about the relations between producing something, bringing it about, and causing it to exist or occur. All of this I will put aside.

---

[21] McKibben 1989. In one sense this claim is obviously false, since there is virtually no human influence on most of the universe (or even on much of the Earth, if we include its core and mantle), but I will put aside this uncharitable understanding.

Even so, the distinction between *X* affecting *Y*, and *Y* being a product of *X*'s influence, is undeniably both vague and a matter of degree. Since we live in a world of vague concepts (e.g. wealth, baldness, intelligence, etc.), I will set aside this concern too (and the interesting issues that follow).

What matters is this: naturalness is a matter of degree and this is reflected in our language. We often say such things as that one region (e.g. the Canadian Rockies) is more natural than another region (e.g. the Adirondacks). Indeed, often what we are most interested in is such comparative judgments: how natural one thing is compared to another.

In some circles it is fashionable to dismiss the idea of natural values as romantic nonsense, or even to dismiss the concept of nature altogether. Nature and the natural, on this view, are social constructions. They exist only as expressions of human culture rather than as features of the world. The clarifications we have just made help us to understand why one influential argument for this view fails.

This argument involves pointing out that humans have been modifying their environments as long as they have existed. The idea is, presumably, that for something to be natural it must not have been affected by humans, and since humans have affected everything, nothing (on the Earth's surface anyway) is natural. This argument simply recapitulates the mistake of conflating *X* affecting *Y* with *Y* being a product of *X*'s influence. It doesn't follow from the fact (if it is one) that humans have been affecting their environments since time immemorial, and now no part of the Earth can be said to be unaffected by humans, that nothing is natural. What threatens the claim that something is natural is not that it is affected by humans, but that it is a product of human influence.

A second argument for a similar conclusion has been most fully developed concerning wilderness, but can easily be extended to nature and the natural. This argument holds that wilderness (or nature or the natural) is a social construction because the concept has a history: not everyone everywhere has always had this concept; and among those who have the concept, it has not always had the same content; and even those who share the concept and agree about its content may have different attitudes towards wilderness (or nature or the natural).[22] Most aboriginal peoples, for example, do not think of themselves as living in a wilderness or perhaps even as living in nature.

[22] Cronon 1996.

The Puritan colonizers of New England knew that they lived in a wilderness, but this meant something quite different to them than it does to us. For them it meant living in a "wild and howling land," "bringing forth no fruit to God, but wild fruits of sin."[23] While many of us value wilderness, the Puritans and many other colonizers of North America viewed wilderness as something to avoid or to improve.

While these observations are true and interesting, the fact that ideas, concepts, and words have histories doesn't in any way show that their referents have no existence independent of human artifice. People lived in the solar system before they knew anything about it. Ecosystems existed before Tansley coined the term. There are facts that can reasonably be seen as social constructions (e.g. the gross domestic product of Tanzania). There are also philosophers (typically called "idealists") who have argued that the structure of our concepts determines the structure of the world, but this is a hard row to hoe and requires some sophisticated work in metaphysics. This argument, however, reflects not some subtle piece of reasoning but rather a failure to attend to some basic distinctions. This argument confuses the concept of the natural, which is a social construction, with the fact of naturalness, which is not.[24]

Returning to the main point, my claim is that, for many people, the quality of being natural contributes to nature's value. Imagine a case in which we are out hiking and we see a landscape filled with amazing mud-covered mounds of a sort you have never seen. You have been reading guidebooks, and you know that this region of Australia is well known for its fantastically large termite mounds. You are beside yourself with admiration. But when I tell you that these are fake termite mounds, put up by the local chamber of commerce to amuse people who aren't interested in bush-walking, your face falls. What you had thought was natural, you now see as the product of human influence.

We might wonder why people see being natural as contributing to nature's value. One response would be to say, "They just do." Why do people find pleasure or kindness valuable? At some point explanation just gives

---

[23] The first quotation is from Roger Williams and the second is from William Bradford; both are taken from a lecture by Carolyn Merchant, available on the web at <http://nature.berkeley.edu/departments/espm/env-hist/espm160/outlines/3.1.htm>. Generally on this subject, see Nash 2001.

[24] For more on social constructivism, see Hacking 1999.

out. Still, in this case, there may be other values that we can identify that lie behind our attraction to what is natural.

We have an urge to control our environments as individuals, communities, and perhaps even as a species. There are many obvious reasons why it benefits us to do so, and it may also reflect our evolutionary history. At least one recent book claims that rather than being distinguished by their hunting prowess, our forebears were much more commonly prey than predator.[25] Animals who are used to being prey may not want to leave their environments to chance.

At the same time there is a kind of loneliness about life in an environment that you dominate (imagine Elvis at Graceland). Part of why we enjoy human companionship is because we get tired of ourselves. We want to be with people who have minds and lives of their own, and are not just extensions of ourselves. Of course, some people prefer to be surrounded by sycophants, but they suffer from being politicians or from some other disorder.

What I am suggesting is that we value what is natural because we value nature's autonomy. That is not to say that we think of nature as a moral agent, accountable to us for her actions (except perhaps metaphorically). Rather, what we value in nature is that she "does her own thing" and is largely indifferent to us. In chapter 5 of the *Tao Te Ching*, attributed to the sixth-century BCE Taoist sage Lao-Tse, we find the following words: "Heaven and Earth are impartial; they treat all of creation as straw dogs." In ancient Chinese rituals, straw dogs were burned as sacrifices in place of living dogs. What is being asserted here is that nature is as indifferent to human welfare as humans are to the fate of the straw dogs they use in ritual sacrifice. For many of us, the indifference of nature can be a welcome relief from life in the human-dominated world.

At its most extreme, nature's autonomy is expressed in wildness. While it is difficult to define this notion precisely, it is easy enough to roughly characterize it, at least negatively. What is wild is not dominated by others; it is free from external control. Thoreau characterized what is wild as that which is self-willed. The contemporary poet, Gary Snyder, tells us that some definitions of 'wild' "come very close to how the Chinese define the term 'Dao', the way of Great Nature . . . eluding analysis, beyond categories, self-organizing . . . independent . . . unmediated . . . self-willed."[26]

---

[25] Hart and Sussman 2005.   [26] Snyder 1990: 10.

He goes on to say that these meanings are not far from the Buddhist term '*dharma*', with its original senses of forming and firming.

These observations chime with the fact that the wildness of nature has often been seen as the correlate to the wildness within us. Snyder asserts that "our bodies are wild," pointing to the "involuntary quick turn of the head at a shout, the vertigo at looking off a precipice, the heart-in-the throat in a moment of danger, the catch of the breath, the quiet moments of relaxing, staring, reflecting – all universal responses of this mammal body."[27] As many have thought, we do not go into the wildness to escape our lives, but to return to them.[28]

While a concern with autonomy and even wildness may be part of why many people value what is natural, it is important to recognize that these are distinct concepts. I have already pointed out that the sense in which people are autonomous is not the same as the sense in which we might say that nature is autonomous. Nor would it be correct to think that in all cases what is natural is also wild. A tame animal is natural, while humans and their creations can be wild (e.g. parties, wars, and generally their behavior).

Another value that people often claim to appreciate in nature is its diversity. While its most familiar form is species diversity, biological diversity (or "biodiversity") comes in other forms as well, and also occurs at various levels. In addition to species diversity there is genetic diversity, ecosystem diversity, anatomical diversity, morphological diversity, and so on. In addition to biological diversity, nature offers us other forms of diversity, such as geological diversity, The Earth is characterized by both seas and land masses. Its land forms range from deserts and plains to mountains and plateaus. Many people find our diverse world fascinating, inspiring, and even admirable simply in virtue of expressing this feature. When the Norwegian philosopher. Arne Naess, and his American follower, George Sessions, codified the eight basic principles of deep ecology on John Muir's birthday in April 1984, they spoke for many when they stated the second principle in this way: "Richness and diversity of life forms contribute to the realization of these values and are also values in themselves."[29]

Despite the fact that many philosophers have held diversity to be of utmost value (e.g., the seventeenth-century philosopher Leibniz and the nineteenth-century philosopher Brentano), it is not easy to explain and

[27] Snyder 1990: 16.   [28] See Turner 1996.
[29] Available on the web at <www.deepecology.org/deepplatform.html>.

justify such claims.[30] Moreover, promoting diversity can conflict with promoting wildness and naturalness. It has been recognized for some time that some biodiversity is human-dependent. In one classic study the biodiversity of an oasis in the Organ Pipe National Monument in Arizona was compared to that of another Sonoran desert oasis in Mexico. The American oasis is managed as a park while the Mexican oasis is used by Papago farmers in traditional ways. Even though the American oasis is wilder, the Mexican oasis has more biodiversity.[31] Biodiversity can also conflict with naturalness. If our only goal is to produce as much biodiversity as possible, then genetic engineering would be a strategy superior to environmental preservation. What most environmentalists want is naturally produced biodiversity, not diversity brought to you by Monsanto.

In the background of these conflicts is what Bernard Williams calls the "paradox" of using "our power to preserve a sense of what is not in our power."[32] If we value what is natural and wild, how can we protect it without defeating what we value? Can we legislate the boundaries of the wild without undermining the very wildness we seek to protect? According to Williams, "a nature which is preserved by us is no longer a nature that is simply not controlled," for "anything we leave untouched we have already touched."

In addition to these conflicts and questions, natural values can conflict with prudential and aesthetic values. A garden may be more aesthetically pleasing than a natural landscape. An irrigated field may serve our interests better than one that is left natural. These conflicts seem to become even more severe when we bring the values of nature together with the concerns about non-human animals that we discussed in the previous chapter.

6.5 Conflicts and trade-offs

In this chapter and the previous one we have been exploring the value of non-human nature. In chapter 5 we examined the case for supposing that all sentient beings or all subjects of a life have intrinsic value in the second sense of being morally considerable. In this chapter we have investigated

---

[30] For a review, see Rosa 2004.
[31] Nabhan *et al.* 1982. Further examples and discussion can be found in Sarkar 2005.
[32] Williams 1995: 240.

whether all living things or ecosystems might also have intrinsic value in this sense. Even if they do not, many people find aesthetic or natural values in nature, in addition to having prudential reasons for valuing nature. However, recognizing values in nature is just part of the task of constructing an environmental ethic. As we have seen, conflicts can occur not only among plural values, but even when we seek to apply a single value in different circumstances. There is an important lesson here. Too often environmentalism is viewed as an ideology whose adherents move in lockstep, obeying the directives of some green politburo. But values can conflict. There are resources in normative ethics for resolving some of these conflicts, but, as we have seen, reasonable people can disagree about which normative views are the most plausible and how to bring theoretical considerations to bear on practical problems. Even if people agree about normative matters, it will not always be obvious what the right thing to do is, given the murky nature of the world in which we live. This will become clear in the following case studies of values in conflict.

6.5.1   Sierra Nevada Bighorn Sheep versus mountain lions

Sierra Nevada Bighorn Sheep[33] are a genetically distinct subspecies of Bighorn Sheep, a species descended from sheep that crossed the Bering land bridge from Siberia to North America during the Pleistocene. Before European contact, there were at most several thousand of these sheep. After European contact, the population dropped dramatically due to hunting and diseases transmitted from domestic sheep. Despite being granted legal protection in 1878, only about 250 Sierra Bighorn Sheep remained by the 1970s. In the 1980s the population spiked upward by 25 percent, but then collapsed to about 100 in 1995. The Sierra Nevada Bighorn Sheep was the first species to be listed as endangered by the federal government in the twenty-first century.

It is generally agreed that predation by mountains lions was the main cause of the population collapse during the 1990s. Between 1976 and 1988, 49 mountain lion kills were documented, and 72 have been documented altogether. Almost all of these attacks took place while the Bighorns grazed

---

[33] For information about this case visit <www.sierrabighorn.org/index.htm> and <www.mountainlion.org>.

in their winter ranges. The result was that the Bighorns stopped coming
down from their high mountain refuges, which are generally over 10,000
feet (3,000 metres). In addition to putting themselves at increased risk of
avalanches, they also lost access to the grasses that constitute an important source of nutrients. Mountain Lions mainly feed on deer, and not all
mountain lions will prey on sheep. The ones that do, however, can kill up
to four sheep per year. In the winter of 1999–2000, two mountain lions
were killed because they were considered serious threats to the sheep. Now,
mountain lions who are found near Bighorn populations are radio-collared
and tracked. By 2001 the Bighorn population had doubled to about 250, and
today it stands at about 350–400.

Mountain lions have not had an easy life in California. In 1907 the state
placed a bounty on them, and this policy was in place until 1963. Trophy-
hunting continued until 1972, when a law was passed that protected them
unless they killed or threatened livestock or pets. In response to repeated
attempts by the California Department of Fish and Game to reinstitute hunting, in 1990 voters passed Proposition 117, which declared mountain lions
as a (the only) "specially protected" species, and required a four-fifths vote
of the legislature to change any provision of the law protecting them. An
attempt six years later by sport hunters and conservative legislators to over-
turn this special protection was summarily rejected by the voters.

No one knows what the mountain lion population of California was
before European contact, but in 1920 a rough estimate put the population
at 600. After hunting ceased in the 1970s there were more than 2,000 Mountain Lions, and today there are 4,000–6,000. Since the Grizzly became extinct
in California in the 1920s, the mountain lion has had no natural predators.
Attacks on pets and livestock have become increasingly common, due in
part to the increasing human population in mountain lion habitat. There
have been only thirteen recorded mountain lion attacks on humans, four
fatal, the most recent being 2004.

How should we think about this conflict between two animals, both of
which have populations that have been severely impacted by human action?
Is mountain lion predation simply a matter of wild nature taking its course?
Is it permissible to kill mountain lions because sheep are endangered? Does
it matter that the sheep are not an ecologically important subspecies? Does
predation have any aesthetic value? Do mountain lions have rights to life?
Should we worry that killing mountain lions to protect sheep may put us

on a slippery slope back to the days when there were bounties on mountain lions?

Here is what a senior editor of the Sierra Club magazine thinks:

> For many conservationists, it is a bitter draught to contemplate the killing of a noble creature they once fought to protect. Yet once we start playing God – by exterminating grizzlies, introducing exotic breeds of sheep, or granting special protection to mountain lions – we seem obliged to continue. To so alter the natural balance and then throw up our hands and say, "Let nature take its course," might erase the Sierra Nevada bighorn from the book of life . . . Here we teeter, as ever, trying to restore the order we have disturbed, trying, when in danger, not to run away, but to move up.[34]

But what is being presupposed here? Is there such a thing as a "natural balance"? Is there an "order" we ought to be trying to restore? Perhaps the most important challenge about cases such as this is to figure out exactly what is the most important question and what bears on answering it.

This case involves a conflict between animals, but human action is always in the background setting the terms. Despite the sheep's listing as an endangered species, the United States Forest Service continues to allow ranchers to graze domestic sheep and goats on public land in Bighorn Sheep habitat. Domestic sheep not only compete for food but can spread diseases such as scabies and pneumonia to Bighorns. Historically, diseases transmitted from domestic sheep have been a major cause of the Bighorn's decline. State wildlife managers say they might have to kill any Bighorns that are exposed to domestic flocks in order to protect the rest of the herd. In reply to criticism, a government official points out that there has been no documented contact between domestic sheep and the Sierra Bighorn for 25 years, and what "caused these sheep to decline over the past 15 years was apparently an unacceptably high level of mountain lion predation that developed in the 1980s, and nothing else." So it appears that from the point of view of the government, it is the livelihoods of the mountain lions that must be managed rather than those of the sheep-ranchers.

---

[34] This and the following quotation are from Paul Rauber, "The Lion and the Lamb: What Happens When a Protected Predator Eats an Endangered Species?," *Sierra Magazine*, March/April 2001, available on the web at <www.sierraclub.org/sierra/200103/sheep_printable.asp>.

6.5.2   Feral goats versus endemic plants

When we consider the question abstractly, most of us would probably say that the interests of animals should take precedence over those of plants. After all, animals are sentient and plants are not. Even if there are other values that we think are important, that difference seems pretty important. But consider the following case.

San Clemente Island, located off the coast of southern California, was first inhabited by humans about 10,000 years ago. Early in the nineteenth century its indigenous inhabitants were moved to missions on the mainland. Until the early twentieth century the island was the intermittent site of hunting for sea otters and seals, whaling, sheep-ranching, smuggling, and the Chinese abalone industry. In 1934 the United States Navy took custody of the island and has subsequently used it for training.

In 1977 seven endemic species (those which are native and exist naturally nowhere else) were listed as endangered under the Endangered Species Act. Four plant species, which were the first to be listed under the Act, provide shelter to two species of bird and one species of lizard. The listing obliged the Navy to develop a recovery plan, and their attention turned immediately to the feral goats who had inhabited the island since the seventeenth century. The goats had severely degraded the native ecosystems and it was clear that they were a major threat to the existence of these species. By 1979 the Navy had removed 16,500 goats from the island, but about 3,000 remained in steep, rugged, canyons. The Navy then proposed a shooting program to be conducted from helicopters, but was blocked in court by the Fund for Animals. A series of negotiations led to the Fund using helicopters and nets to capture some of the goats, taking them off the island, and finding homes for them across the country. However, the conflict continued, and in 1990 the last goat on the island was shot. While accurate numbers are hard to come by, one estimate is that about 27,000 goats were shot and about 4,000 were airlifted to safety.

This case seems to present us clearly with questions about the value of sentient but common animals versus the value of highly endangered but insentient plants. Someone who endorses biocentrism or believes that bio-diversity should never be reduced, even slightly, might think that morality demands killing the goats. Someone who takes sentience or animal rights more seriously would find this conclusion almost impossible to swallow.

Both sides face a series of further questions, including these: How many sentient animals is a single plant worth? How much environmental degradation must we sustain before a single goat can be killed?

An initial reaction that many have is that the airlift organized by the Fund for Animals was a good compromise. Goats were removed, as the Navy wanted, but they escaped harm, as the Fund wanted. But imagine how much this evacuation cost! What else could have been done with this money to protect nature and to reduce animal suffering? Moreover, there is only so far that the Navy could have gone in this direction. When it comes to eradicating goats, a miss is as good as a mile. If there are a few goats left, it won't take long for them to breed up again to the same level that was threatening the endangered plants. And, unfortunately, it was never going to be possible for the Fund to capture all the goats. After seeing what was happening to their companions, the goats began to hide and to retreat to parts of the island that were inaccessible to their rescuers. So we seem to be left with the simple but profound question of whether our environmental ethic tells us to prefer endangered plants to common animals, or the other way round.

While it is important to think this question through, the world is always more complicated than philosophers' examples. This case, which is so easy to cast as "endangered plants versus common animals", carries some surprises. The first is that the San Clemente Island goats have been revalued from feral animals no one wants, to a highly prized rare breed. They are officially registered with the American Livestock Breeds Conservancy, which lists their status as "critical" on their conservation priority list. The initial adoption agreements required that the animals be sterilized so that no more unwanted goats would be produced. As a result, only about 200 individuals exist. Several zoos have joined the struggle to preserve the San Clemente Island goat, exhibiting them in their collections. Ironically, it turns out that the Fund for Animals wasn't just protecting animal welfare but was also acting to preserve biological diversity. From our present perspective the choice was not between endangered plants and common animals, but between endangered plants and rare animals.

What has become of the endangered plants and animals since the goats' removal? While it is widely agreed that removing the goats has improved the ecological condition of the island, there are now nine endangered species on the island. Two more plant species have been added to the list, and none has been declared recovered.

In recent years it is an animal species that has received the most attention. The San Clemente Island Loggerhead Shrike was first listed as endangered along with those four plant and two other animal species in 1977.
Even after the removal of the goats, its population continued to decline. By
the mid-1990s, the shrike was on the verge of extinction, and a coalition of
environmental groups threatened to sue the Navy. In order to forestall the
suit, the Navy built a shrike captive breeding facility, implemented a year-
round predator control program, improved the fire management plan, and
improved the system for coordinating military activities on the island with
shrike conservation and research. It also created a consortium of wildlife
agencies to manage the shrike's recovery. In 1998 only 13 of the birds
remained; today there are as many as 160.

You might wonder what the Navy uses the island for. While it serves
various training functions, a recent headline from the *San Diego Union* newspaper says it best: "Endangered loggerhead shrike lives on island Navy uses
for target practice."[35] The Navy describes its activities in a more nuanced
way:

> SCI [San Clemente Island] is a very unique combination of airfields, airspace
> and ranges unlike any other facility owned by the Navy. It is the only
> location in the Pacific where surface ships, submarines, aircraft and Navy
> expeditionary forces can train in all warfare areas simultaneously using
> shore gunnery, bombardment, air defense, anti sub and electronic
> warfare . . . Training on the island has increased 25% since the terrorist
> attacks of September 2001. The Department of Defense began construction
> in July 2002 of a $21-million simulated U.S. embassy compound to train
> troops in rescuing Americans.[36]

While using the island for target practice, the Navy has also been spending $2.4 million per year on its shrike recovery program, which employs
about fifty people. During the shrike's breeding season, the Navy closes its
bombing range four days a week, and during the fire season it reduces one
of its firing ranges by 90 percent and the other by 50 percent. In 2002, Joel
Hefley, a Colorado Republican who was then chairman of the subcommittee
on military readiness, wondered at hearings on the subject where it would
end: "How many shrikes must be reintroduced into the wild and maintained

[35] <www.signonsandiego.com/news/science/20060426-9999-lz1c26shrike.html>.
[36] <www.nbc.navy.mil/index.asp?fuseaction=NBCInstallations.NALFSCI>.

on San Clemente Island before we can say that the Navy can once again devote its complete attention and dollars to its primary mission of preparing our military forces to ensure national security?"[37]

There are (of course) other complications. In its efforts to protect the shrike, the Navy's predator control program was eliminating not only introduced species such as rats and feral cats, but also native species such as ravens and kestrels, and even another rare species, the Channel Island Fox. Indeed, one group of scientists at New Mexico State claimed that "*The momentum* . . . for conservation of the shrike has led to an endangered species conflict that has contributed to the endangerment of the endemic island fox." They went on to question whether the shrike really is a distinct subspecies worthy of protection.[38] This latter challenge appears to have been answered, and the Navy is no longer killing foxes, but the complications and ironies are not so easily dismissed.[39]

6.5.3 Natives versus exotics

In the background of the previous case was a conflict between native and exotic species. The main reason for preferring the plants to the goats on San Clemente Island is that the plants are endemic while the goats are exotic. If there is one policy that seems to unite most environmentalists it is that native plants and animals should be preferred over ones that are exotic. But what exactly is the difference between native and exotic species? It turns out to be surprisingly difficult to say.

One intuitive characterization finds human action at the center. A species is exotic in an environment if it would not be in that environment without human action.[40] This definition seems to fit a range of cases that come readily to mind: the intentional introduction of European domesticated animals all over the world; the Norwegian rats that tagged along on most European voyages of discovery; and even the coyotes who have spread throughout North America, filling the ecological niche opened by the extermination of wolves. However, this definition is both too strong and too weak: it counts

---

[37] <www.house.gov/hefley/state_floor9.htm>.

[38] Roemer and Wayne 2003. This last challenge seems to have been put to rest by Eggert *et al.* 2004.

[39] For a final irony, visit <www.ptreyeslight.com/stories/june26/goats.html>.

[40] Noss and Cooperrider 1994.

some species as native that appear to be exotic, and counts other species as exotic that appear to be native.

An example which may show that the definition is too weak is the case of "saltcedar" (genus *Tamarix*), which was first introduced to the United States as an ornamental plant, and by the late nineteenth century was ubiquitous in the desert Southwest. While there are taxonomical disagreements, some biologists claim that new species have evolved since the genus has been in the United States. If that is the case, then this definition would count them as exotic, since they would not be in the United States were it not for the fact that humans introduced their ancestors. Still, it would be hard to deny that they are native (indeed endemic) to the United States, since this is in fact where they evolved. In this strange case we appear to have a native species which belongs to an exotic genus.[41]

A clearer example of a native species which would not be present in a particular environment were it not for human action is the case of the wolf in Yellowstone. Wolves roamed this area for hundreds of thousands of years before the last one was killed in 1943. Little more than half a century later, in 1995, they were reintroduced. Were it not for the reintroduction, there would probably be no wolves in Yellowstone, yet this clearly seems to be a case of reintroducing a native species.

Cases in which exotics are introduced to new environments without human assistance show that the definition is too strong. Ten thousand years ago, when the first finches made their way to the Galapagos Islands from the South American mainland, they were exotics, yet this definition would count them as native.

The fundamental problem with this definition is that it draws an unreasonably sharp distinction between human and non-human causes. A plant species is exotic if its seeds hitch a ride with a backpacker, but not if it is introduced by a bird. The finches are native if they get to the Galapagos in any way except with the help of humans. This does not seem to get to the heart of what makes a species exotic.

A second definition claims that organisms are exotic when they occur outside of their historical range. Thus, on this account, the endemic saltcedar is

---

[41] Another interesting case is that of *Spartina*, which quickly and successfully hybridizes when introduced into new environments. The evolution of exotics is currently an intensive area of research. See e.g. Maron *et al.* 2004.

native and the first finches in the Galapagos are exotic. This definition also seems to account for the clear examples with which we began: introduced domesticated animals, Norway rats, and coyotes occupying wolf habitat, all count as exotic species on this definition.

However, the idea of a species' historical range is vague and often difficult to determine. In the program currently under way to introduce lynx to southern Colorado, one of the main points of contention is whether southern Colorado was in fact part of the lynx's historical range. The evidence on both sides is quite speculative. In addition to the difficulty of answering such empirical questions, there are also conceptual questions about this definition. How far back in time do we go in assessing a species' historical range? Various species of camels, elephants, and cheetahs existed in North America, but were driven to extinction about 13,000 years ago during the Pleistocene. If we were to introduce their African and Asian cousins to North America, would they count as native species reclaiming their historical range or would they count as exotics?[42] I suspect most of us would count them as exotics on the grounds that while they are close relatives of the extinct species, they are genetically distinct. But when populations are small, genetically distinct populations are often mingled in captive breeding programs (e.g. in the Galapagos Tortoise breeding program). A striking example is the highly regarded program that returned the Peregrine Falcon to North America, which used captive-bred birds from seven subspecies on four continents.[43] These are cases in which members of different subspecies are bred, while introducing camels, elephants, and cheetahs to North America would involve using species different from the ones that were driven to extinction. Still, the line between species and subspecies is often not clear, and the relationships between species can also be complex and various. Does it matter to the policy of introducing camels to North America that all existing camels are descendents of the extinct North American camel? Would it matter if the introduced species were to play the same ecological role as the one which became extinct?

Even if a species has not become extinct (locally or otherwise), its historical range can shift. Once there were palm trees in the Canadian Arctic,

---

[42] Such a policy has been advocated by a number of scientists and environmentalists. See Donlan et al. 2005, and visit <www.eeb.cornell.edu/donlan/deeptime.htm>. For discussion, see Atkinson 2001.

[43] Donlan et al. 2005.

and aspens grew at relatively low elevations in Baja California. Yet it is hard to resist the idea that someone who planted a palm tree in the Canadian Arctic or an aspen in San Diego would have planted an exotic species.

A third definition seems to capture all of the cases discussed so far, including the case of the Arctic palm and the San Diego aspen: a species is exotic if and only if it is not well integrated into the ecological community. In general, however, this criterion seems vaguer and more difficult to apply than the previous one. As we have seen, the concept of an ecosystem or ecological community is not all that clear in the first place, and it is even less clear what it means for a species to be well integrated. One thought might be that being well adapted to an environment is sufficient for being well integrated. But the goats of San Clemente Island were well adapted in the sense that they enjoyed high levels of reproductive success. Yet it seems clear that they were not well integrated into the ecosystem. Even if we reject the idea that there is any connection between being well adapted and being well integrated, we must still contend with the fact that exotic organisms often have no demonstrable impact on ecosystems.[44] There are a number of theories about why this is the case, one of which holds that exotics often take advantage of available unused resources (such as soil nutrients) rather than competing with other organisms.[45] On this view, exotics often tap into an unrealized niche and become just another part of the ecosystem. In these cases it seems clear that what we would consider an exotic organism in fact successfully integrates into the ecological community. Even if exotics do not integrate successfully immediately, over time they can transform an ecosystem into one in which they are well integrated. Many cases of what is called "naturalization" are like this. Assuming that they did not become extinct, at some point the San Clemente Island goats would have naturalized and become native (like the finches of the Galapagos). Since many organisms are native but not endemic, the transformation from exotic to native must be common. What exactly are the conditions for this, however, is difficult to say.

There are also cases in which native species do not seem well integrated into ecological systems. The Asian Long-Horned Beetle (*Anoplophora*

---

[44] James Carlton warns us to be cautious about such statements, since the impact of most exotics has not been scientifically studied. I have benefited from correspondence with him on these topics.

[45] Davis 2003. See also Westman 1990.

glabripennis), which seriously damages trees in Chicago, does the same in parts of it its native range. *Pfiesteria piscicida*, a one-celled microorganism (dinoflagellate), is believed to have been widely dispersed in the environment for millions of years. However, since being discovered in 1988, it has become highly toxic, killing more than one billion fish.[46]

Let us take stock of where we are. We began with an intuitive distinction between exotic and native organisms, and then reviewed several definitions that aim to show what the distinction consists in. Although there must be a vast number of examples that conform to these definitions, none of them succeeds in providing either necessary or sufficient conditions for an organism's being exotic. What this shows is that, however useful these accounts may be in generalizations or as rules of thumb, they do not succeed in giving us a definition of the term or a precise analysis of the concept. This has led some philosophers to claim that the concepts of an exotic and a native are "cluster concepts" that typically exhibit various traits, no one of which is sufficient. Others have claimed that these concepts are vague and admit of degree.[47] In my view it is the value-ladenness of judgments about what is exotic and what is native that accounts for the difficulty of specifying precise conditions for the applications of these concepts. This may also explain why managers increasingly speak of "invasive" rather than exotic species, variously using the expression to refer to all species that we regard as damaging, as a synonym for 'exotic species', or as referring to a subclass of exotic species (as in the phrase 'invasive exotic species'). Something that is invasive is clearly bad; what is exotic may be dangerous, but also fun.

Since the concept of an exotic species is value-laden and management decisions often occur in highly complex circumstances, there are unlikely to be any categorical rules that apply in such cases. Decisions about managing (and even identifying) exotics are likely to involve conflicts of value reflecting such concerns as animal welfare, prudential values, aesthetic values, and natural values. In light of these considerations, eliminating what are regarded as exotics may, in many cases, be worse than tolerating them.

A recent article by Tim J. Setnicka, the former Superintendent of the Channel Islands National Park (which includes San Clemente Island), makes

---

[46] Barker 1997.

[47] See Woods and Moriarity 2001 for the former view, and Hettinger 2001 for the latter. This section is greatly indebted to their work.

clear what can be at stake in trying to eradicate exotic organisms. He writes "that a large portion of the park's history revolved around killing one species to save another." He tells of killing tens of thousands of animals in his thirty-year career. Mules, rabbits, and pigs were shot; rats were poisoned; pigs were stabbed. He sprayed herbicides and he set fires. His description of pig eradication is especially graphic:

> While hunting in such conditions, we frequently gut shot and wounded pigs who escaped. When sows were shot, their piglets were caught by dogs or we chased them down on foot. The dogs frequently chased down and cornered pigs. They would often tear into and mangle the smaller pigs. The larger pigs would fight the dogs, occasionally injuring or killing one. Due to the close quarters, pigs were caught by their hind legs and then were knifed or beaten to death. The terms "squealing like a stuck pig" or "bleeding like a stuck pig" are given graphic definition. Watching an animal bleed to death after sticking a knife in their jugular vein is a horrendous sight. You watch the life drain out of their eye which becomes dull as they die.[48]

This is a picture that would make many environmentalists squirm. The fact is that in the everyday trenches of conservation biology the romantic idea of "saving nature" often becomes a war against the unwanted.

In this section we have explored some conflicts of value that are at the heart of environmental ethics. What begins as a clear conflict between common animals and rare plants, for example, often winds up in a miasma of ever more complex issues. For what we often discover is that it is the hand of man that is behind such conflicts. In order to face up to our responsibilities, we must think clearly about the values that are at stake, for the world of the future will be the one that we make. The real final examination will not be a test at the end of the semester, but how we choose to live. In the next chapter we will discuss some of the forces that are shaping nature's future and the decisions that we face.

---

[48] "Ex-Park Chief Calls for Moratorium on Island 'Hunt': Commentary," Tim J. Setnicka, *Santa Barbara News Press*, March 25, 2005; available on the web at <www.idausa.org/campaigns/wildlife/pdf/call_for_ moratorium_on_island_hunt.pdf>.

7   Nature's future

7.1   Travails of the biosphere

Nature is in trouble: biodiversity is under siege, the climate is changing, and the ozone hole has not yet healed. The quality of human life is at risk from new infectious diseases, from pollution of air, food, and water, and from the loss of wildness and connection to nature.

While many people are aware of some or all of these problems, there is a tendency to see them in isolation. Environmental science texts give long lists of maladies, as if each entry were the name of a separate plague that is befalling us. Environmental organizations often specialize in a single issue while ignoring its neighbors. Government officials charged with protecting the environment issue reports and commission studies instead of writing regulations and enforcing laws, while their colleagues in other agencies do everything they can to encourage drilling and digging, as if these activities had no environmental consequences. Even the newspaper reinforces this separation among environmental problems and between environmental and other human concerns. While the science section tells us that fossil-fuel-driven climate change threatens both nature and human societies, the business section treats modest increases in the price of oil as if they were the catastrophes. Meanwhile the opinion sections opine about the political fallout of climate change or higher oil prices, rather than educating us about how we should act as citizens. In such social and political circumstances, it is no wonder that it is difficult for us to think clearly about nature's future.

In the 1980s a new way of thinking about environmental problems began to emerge.[1] Instead of seeing environmental problems as a heterogeneous list of insults, scientists and theorists began to see them as exhibiting

---

[1] There were many who anticipated this way of thinking, the most important of which was the nineteenth-century American lawyer, farmer, manufacturer, congressman, diplomat,

important unifying themes. They began to see these problems as systemic, with human action as their main driver.

This insight began to gain influence at the same time as a new picture of the Earth system was emerging. Rather than seeking equilibrium and being in love with stability, it turns out that Mother Nature is a restless old lady. Not only is environmental change inevitable and ubiquitous, but it is often quite dramatic. Indeed, were it not for extreme events such as the life-killing meteor that crashed into the Yucatan Peninsula about 65 million years ago, the dinosaurs might still be running the show. Only in the last 10,000 years have human life and society as we know it emerged, and the evidence is increasingly clear that this coincided with an unusually quiet and stable period in Earth's history. We seem to have mistaken the special conditions that allowed us to rise and dominate the Earth with necessary features of the Earth system. This is a dangerous mistake.

The primary challenge we face is not to preserve and protect stable, equilibrium-seeking systems, but rather to cope with change. The irony is that the most dramatic changes that are now under way are not externally driven, but flow from the heart of our societies. The greatest challenge that we face today is to live with the profound changes that we ourselves are initiating.

In section 6.4.3 we discussed such ideas as "the end of nature," and the claim that there is no such thing as wilderness. While I tried to alert you to the naïveté of such claims and to show how they are often used in fallacious arguments, there is an insight that such claims struggle to express that should be acknowledged. What inspires these claims is a robust appreciation of how thoroughgoing the human transformation of the planet really is.

Before we try to characterize this more precisely, think for a moment about just one of the many amazing scenarios that are now being contemplated by climate scientists. The global warming now under way will be more extreme near the poles than at the mid latitudes. Indeed, both the Antarctic and Greenland ice sheets are already melting faster and showing more signs of instability than most scientists thought possible. If these ice sheets were to melt completely, sea level would rise about 70 meters. A 6 meter sea level rise would destroy much of Florida and the Gulf Coast. It

scholar, linguist, and pioneer conservationist, George P. Marsh, who in 1864 published *Man and Nature; or, Physical Geography as Modified by Human Action.*

would take only a 1 meter sea level rise to inundate all the major cities
on the East Coast of the United States. Because it takes many years for the
impacts of greenhouse gas emissions to be felt, even if emissions had been
stabilized in 2000 we would still be committed to a much greater warming
than we have yet experienced. The volume of the oceans will expand as they
warm, and this alone will increase sea levels by about 25 centimeters.[2] Melting polar ice sheets will probably contribute even more to sea level rise. But
here is the really bad news: rather than stabilizing global greenhouse gas
emissions, the world has actually increased them by more than 9 percent
in just the first three years of this century. If we continue on this "business
as usual" trajectory, we can expect a warming of about 3 °C in this century.
The last time the Earth was this warm, sea levels were more than 24 meters
higher. When we look at all these factors together, the 1 meter sea level
rise that will inundate every major East Coast city looks close enough to
touch. The main point I want to make, however, is not about the credi-
bility of any particular climate change scenario. Rather, it is this: humans
have a profound ability to remake the global environment in ways we do
not fully understand, and such dramatic anthropogenic changes are already
well under way.

   In a 1997 article, a group of distinguished scientists led by Stanford's Peter
Vitousek reviewed the broad range of human impacts on nature. What they
found was that between one-third and one-half of Earth's land surface has
been transformed by human action; carbon dioxide in the atmosphere has
increased by more than 30 percent since the beginning of the Industrial
Revolution; more nitrogen is fixed by humanity than by all other terrestrial
organisms combined; more than half of all accessible surface fresh water
is appropriated by humanity; and about one-quarter of Earth's bird species
have been driven to extinction. Their conclusion was that "it is clear that we
live on a human dominated planet."[3] More recently the Millennium Ecosystem Assessment project issued its final report. This comprehensive analysis,
involving more than 1,000 scientists over a four-year period, concluded that
"human activity is putting such strain on the natural functions of Earth

[2] Meehl *et al.* (2005). The international scientific consensus on climate change is stated in
   a series of reports from the Intergovernmental Panel on Climate Change. The executive
   summary of their latest report on the physical-science basis of climate change is available
   on the web at <www.ipcc.ch/SPM2feb07.pdf>.
[3] Vitousek *et al.* 1997: 494.

that the ability of the planet's ecosystems to sustain future generations can no longer be taken for granted."[4]

There are various ways of measuring the human impact on nature. In 1986 Vitousek and his colleagues approached this problem by calculating the fraction of Earth's net primary production (NPP) that is appropriated by humanity, and thus is not directly available for other forms of life. (NPP is the amount of biomass that remains after primary producers (autotrophic organisms such as plants or algae) have accounted for their respiratory needs.) What they found is that humanity probably appropriates about 40 percent of Earth's terrestrial NPP.[5]

Another approach to assessing the human impact on nature is ecological footprint analysis, pioneered by Mathis Wackernagel and William Rees (1996). The ecological footprint of a nation, community, or individual is the amount of land area required to produce the resources it consumes and to absorb the wastes it generates, given its standard of living and prevailing technology.

With its recognition of the importance of technology and standard of living, ecological footprint analysis can be viewed as a development of the IPAT formula developed by Paul Ehrlich and John Holdren (1972) in dialogue with Barry Commoner. This simple equation, $I = PAT$, expresses impact (I) as the product of population (P), affluence (A), and technology, (T). What is insightful about this is that it recognizes that environmental impact is not a single-variable function; rather, it is a matter of how several variables interact. Because these variables have different values for different nations, communities, and individuals, environmental impacts can have quite different profiles. For example, according to one study, the American footprint is about four times larger than the global average.[6]

This may surprise some people who think of population size as the most important factor in determining environmental impact. It is true that the twentieth century witnessed both the largest increase in environmental destruction and the greatest increase in global population in human

---

[4] *Living Beyond Our Means*, p. 5, available on the web at <www.maweb.org//documents/document.429.aspx.pdf>.

[5] Subsequent studies using different methodologies have produced a range of figures, but Vitousek *et al.*'s (1986) original claim seems roughly correct. For a review, see Field 2001.

[6] <www.rprogress.org/media/releases/021125_efnations.html>. Various websites allow one to compute one's own ecological footprint; visit, e.g., <http://myfootprint.org>.

Table 2. *Countries ranked by population: 2006*

Rank	Country	Population
1	China	1,313,973,713
2	India	1,111,713,910
3	United States	298,444,215
4	Indonesia	231,820,243
5	Brazil	188,078,227
6	Pakistan	165,803,560
7	Bangladesh	147,365,352
8	Russia	142,069,494
9	Nigeria	131,859,731
10	Japan	127,463,611

Note: Data updated August 24, 2006
Source: US Census Bureau, International Data Base

history. The Earth did not have 1 billion inhabitants until 1802, and it was not until 1927, 125 years later, that it added the second billion. By 1961, 34 years later, the Earth's population had reached 3 billion. It took only 12 years to add the fourth billion, and 13 years to add the fifth. By 1999 there were 6 billion people on the planet. Global population now stands at about 6.6 billion and is growing at a rate of about 1.14 percent per year. If this rate continues, the population will double in 61 years. Current projections call for 8 billion people by 2025, with 99 percent of the increase occurring in developing countries. Indeed, 8 of the 10 largest countries are developing countries, as Table 2 shows.

Much of the twentieth-century population increase was caused by declines in mortality rates due to nutrional improvements, the control of infectious diseases, and the creation of public health systems. If global population is going to be stabilized or reduced in a morally acceptable way, voluntary reductions in fertility (the number of lifetime births per woman) are going to have to be the major part of the story.

Fertility has generally been declining since the mid twentieth century. In the 1960s the global fertility rate was about 5 births per woman; it now stands at about 2.6. However, these numbers mask a great deal of national variation. Twelve African countries, Afghanistan, and Yemen have fertility rates greater than 6, while Hong Kong's fertility rate is less than one. In

1950 China and India both had fertility rates of about 6. India's rate is now 2.73 and China's rate is 1.73. By mid-century, India will have the largest population in the world. As for the third-largest country, since reaching its low point in 1972 the American fertility rate has increased. At 2.09 it is significantly higher than that of most other industrialized countries, which have fertility rates ranging from 1.3 to 1.5.[7] It is not entirely clear what controls fertility rates, but economic factors, the status of women, and prevailing cultural values are certainly all involved.

In addition to population, the IPAT formula directs our attention to affluence as another variable that affects an individual's or nation's ecological footprint. Affluence is expressed in consumption, and there are various ways of trying to understand its effects.

Climate-changing greenhouse gas emissions are one mark of consumption and affluence. A large majority of the total greenhouse gas emissions are from rich countries, but some less developed countries are moving up on the list. According to preliminary data from the Netherlands Environmental Assessment Agency, China is now the world's largest single emitter of carbon dioxide. These emissions are driven to a great extent by the fact that China produces many of the goods that are consumed in Europe and North America. On a per capita basis, Americans emit more than four times as much as the Chinese.[8] In general, greenhouse gas emissions are closely associated with national incomes, as we can see from the graph below.[9] On most other measures of consumption and affluence, the same relationship obtains.

The third variable in the IPAT formula is technology, which affects environmental impacts in many different ways. One way is this. Because of their access to better technology, it generally takes rich countries fewer energy inputs than poor countries to produce the same amount of wealth. For example, the United States requires 176 tons of carbon (or its equivalent) to

---

[7] <https://www.cia.gov/cia/publications/factbook/rankorder/2127rank.html>.

[8] <www.mnp.nl/en/dossiers/Climatechange/moreinfo/Chinanowno1inCO2emissionsUSAin secondposition.html>.

[9] The source of this graph is the World Bank Online Database, 2004. It is available on the web at <www.vitalgraphics.net/graphic.cfm?filename=climate2/large/16.jpg>. One way of making the point vivid is to say that CO_2 emissions from using an electric kettle for one year in the UK are equivalent to average person's total annual CO_2 emissions in Nepal ("Nepal's Farmers on the Front Line of Global Climate Change," *Guardian*, December 2, 2006, available on the web at <www.guardian.co.uk/print/0,,329651149-123104,00.html>.

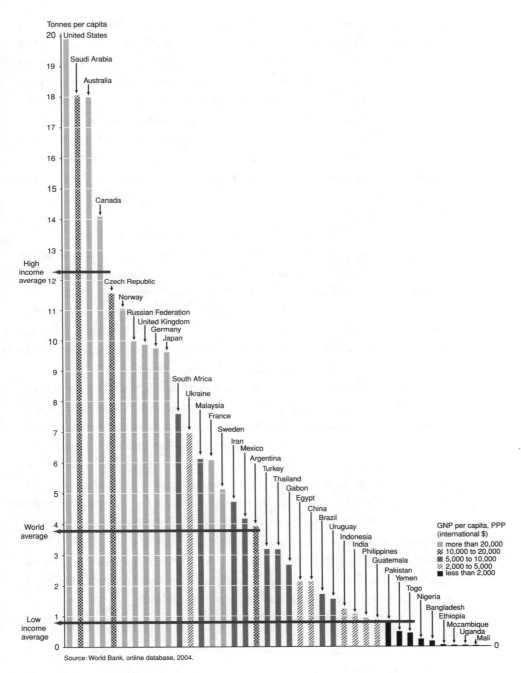

Tonnes per capita

High income average 12

World average 4

Low income average

GNP per capita, PPP
(international $)

- more than 20,000
- 10,000 to 20,000
- 5,000 to 10,000
- 2,000 to 5,000
- less than 2,000

Source: World Bank, online database, 2004.

CO_2 emissions in 2002

produce $1 million in output, while India requires 514 tons and China 749 tons to produce the same $1 million of output. India's efficiency has slipped slightly since 1980, when it took 509 tons of input to produce $1 million of output, while China's efficiency has increased enormously. In 1980 it took the Chinese 2,407 tons of carbon equivalent and the Americans 269 tons to produce $1 million of output, a much larger gap than exists today. American efficiency looks good when compared to the developing world, but it does not fare as well when compared to other industrialized countries. It takes the United Kingdom only 116 tons of carbon equivalent to produce $1 million of output, 100 tons for Italy, 84 tons for Germany, 61 tons for France, and 56 tons for Japan.[10]

How does all this come out in the wash? The simple fact is that in determining the size of a nation's ecological footprint, the vast differences in affluence overwhelm differences in technology and even population. Using measures from the Redefining Progress Foundation, the ecological footprint of the United States is more than twice that of China and more than 6 times that of India.[11] The United States does a little better on measures provided by the World Wide Fund for Nature, with an ecological footprint about 50 percent greater than China's and 3 times greater than India's.[12]

The reason the American footprint is larger than that of China and India is that the per capita footprint of Americans is so much larger than that of Chinese or Indians. While China's population is a little more than 4 times that of the United States, the footprint of each American is 6–9 times greater. In the case of India, the population is a little less than 4 times that of the United States but the per capita footprint is between $\frac{1}{12}$ and $\frac{1}{25}$ as great. While in general there is a large disparity between the footprints of those who live in rich and poor countries, it does not have to be this great. The per capita footprint of Europeans is about half that of Americans.

None of this should surprise us if we look at the lifestyles of Americans. Charles Hall and his colleagues performed a life cycle analysis of the environmental impact of the average American by determining each person's share of the nation's total consumption of various resources.[13] They found that a

[10] See <www.gao.gov/new.items/d04146r.pdf>.

[11] <www.rprogress.org/>.

[12] <www.panda.org/news_facts/publications/key_publications/living_planet_report/index. cfm>.

[13] Hall *et al.* 1995. For another perspective, see Wapner and Willoughby 2005.

single American born in the 1990s will be responsible, over his (or her) lifetime, for 22 million pounds of liquid waste and 2.2 million pounds each of
solid waste and atmospheric waste. He will have a lifetime consumption
of 4,000 barrels of oil, 1.5 million pounds of minerals, and 62,000 pounds
of animal products that will entail the slaughter of 2,000 animals. If an
American wants to minimize his environmental impact, the most effective
thing he can do is to refrain from having children. He can drive around in
an SUV, hang out at McDonald's, take long hot showers and still have much
less environmental impact than if he fathers one, good, green, nature-loving
American child.

There are many complications here that invite further discussion. Various
technical and methodological questions can be asked about how we can
contend with gaps in the data and how we can account for the fact that
much of what we consume is produced elsewhere.[14]

There are also different ways of looking at the significance of these figures. If we view a nation or region as entitled to its natural wealth, then we
might think of the ratio of its ecological footprint to its natural wealth as
an indicator of environmental responsibility. By this measure, rich countries
such as Canada and Australia fare much better than poor countries such as
China and India.[15] If we turn our attention to the fraction of NPP appropriated by humanity and disaggregate this number by region, we find that
North America appropriates 23.7% of NPP while South-Central Asia appropriates 80.4%.[16] This might suggest that North Americans are more environmentally responsible than South-Central Asians since they have less impact
on nature. Against this it might be claimed that rather than being a sign of
environmental responsibility, the relatively low proportion of NPP appropriated by North Americans is the result of their good luck in inhabiting a con-
tinent that is much more biologically productive than South-Central Asia.
But in response it might be pointed out that biological productivity is not
only a matter of luck; it is also a function of land use practices and environmental policy. To this it might be said that we cannot understand the comparative biological impoverishment of South-Central Asia without reflecting
on the history of exploitation and imperialism to which this region was

[14] For discussion of these and other issues, see e.g. Van den Bergh and Verbruggen 1999.
[15] <http://assets.panda.org/downloads/asialpr2005.pdf>.
[16] <http://ecophys.plantbio.ohiou.edu/HumanNPP_nature04.pdf>.

subjected. Moreover, it might be said, much of the NPP appropriation that is at the foundation of North American and European lifestyles occurs off-shore, and thus counts against those countries whose biological wealth is being exported for use by others. Obviously, there is much more to say and the argument can go on. I will only note the interesting further point that it is South America and Africa that appropriate the lowest percentage of their NPP (6.1% and 12.4% respectively), while Western Europe is second only to South-Central Asia in its high exploitation of NPP (72.2%).

Whatever we think about these disputes, the bottom line is clear. According to WWF's *Living Planet Report*, some time in the late 1980s humanity began to consume resources faster than the Earth can regenerate them, and this gap is increasing every year. The planetary impacts of the highly consumptive lifestyles practiced in the industrialized world cannot be generalized: the fact is that the planet simply cannot stand many people who consume like Americans, and this raises important questions of justice.

7.2   Questions of justice

The differences in the per capita ecological footprints of people in developed and developing countries are expressions of global inequality and the distribution of poverty. About a sixth of the world (including many people in India and China) live highly consumptive lifestyles like most Americans and Europeans, and about twice as many people in the world face a constant challenge in meeting even their basic nutritional needs. With so many people living on the edge, humanitarian disasters triggered by wars or other extreme events are a predictable fact of life. Environmental disruptions and extreme events have always, everywhere, affected the poor more than the rich. This was true during the "little ice age" that occurred in Europe from about 1300 to 1850, and it was true when Hurricane Katrina struck the Gulf Coast of the United States in 2005. If aggressive action is not taken soon to mitigate climate change, hundreds of millions of additional people will slip over the edge and be at risk from hunger, malaria, flooding, and water shortages.[17] Most of those who will suffer, and those who will suffer most, are not our poor contemporaries but poor people who will live in the future.

---

[17] Parry *et al.* 2001.

Most of us claim to care about future generations. Indeed, some studies indicate that this is the primary motivation for environmental concern.[18] However, the term 'future generations' obscures the distinction between those who are near us in time and those who are remote.

We care about many of those who are near us in time because we are directly related to them or because shared circumstances and experiences give us a sense of identification with them. Something like "sentimental transitivity" may extend this concern a little further into the future. For example, we may care about our children's children because we care about our children, or perhaps because we see our children's children as our own. However, sentimental transitivity fails after about two or three generations. Rather than thinking about future people as identifiable individuals who will carry on projects with which we identify, they start to become an undifferentiated mass who will live in a world that is difficult for us to imagine. Yet these people in the further future will have to live with our nuclear waste and the climate change that we are causing.

Some are skeptical about whether we have strong duties to those who will live in the further future. Economists typically assume that people will become progressively better off, since later generations benefit from the investments of those that precede them. Any sacrifice that we would make for those in the further future would thus be seen as a transfer from those who are worse off to those who are better off. Others are skeptical that we can anticipate the preferences of those who will live in the further future. How can we be sure that they will be interested in whales or wilderness rather than in virtual reality or some other form of satisfaction that is now beyond our imagination? Sacrificing to preserve energy sources or limited commodity stocks would be foolish if technological changes result in cheap substitutes for them.

The most important reasons for being skeptical about our duties to the further future flow from the fact that our relations with these people are largely asymmetric: we have enormous causal power over them, but they have little causal power over us. (However, they do have some power over us; for example, they can frustrate my desire that my grave always be kept clean.) This asymmetry manifests in several important ways.

[18] Kempton *et al.* 1995.

Reciprocity is central to our moral consciousness and motivation, yet the asymmetry of our relationships with those who will live in the further future makes it impossible. We gift them our accumulated capital, yet we receive nothing in return, not even so much as a "thank you." As Groucho Marx once said, "Why should I do anything for posterity? What has posterity ever done for me?"[19]

What we bequeath to people in the further future is not just capital, but the very world in which they make the choices that make their lives meaningful. Consider an example. In the space of a few centuries Manhattan was transformed from a verdant natural paradise to the vibrant, architecturally impressive, culturally rich and diverse city that it is today. Was this transformation of Manhattan good or bad for me? It is not only that I do not know the answer to this question; it is rather that I do not know how this question could be answered. Much of what makes my life go better or worse presupposes Manhattan as it currently exists. How can I compare this life which I actually lead to the one that I would have lived in the Manhattan that was a wilderness? This is not to deny that there is room to argue that this transformation of Manhattan was, all things considered, good or bad, or that the actions or policies that produced this transformation were right or wrong. What I cannot see is how it can be argued that this transformation was good or bad for me. If this is true with respect to the transformation of Manhattan and me, it is certainly true of the transformation of the Earth that will create the conditions of life that will be presupposed by those who will live in the further future.

Moreover, the very existence of people in the further future depends on our actions. We could prevent their existence by causing a nuclear holocaust or engaging in massive, voluntary birth control. Even if we assume that there will be people in the further future, different individuals will exist depending on what policies we adopt. For example, if we decide to conserve energy rather than following a "business as usual" policy, people may go to bed earlier in order to stay warm and save electricity. Since the origin of each person is in the highly improbable union of a particular sperm and egg, conceiving a child at different times will almost certainly result in different people coming into existence. People who exist on one scenario (e.g. conservation) but who would not have existed on the other scenario

---

[19] <http://quotations.about.com/od/funnymovieandtvquotes/a/grouchomarx1.htm>.

(e.g. business as usual) will go on to make babies with people who would have existed on either scenario. Their offspring would not have existed had we adopted a different policy, since one of their parents would not have existed. We do not have to go through many generations in order to reach an entire population that would not have existed had we adopted a different policy. So long as these people have lives worth living, it is hard to see how they can complain about whatever policies we have followed. For if we had not followed the policy that we did, these particular people would not have existed.[20]

Despite these arguments, most of us think that we do have duties to those who will live in the further future, even though our motivation to fulfill them may sometimes flag. The human ecologist, the late Garrett Hardin, drew an uncomfortable conclusion from this commitment. He wrote that "to be generous with one's own possessions is one thing; to be generous with posterity's is quite another."[21] A concern for justice for our poor contemporaries, he claimed, has the effect of destroying the environment and cheating future generations.

Hardin rejected Boulding's analogy of the Earth as a spaceship, for this implies sharing resources without assigning individual responsibilities, and this, he thinks, is a prescription for disaster. The sharing ethic suggested by the spaceship analogy leads to the "tragedy of the commons", which, according to Hardin, is the source of most of our environmental problems, including pollution, land destruction, and fishery collapse. In a very influential paper[22] he illustrated the tragedy of the commons by asking us to imagine a pasture shared by herders. Each herder individually benefits from grazing an animal, while the costs are spread over all the herders in the slight degradation of the pasture caused by the animal. Thus, each herder has an incentive to keep adding animals, since he gains all the benefits but shares the costs. The result is overgrazing and the degradation of the pasture.

---

[20] Indeed, this magnifies the problem discussed in the previous paragraph: would it even have been possible for me to exist in the verdant, natural paradise of Manhattan? Of course, to some extent this depends on what we mean by 'possible', a question that has exercised philosophers for millennia.

This "non-identity problem" was developed by Parfit (1984: ch. 16). Schwarz (1978), but not Parfit, develops it as an argument against the idea that we have duties to those who will live in the further future.

[21] Hardin 1974.   [22] Hardin 1968.

Instead of the camaraderie of the spaceship, Hardin proposes the more desperate analogy of the lifeboat, whose maximum capacity is 60 people, already occupied by 50 people, and surrounded by 100 people who will drown if they cannot get in. There are three possible responses. We could put everyone in the boat, which would result in everyone drowning. We could admit ten more people, thus losing the boat's safety factor and raising the question of which ten to admit. Or we could admit no one to the boat and fight off those who try to get on board. Hardin advocates the latter response.

According to Hardin, food aid to those who are hungry displays the same flawed logic as that of the unregulated commons. It provides benefits to individuals without imposing responsibilities. The result is that a population that receives food aid will breed up to the next crisis point at which it will again require food aid. This cycle will continue until food aid cannot or will not be provided. At this point, the population will starve. The number of people who will die is a function of the amount of food aid provided. More food aid means that more people will be brought into existence who will eventually starve to death. In effect, what Hardin gives us is a utilitarian argument for denying food to those who are hungry.

In response, we might want to distinguish food aid, which is a matter of charity, from redistribution, which is a matter of justice. We might say that poor people and countries are entitled to resources and that rich people and countries wrong them if they fail to respond. Hardin admits that the existing global order is based on injustices, but he insists that they cannot be rectified and we must proceed from where we are, not where we should be. Even if it would be unjust for us to deny people food (or a place in the lifeboat) we should do so anyway. More people will die if we respond to their demands than if we deny them, and responding may even put our own survival at risk. These are good reasons, in Hardin's view, for spurning even demands of justice. Hardin's view is dark and unrelenting, but it is an honest challenge that must be met.[23]

In the 1980s a powerful movement emerged that was directed towards both protecting the global environment and satisfying the demands of justice on behalf of our poor contemporaries and future generations. In 1983 the General Assembly of the United Nations created the World Commission

---

[23] For responses, see O'Neill 1986 and Singer 1993: 236–41.

on Environment and Development, known as the Brundtland Commission after its Chair, the Norwegian politician and physician, Gro Harlem Brundtland. The charge of the Commission was to "propose long-term environmental strategies for achieving sustainable development by the year 2000 and beyond . . . and to recommend ways concern for the environment may be translated into greater co-operation among . . . countries at different states of economic and social development."[24]

Their results were published in a 1987 book, *Our Common Future*, which defined sustainable development as "meeting the needs of the present without compromising the ability of future generations to meet their needs," and discussed how it might be implemented in such areas as population, food security, species and ecosystem preservation, and so on.[25]

For a brief period it seemed that *Our Common Future* might be prophetic. In 1985 Mikhail Gorbachev came to power in the Soviet Union and for the first time that country began to play an active role in addressing global environmental problems. He proposed turning the United Nations Trusteeship Council, which had supervised the transition to independence of eleven former colonies, into an institution for managing the global commons (i.e. oceans, atmosphere, biodiversity, and climate). In a speech to the Global Forum for the Survival of Humanity in 1989, Gorbachev proposed a new organization which would respond to environmental problems that transcend national boundaries by applying the medical emergency model of the Red Cross to ecological issues. In the United States, after a failed bid for the presidency in 1988, Al Gore began writing *Earth in the Balance: Ecology and the Human Spirit*, in which he asserted that "we must make the rescue of the environment the central organizing principle for civilization."[26] By the late 1980s the entwined problems of environment and development were the subject of countless international meetings and were on the front pages of newspapers around the world.

This activity culminated in the 1992 United Nations Conference on Environment and Development, held in Rio de Janeiro, Brazil. This meeting, popularly known as the "Rio Earth Summit," was the largest gathering of national leaders ever held. Thousands of people came to Rio to make their voices heard and to be part of history. Expectations were high that Rio would

---

[24] World Commission on Environment and Development 1987: ix.
[25] World Commission on Environment and Development 1987: 43.   [26] Gore 1992: 269.

change the world. Agreements would be made to curb global warming, preserve biodiversity, and protect the world's forests, in addition to taking concrete steps to reduce global poverty. An Earth Charter would be adopted that would serve as a new, global code of ethics governing human relationships with nature.

In some ways the meeting was a success, but on the whole it was a disappointment. The Framework Convention on Climate Change was adopted, but American and Russian opposition prevented the inclusion of binding commitments to emissions reductions in the treaty. The Convention on Biodiversity was adopted, but the United States refused to sign it, and although it was later signed by President Clinton, the US Senate has refused to ratify it. The attempt to create a global convention to protect forests failed due to the opposition of developing countries led by Malaysia; instead, a nonbinding Statement of Forest Principles was adopted. Agenda 21, an impressively detailed program for integrating environmental protection and development, was adopted, but it too was non-binding, and has subsequently been ignored. The nations of the world were unable to agree on an Earth Charter, instead adopting the Rio Declaration, an incoherent statement of fairly innocuous principles. The question of population was never on the table because of a coalition of the United States and Muslim, Catholic, and developing countries. In retrospect, we can see that the window that had briefly opened in the 1980s that might have allowed action on these issues was closing very rapidly by the time of the Rio Earth Summit. The first Gulf War broke out in 1990, and Gorbachev was replaced by a coup in 1991. The issues that have subsequently dominated the world's attention were already moving to center stage.

7.3   Visions of the future

In my opinion, there are three broad scenarios for what the future may bring: environmental catastrophe; continuing and increasing global inequality and environmental degradation; or a change in the way of life of the world's most privileged people. These three scenarios are not clear-cut, nor are they mutually exclusive. To some extent we are living in the midst of each of them right now, and the future may hold more of the same.

Consider first environmental catastrophe. Green rhetoric about "saving the planet" seems to suggest that if we don't change our ways the planet will be in trouble. But while there is some chance that we may destroy ourselves and most other forms of life, there is little chance that we will destroy the planet. The planet will survive nuclear war, a runaway greenhouse effect, or continuing ozone depletion. It will continue in its orbit until it collides with a bolide, falls into the sun, or the universe collapses. What we mean by an environmental catastrophe is a catastrophe for us and other living things, not for the planet.

Catastrophes don't arrive announcing themselves as such. As things now stand, everyday environmental problems cause death and destruction to vast numbers of humans and other animals. Yet most us do not think of ourselves as living through a catastrophe. Some of this is a matter of perception and some is a matter of where we are located. There is not much question that those who depend on the Aral Sea for their livelihood are living through an environmental catastrophe, as are the Great Apes who are being hunted for bush meat in Africa. However, it is more difficult to say this of those who live in the tony suburbs of Australia or North America. They are doing just fine.

What counts as an environmental catastrophe also depends on what one values. Many ecologists feel that the species extinctions and biodiversity losses that are now under way are the early stages of an environmental catastrophe, but not everyone thinks that these things matter. Commenting on the highly endangered Northern Spotted Owl, American political commentator Rush Limbaugh once said, "If the owl can't adapt to the superiority of humans, screw it."[27] Even if many species become extinct, many people will continue to have quite good lives by their own lights.

Yet having said all this, because of the increasing consumption and population reviewed in the first part of this chapter, we may well be headed for what would be an environmental catastrophe that would be difficult to deny. Even though the number of people living in utter poverty does not seem to budge, an increasing number of people in developing countries are living like those in developed countries. Energy consumption, meat production, automobile ownership and the other markers of affluence are increasing dramatically in such countries as China and India. Where will it end? According to one study, if everyone lived the same way as the average American, we would need 5.3 planets with the resources of Earth.[28]

[27] <www.ontheissues.org/Celeb/Rush_Limbaugh_Environment.htm>.
[28] <www.farces.com/index.php/how_many_planets_are_needed_to_support_your_lifestyle/>.

This leads to the second scenario, in which global inequality and environmental degradation continue and increase. On this scenario, we prevent the environmental catastrophe implied by everyone living in the same way as the average American by making sure that they do not: the rich continue to be rich, and the poor continue to be poor.

In addition to being morally indefensible, this is probably not a viable long-term strategy. Developing countries are quite sensitive to the possibility that their development prospects are being intentionally thwarted in order to protect the quality of life in already developed countries. They will not accept this without a struggle. Consciously adopting the strategy of preventing third-world development would guarantee that tensions and conflicts between the rich and poor countries would be a permanent feature of life. As weapons of mass destruction increasingly proliferate, this is a foreboding prospect. Moreover, there is only so much rich countries can do to keep down developing countries. There is no question that China's development is well under way. If the Chinese do not gain access to more efficient and environmentally friendly technologies, they will fuel their development with their vast reserves of coal. There are already more than 500 new coal-powered electricity generating plants in various stages of development in China. If they come on line, the result will be devastating for the global environment. This is not the result that the Chinese want, but there is little doubt that they prefer it to remaining poor.

The truth is that the developing world is in a position to do a great deal of damage to the rich countries and the things that they value. In addition to their ability significantly to increase and accelerate climate change, developing countries are also the custodians of much of the world's biodiversity. Without the active cooperation of countries in Africa, South America, and Asia, much of it will be lost for ever, including some of the animal species that we most love and admire. Moreover, nine developing countries still manufacture ozone-depleting chemicals. They are supposed to stop by 2010, but if they do not, ozone depletion will again take center stage as our most threatening environmental problem.

Because developing countries have the ability to threaten what those in the developed world cherish, there is the possibility of a deal. For their part, developing countries would develop in a way that "leapfrogs" the highly polluting, resource-intensive development model that was followed by Europe and North America, and move directly to the highly efficient, sustainable technologies of the future. In return, the rich countries must set an example by reducing their own consumption and moving towards sustainability. To a great extent they must also develop, provide, and pay for the new technologies that the developing countries need in order to make this transition. It was the recognition of this convergence of interests that brought hope to people in the 1980s that real progress could be made on healing the global environment and addressing the problems of poverty. What are the chances of such a deal today?

There is reason to think that much of the developing world is still interested. As Zhou Dadi, of Beijing's Energy Research Institute, told the BBC: "We need a new model of development that means high-level living standards with lower emissions per capita. If we can find such a model, China will follow that."[29] Most European countries have also shown their willingness to move in a different direction. For example, by committing themselves to reducing greenhouse gas emissions, they have put themselves at a competitive disadvantage with respect to the United States, which refuses to control its own emissions. European countries have also adopted a variety of important environmental laws, from Germany's extended producer responsibility laws, which require manufacturers to be responsible for their products throughout their entire life cycles, to London's congestion pricing system, which has reduced traffic and air pollution. This brings us to the most important question about the future. Can we imagine the United States reducing consumption, increasing efficiency, and moving towards sustainability?

There are reasons for being pessimistic. The United States today is a remarkably materialistic society. One indication of this is the talismanic role played by economic indicators, statistics, and projections in the public life of the nation. Information that used to be confined to the business section of the newspaper has increasingly colonized the news pages. A random glance at today's *New York Times*, for example, shows that a speech by a minor Federal Reserve official is treated as more newsworthy than 100 elephants poached in Africa and the latest Israeli raid in Gaza. It is difficult to imagine another national leader imploring his country, as President Bush did in the wake of the September 11 attacks, to go shopping as a way of defeating terrorism. While the state of the economy is an important political issue in every nation, it is hard to imagine another political campaign as

[29] <http://news.bbc.co.uk/2/hi/programmes/newsnight/4330469.stm>.

self-consciously guided by the mantra "It's the economy, stupid," as President Clinton's was in 1992. Environmental concern often loses out in America because it is seen as inconsistent with economic growth or the comforts it is supposed to deliver. President Reagan spoke for many Americans when he said that "conservation means that we'll be hot in the summer and cold in the winter."[30] Perhaps the clearest statement of the American commitment to a high-consumption lifestyle was made by the first President Bush, when he told representatives from several third-world countries during the 1992 Rio Earth Summit that "the American way of life is not negotiable." The obsession with wealth makes it difficult for the United States to act on environmental issues. When the economy is weak, the nation feels too poor to take aggressive action; when the economy is strong, the risks are too great. The result is that the richest country in the history of the world feels too economically constrained to take aggressive action to protect the environment.

As I mentioned, Western Europe has become the environmental leader of the world. Although there are "win/win" synergies between economic growth and environmental protection, the brute fact is that Western Europeans have sometimes chosen to promote values other than unbridled economic growth. For example, they have traded increments of economic growth for goods such as greater leisure, more equality, less poverty, and greater provision of public goods. The statistic that has the most symbolic resonance in this regard is that Western Europeans work about 20 percent less than Americans. Many have a legal right to at least one month of paid vacation each year, while the average American takes little more than two weeks' vacation, this at the discretion of his employer, and sometimes without pay. Various explanations have been given for these differences between the United States and Western Europe, but at heart they express a difference of values.[31]

The case for prioritizing economic growth over other values must in the end rest on its supposed special relationship to human happiness. Yet it is surprisingly difficult to make the case for this. It is increasingly clear

---

[30] Reported on the front page of the *New York Times*, January 4, 1981.

[31] While there are different studies and different methodologies, evidence for European leadership can be found in the Environmental Sustainability Index, which ranks the United States seventeenth among OECD countries. For details, visit <www.yale.edu/esi/ESI2005_Main_Report.pdf>.

that wealth is not a good indicator of happiness, either for countries or for individuals.[32] The evidence is mounting that wealth past a fairly basic level does not make people happy. What does make people happy is love, companionship, and engaging in meaningful activities. The psychologist, Edward Diener, summarizes what is known in this way:

> Once basic needs have been met . . . increases in income do little
> to affect happiness. If a nation has achieved a moderate level of economic
> prosperity, little increase in subjective well-being is seen as that society
> grows richer still. Research on groups living a materially simple lifestyle –
> from the Maasai in Kenya, to the Amish in America, to the seal hunters in
> Greenland – shows that these societies exhibit positive levels of subjective
> well-being despite the absence of swimming pools, dishwashers, and Harry
> Potter. In fact, a growing body of research suggests that materialism can
> actually be toxic to happiness. In one such study, people who reported that
> they valued money more than love were less satisfied with their lives than
> those who favored love. In the end, having money is probably mildly beneficial
> to happiness, while focusing on money as a major goal is detrimental.[33]

Philosophers for a long time have said that treating wealth or economic growth as a surrogate for happiness is a mistake. The nineteenth-century British philosopher, John Stuart Mill, argued for a stationary state economy in order to avoid a world in which

> solitude is extirpated . . . [since it] is essential to any depth of meditation or
> of character; and solitude in the presence of natural beauty and grandeur,
> is the cradle of thought and aspirations . . . Nor is there much satisfaction
> in contemplating the world with nothing left to the spontaneous activity of
> nature; with every rood of land brought into cultivation . . . every flowery
> waste or natural pasture ploughed up, all quadrupeds or birds which are
> not domesticated for man's use exterminated . . . every hedgerow or
> superfluous tree rooted out, and scarcely a place left where a wild shrub or
> flower could grow without being eradicated as a weed in the name of
> improved agriculture.

[32] More precisely, it is not a good indicator of subjective reports of happiness. While the question of what happiness consists in is a deep and important philosophical question, it would be mad (or at least implausible) to suppose that it had no interesting relation to what people say about their happiness.

[33] In Biswas-Diener 2004; available on the web at <www.findarticles.com/p/articles/mi_qa3671/is_200404/ai_n9394174/pg_3>.

He went on to point out that

> a stationary condition of capital and population implies no stationary state
> of human improvement. There would be as much scope as ever for all kinds
> of mental culture, and moral and social progress; as much room for
> improving the Art of Living, and much more likelihood of its being
> improved.[34]

Still, it might be thought that even if this is true, the sort of simplicity that Mill advocates is un-American; materialism, it might be said, is as
American as apple pie; there is no getting away from it and we should just
get used to it.

This may be true, but it is important to recognize that the degree and
extent of materialism that we see in the United States today are a relatively
recent phenomenon. If we go back to the founders of the American republic
we will find an enormous emphasis on such virtues as thrift, prudence, and
simplicity. In *The Art of Virtue*, a book that he projected when he was a young
man but was only published recently, Benjamin Franklin lists frugality as a
virtue, and characterizes it as to "make no expense but to do good to others
or yourself; i.e. waste nothing."[35] The "greatest generation" is legendary for
its sacrifices in fighting a faraway war for democracy in Europe and in the
Pacific. Even in the 1960s many people took pride in minimal rather than
conspicuous consumption. In the 1970s environmentalists popularized such
slogans as "Small is beautiful" and "Live simply so that others may simply
live."[36] Perhaps it is symbolic of how the United States has changed that if
you google "simple life" you will come up with the reality TV show starring
Paris Hilton and Nicole Ritchie. It is important to recognize, however, that
the celebration of consumption is relatively recent, and arguably a depar-
ture from the main themes of American life and history. Indeed, even the
fissures between the United States and Europe on environmental protection
are largely a product of the last decade or two. Until sometime in the 1980s
it was the United States, not Western Europe, that was the leading advocate
for protecting the global environment.

---

[34] As quoted in Gruen and Jamieson 1994: 30.

[35] Franklin 1996: 42; available on the web at <www.fordham.edu/halsall/mod/franklin-
virtue.html>.

[36] The phrase "Small is beautiful" is from Schumacher 1973. "Live simply so that others
may simply live" is often attributed to Ghandi. See also Elgin 1998.

Whatever is true of the history, the question remains of whether it is possible for the United States to move in the direction of reducing consumption and increasing efficiency. Even with the best of intentions it would be very difficult. High resource loads are built into virtually everything that is consumed in the United States, from housing to food, transportation, and clothes. Recycling and volunteerism are not enough.

There are also serious political difficulties in moving in this direction. The costs of present lifestyles are currently pushed on to future generations, offshore on to other nations, or on to nature. Those who would lose from a transition to sustainability are well organized and well represented, while those who would benefit are not. For example, any serious attempt to move away from fossil fuels to renewable energy immediately incurs the wrath of the oil companies and car-makers, which include ten of the eleven largest corporations in the world. The new businesses that would be created by such a change do not yet exist, so they are not at the table advocating their interests. Moreover, the American political system is quite conservative in its bias towards incumbents. According to reporter Juliet Eilperin (2006), the old Soviet Politburo had more turnover than the American congress.

Still, change does occur, often with surprising rapidity, in ways that we do not understand. The wave of "people power" movements that brought down communism in the late 1980s and early 1990s caught the experts by surprise. The movement to ban smoking in public places has also been surprising and difficult to predict. The carcinogenic effects of tobacco smoke were strongly suspected as early as the 1920s, and by 1964 the Surgeon General of the United States had published a report showing that smoking is linked to lung and other forms of cancer, heart disease, emphysema, bronchitis, and a number of other illnesses. Yet it was not until the 1990s that a powerful movement began to develop to ban smoking in public places. Why then? Why not sooner? If not then, why ever?

If the United States is to move towards sustainability, action at many different levels is important. Individual action is important for many reasons, including the fact that through their actions individuals signal to politicians and decision-makers that they will not be punished for changing law and policy. In an interest-group democracy like that of the United States, churches, environmental organizations, the media, and other institutions of civil society are important for mobilizing individuals and carrying messages. In the end, however, government action is important both because of its regulatory power and because of its ability to affect market behavior. Markets are extremely important because by coordinating behavior they can magnify the effects of change.

A good example of markets having this effect is the case of ozone-destroying chlorofluorocarbons (CFCs). When consumers and environmentalists began campaigning against the use of these chemicals, the manufacturers began looking for alternatives. When alternatives came into view, the government was freer to support a ban. Even so, the initial agreement signed in 1987 would have restricted but not banned CFCs. But once these substances were being controlled and alternatives were becoming available, the smart money started going elsewhere, and it was relatively easy to move to an outright ban.[37] While controlling greenhouse gases is much more complicated, there is no reason why the same general story could not be repeated. Once there is a price on carbon, markets may begin to move quickly towards alternatives.

Of course, there is no guarantee that things will go this way. The United States has rejected the current regime for managing greenhouse emissions, and that regime is not very effective anyway. It remains to be seen what the future holds. Will it be environmental catastrophe, continuing and increasing global inequality and environmental degradation, a change in the way of life of the world's most privileged people, or some combination of the three?

7.4 Conclusion

We have covered a great deal of ground in this book, from the foundations of morality to the threats against nature. This has taken us from the writings of philosophers to the calculations of environmental scientists. We have considered the problem of global poverty and pondered the motivations of the world's richest people. We have looked to the past in an effort to explain why we have the problems that we do, and we have also speculated on possible futures.

Very little has been said in this book that is incontrovertible. I have spelled out some arguments, sketched some more, and alluded to many others. In critically reading this book, I hope that you have taken these

[37] For an account, see Benedick 1991.

accounts further, and thought of some important points that have escaped my attention. We have reached the end of this book, but not the end of the road.

One theme that I have urged is that our future is entwined with nature's; for all sorts of reasons, both conceptual and empirical, they cannot be pulled apart. What happens next depends on us. Not entirely, of course, for Mother Nature will make herself felt. But in the end she cannot say what gives our lives meaning. She can lay down the law but it is up to us to choose how to live. Whether through action or inaction, we will chart the course for life on Earth.

References

Agar, Nicholas. 2001. *Life's Intrinsic Value: Science, Ethics, and Nature*. New York: Columbia University Press.

Anscombe, G. E. M. 1958. "Modern Moral Philosophy," *Philosophy* 33: 1–19.

Atkinson, I. A. E. 2001. "Introduced Mammals and Models for Restoration." *Biological Conservation* 99: 81–96.

Attfield, Robin. 1987. *A Theory of Value and Obligation*. London: Croom Helm.

Ayer, A. J. 1946. *Language, Truth, and Logic*. London: Gollancz. (1st edn. 1936.)

Baier, Kurt. 1958. *The Moral Point of View: A Rational Basis of Ethics*. Ithaca, NY: Cornell University Press.

Baranzke, Heike. 2004. "Does Beast Suffering Count for Kant? A Contextual Examination of §17 in *The Doctrine of Virtue*," *Essays in Philosophy* 5/2 (available at <www.humboldt.edu/~essays/baranzke.html>).

Barker, Rodney. 1997. *And the Waters Turned to Blood: The Ultimate Biological Threat*. New York: Simon & Schuster.

Benedick, Richard E. 1991. *Ozone Diplomacy*. Cambridge, MA: Harvard University Press.

Bentham, Jeremy. 1827. *Rationale of Judicial Evidence, Specially Applied to English Practice*, ed. John Stuart Mill. 5 vols. London. (Reprinted in *The Works of Jeremy Bentham*, ed. J. Bowring, Edinburgh, 1838–43.)

Biswas-Diener, Robert, Ed Diener, and Maya Tamir. 2004. "The Psychology of Subjective Well-Being." *Daedalus* 133: 18–25.

Blackburn, Simon. 1993. *Essays in Quasi-Realism*. Oxford: Oxford University Press. 1998. *Ruling Passions*. Oxford: Clarendon Press.

Boulding, Kenneth. 1966. "The Economics of the Coming Spaceship Earth." In *Environmental Quality in a Growing Economy: Essays from the Sixth RFF Forum*, ed. Henry Jarrett. Baltimore, MD: Johns Hopkins University Press, for Resources for the Future: 3–14.

Boyd, Richard. 1988. "How to Be a Moral Realist." In *Essays on Moral Realism*, ed. Sayre McCord. Ithaca, NY: Cornell University Press.

Brennan, Scott, and Jay Withgott. 2005. *The Science Behind the Stories*. San Francisco: Benjamin Cummings.

Brink, David. 1989. *Moral Realism and the Foundations of Ethics*. New York: Cambridge University Press.

Brown, Peter, *et al.* 2004. "A New Small-Bodied Hominid from the Late Pleistocene of Flores, Indonesia." *Nature* 431: 1055–61.

Cafaro, Philip, and Ronald Sandler, eds. 2005. *Environmental Virtue Ethics*. New York: Rowman & Littlefield.

Callicott, J. Baird, ed. 1980. "Animal Liberation: A Triangular Affair." *Environmental Ethics* 2: 311–38.

   1989. *In Defense of the Land Ethic*. Albany, NY: State University of New York Press.

Carlson, Allen. 2000. *Aesthetics and the Environment: The Appreciation of Nature, Art and Architecture*. London: Routledge.

Carnap, Rudolf. 1937. *Philosophy and Logical Syntax*. London: Kegan Paul, Trench, Trubner.

Chandroo, Kris P., Ian J. H. Duncan, and Richard D. Moccia. 2004. "Can Fish Suffer? Perspectives on Sentience, Pain, Fear and Stress." *Applied Animal Behaviour Science* 86: 225–50.

Commoner, Barry. 1971. *The Closing Circle: Nature, Man, and Technology*. New York: Knopf.

Copp, David. 1995. *Morality, Normativity, and Society*. Oxford: Oxford University Press.

Costanza, Robert, Ralph d'Arge, Rudolf de Groot, Stephen Farber, Monica Grasso, Bruce Hannon, Karin Limburg, Shahid Naeem, Robert V. O'Neill, José Paruelo, Robert G. Raskin, Paul Sutton, and Marjan van den Belt. 1997. "The Value of the World's Ecosystem Services and Natural Capital," *Nature* 387/6230: 253–60.

Cowen, Tyler, with Derek Parfit. 1992. "Against the Social Discount Rate." In *Justice Across the Generations: Philosophy, Politics, and Society*, 6th series, ed. Peter Laslett and James Fishkin. New York: Yale University Press: 144–61.

Cronon, William. 1996. "The Trouble with Wilderness, or, Getting Back to the Wrong Nature." In *Uncommon Ground: Rethinking the Human Place in Nature*, ed. William Cronon. New York: Norton.

Damasio, Antonio R. 1994. *Descartes' Error: Emotion, Reason, and The Human Brain*. New York: Putnam.

Davis, Mark A. 2003. "Biotic Globalization: Does Competition from Introduced Species Threaten Biodiversity?" *Bioscience* 53: 481–9.

de Waal, Frans, Stephen Macedo, and Josiah Ober, eds. 2006. *Primates And Philosophers: How Morality Evolved*. Princeton: Princeton University Press.

Dombrowski, Daniel. 1997. *Babies and Beasts: The Argument from Marginal Cases.* Champaign: University of Illinois Press.

Donlan, C. Josh, Harry W. Greene, Joel Berger, Carl E. Bock, Jane H. Bock, David A. Burney, James A. Estes, Dave Forman, Paul S. Martin, Gary W. Roemer, Felicia A. Smith, and Michael E. Soulé. 2005. "Re-wilding North America." *Nature* 436: 913–14.

Easterbrook, Gregg. 1996. *A Moment on the Earth: The Coming Age of Environmental Optimism.* New York: Viking.

Edelman, Pieter D., Douglas C. McFarland, Vladimir A. Mironov, and Jason G. Matheny. 2005. "In Vitro Cultured Meat Production: Commentary." *Tissue Engineering* 11/5–6: 659–62.

Edelstein, Michael R., and William J. Makofske. 1998. *Radon's Deadly Daughters: Science, Environmental Policy, and the Politics of Risk.* New York: Rowman & Littlefield.

Eggert, Lori S., Nicholas I. Mundy, and David S. Woodruff. 2004. "Population Structure of Loggerhead Shrikes in the California Channel Islands." *Molecular Ecology* 13/8: 2121–33.

Ehrlich, Paul and John Holdren. 1972. "A Bulletin Dialogue on the 'Closing Circle' Critique: One-Dimensional Ecology." *Bulletin of Atomic Science* 28: 16–27.

Eilperin, Juliet. 2006. *Fight Club Politics.* New York: Rowman & Littlefield in co-operation with the Hoover Institution.

Eisnitz, Gail A. 1997. *Slaughterhouse: The Shocking Story of Greed, Neglect, and Inhumane Treatment Inside the U.S. Meat Industry.* Buffalo: Prometheus.

Elgin, Duane. 1998. *Voluntary Simplicity: Toward a Way of Life That Is Outwardly Simple, Inwardly Rich,* rev. edn. New York: Harper Paperbacks. (1st edn. 1981.)

Elliot, Robert. 1985. "Metaethics and Environmental Ethics." *Metaphilosophy* 16: 103–17.

——— 1997. *Faking Nature: The Ethics of Environmental Restoration.* London: Routledge.

Elliot, Robert, Gidon Eshel, and Pamela A. Martin. 2006. "Diet, Energy, and Global Warming." *Earth Interactions* 10: 1–17.

Evans, Patrick D., Nitzan Mekel-Bobrov, Eric J. Vallender, Richard R. Hudson, and Bruce T. Lahn. 2006. "Evidence that the Adaptive Allele of the Brain Size Gene Microcephalin Introgressed into Homo Sapiens from Anarchaic Homo Lineage." *Proceedings of the National Academy of Sciences* 103: 18178–83.

Falk, W. D. 1986. *Ought, Reasons, and Morality: The Collected Papers of W. D. Falk.* Ithaca, NY: Cornell University Press.

Field, Christopher B. 2001. "Sharing the Garden." *Science* 294: 2490–1.

Fiskesjo, Magnus. 2003. *The Thanksgiving Turkey Pardon, the Death of Teddy's Bear, and the Sovereign Exception of Guantanamo.* Chicago: Prickly Paradigm Press.

Franklin, Benjamin. 1996. *Benjamin Franklin's The Art of Virtue: His Formula for Successful Living*, ed. George L. Rogers, 3rd edn. Battle Creek, MI: Acorn Publishing. (1st edn. 1986.)

Freuchen, Peter. 1961. *The Book of the Eskimo*. Cleveland, OH: World Publishing.

Geach, Peter. 1965. "Assertion." *Philosophical Review* 74: 449–65.

Gibbard, Allan. 1990. *Wise Choices, Apt Feelings*. Cambridge, MA: Harvard University Press.

Godwin, William. 1985. *An Enquiry Concerning Political Justice*. Harmondsworth: Penguin. (First published 1793.)

Goldburg, Rebecca, and Rosamond L. Naylor. 2005. "Future Seascapes, Fishing, and Fish Farming." *Frontiers in Ecology and the Environment* 3/1: 21–8.

Goodin, Robert. 1992. *Green Political Theory*. Cambridge: Polity Press.

Goodman, Nelson. 1978. *Ways of Worldmaking*. Indianapolis: Hackett Publishing Company.

Goodpaster, Kenneth. 1978. "On Being Morally Considerable." *Journal of Philosophy* 75: 308–25.

Gore, Albert. 1992. *Earth in the Balance: Ecology and the Human Spirit*. Boston, MA: Houghton Mifflin.

Gregory, Neville G., and Steve B. Wotton. 1986. "Effect of Slaughter on the Spontaneous and Evoked Activity of the Brain." *British Poultry Science* 27: 195–205.

Gruen, Lori, and Dale Jamieson, eds. 1994. *Reflecting on Nature: Readings in Environmental Philosophy*. New York: Oxford University Press.

Hacking, Ian. 1999. *The Social Construction of What?* Cambridge, MA: Harvard University Press.

Hall, Charles A. S., R. Gil Pontius, Jr., Lisa Coleman, and Jae-Young Ko. 1995. "The Environmental Consequences of Having a Baby in the United States." *Population and Environment* 15/6: 505–23.

Hardin, Garrett. 1968. "The Tragedy of the Commons." *Science* 162: 1243–8.

—— 1974. "Living on a Lifeboat." *BioScience* 24/10: 561–8 (available at <www.garretthardinsociety.org/articles/art_living_on_a_lifeboat.html>).

Hare, Richard M. 1952. *The Language of Morals*. Oxford: Clarendon Press.

—— 1963. *Freedom and Reason*. Oxford: Oxford University Press.

—— 1981. *Moral Thinking: Its Levels, Method, and Point*. Oxford: Oxford University Press.

Harrison, Ross. 1983. *Bentham*. London: Routledge.

Hart, Donna, and Robert W. Sussman. 2005. *Man the Hunted: Primates, Predators, and Human Evolution*. Boulder, CO: Westview Press.

Heath, John. 2005. *The Talking Greeks: Speech, Animals, and the Other in Homer, Aeschylus, and Plato*. Cambridge: Cambridge University Press.

Hettinger, Ned. 2001. "Exotic Species, Naturalization, and Biological Nativism." *Environmental Values* 10/2: 193–224.

Hill, Thomas, Jr. 1983. "Ideals of Human Excellence," *Environmental Ethics* 5: 211–24.

Hoebel, E. Adamson. 1954. *The Law of Primitive Man: A Study in Comparative Legal Dynamics*. Cambridge, MA: Harvard University Press.

Holland, Alan. 1984. "On Behalf of a Moderate Speciesism." *Journal of Applied Philosophy* 1/2: 281–91.

Hume, David. 1965. *Of the Standard of Taste*. Indianapolis: Bobbs-Merrill. (First published 1757.)

   2000. *A Treatise of Human Nature*, ed. David Fate Norton and Mary J. Norton. Oxford and New York: Oxford University Press. (First published 1740.)

Hurka, Thomas. 1992. "Future Generations." In *Encyclopedia of Ethics*, ed. Lawrence C. Becker. New York: Garland Publishing: 391–4.

Hursthouse, Rosalind. 1999. *On Virtue Ethics*. Oxford: Oxford University Press.

Jamieson, Dale. 1990. "Rights, Justice and Duties to Aid: A Critique of Regan's Theory of Rights." *Ethics* 100: 349–62.

   ed. 1999. *Singer and the Practical Ethics Movement*. Oxford: Blackwell.

   ed. 2001. *A Companion to Environmental Philosophy*. Oxford: Blackwell.

   2002. *Morality's Progress: Essays on Humans, Other Animals, and the Rest of Nature*. Oxford: Oxford University Press.

Jenni, Kathie. 2005. "The Power of the Visual." *Animal Liberation Philosophy and Policy Journal* 3: 1–21.

Kant, Immanuel. 1996. *Practical Philosophy*, trans. and ed. Mary Gregor. Cambridge: Cambridge University Press.

   1997. *Lectures on Ethics*, trans. Peter Heath, ed. Peter Heath and Jerome B. Schneewind. Cambridge: Cambridge University Press.

   2006. *Anthropology from a Pragmatic Point of View*, trans. and ed. Robert Louden. Cambridge: Cambridge University Press.

Kempton, Willett, James S. Boster, and Jennifer A. Hartley. 1995. *Environmental Values in American Culture*. Cambridge, MA: MIT Press.

Korsgaard, Christine M. 1996. *The Sources of Normativity*. Cambridge: Cambridge University Press.

   2005. "Fellow Creatures: Kantian Ethics and Our Duties to Animals." In *Tanner Lectures on Human Values* 25, ed. Grethe B. Peterson. Salt Lake City: University of Utah Press: 77–110.

Kuflik, Arthur. 1998. "Moral Standing." In *Routledge Encyclopedia of Philosophy*, ed. Edward Craig. London: Routledge.

Leopold, Aldo. 1949. *A Sand County Almanac and Sketches Here and There*. New York: Oxford University Press.

Lomborg, Bjorn. 2001. *The Skeptical Environmentalist*. Cambridge: Cambridge University Press.

Lovelock, James. 2006. *The Revenge of Gaia: Why the Earth is Fighting Back – And How We Can Still Save Humanity*. Harmondsworth: Allen Lane.

McCloskey, H. J. 1957. "An Examination of Restricted Utilitarianism." *Philosophical Review* 66/4: 466–85.

McDowell, John. 1985. "Values and Secondary Qualities." In *Morality and Objectivity*, ed. Ted Honderich. London: Routledge & Kegan Paul: 110–29.

McKibben, Bill. 1989. *The End of Nature*. New York: Random House.

Maron, John L., Montserrat Vila, Riccardo Bommarco, Sarah Elmendorf, and Paul Beardsley. 2004. "Rapid Evolution of an Invasive Plant." *Ecological Monographs* 74/2: 261–80.

Martin, Robert D., Ann M. MacLarnon, James L. Phillips, Laure Dussubieux, Patrick R. Williams, and William B. Dobyns. 2006. "Comment on 'The Brain of LB1, Homo floresiensis.'" *Science* 312/5776: 999.

Mather, Jennifer A. 2001. "Animal Suffering: An Invertebrate Perspective." *Journal of Applied Welfare Science* 4/2: 151–6.

Meehl, Gerald A., M. Washington Warren, William D. Collins, Julie M. Arblaster, Aixue Hu, Lawrence E. Buja, Warren G. Strand, Haiyan Teng. 2005. "How Much More Global Warming and Sea Level Rise?" *Science* 307/5716: 1769–72.

Moore, G. E. 1903. *Principia Ethica*. Cambridge: Cambridge University Press.

1922. *Philosophical Studies*. London: Routledge & Kegan Paul.

Morwood, M. J., *et al.* 2004. "Archaeology and Age of a New Hominid from Flores in Eastern Indonesia." *Nature* 431: 1087–91.

Muir, John. 2006. *Steep Trails*. New York: Cosimo. (First published 1918.)

Myers, Ransom A., and Boris Worm. 2003. "Rapid Worldwide Depletion of Predatory Fish Communities." *Nature* 423: 280–3.

Nabhan, Gary P., A. M. Rea, Karen L. Reichhardt, Eric Mellick, and Charles F. Hutchinson. 1982. "Papago Influence on Habitat and Biotic Diversity: Quiotovac Oases Ethnoecology." *Journal of Ethnobiology* 2: 124–43.

Nash, Roderick. 2001. *Wilderness and the American Mind*. 4th edn. New Haven, CT: Yale University Press. (First edn. 1967.)

Naylor, Rosamond L., and Marshall Burke. 2005. "Aquaculture and Ocean Resources: Raising Tigers of the Sea." *Annual Review of Environment and Resources* 30: 185–218.

Norton, Bryan G. 1991. *Toward Unity Among Environmentalists*. New York: Oxford University Press.

2005. *Sustainability: A Philosophy of Adaptive Ecosystem Management*. Chicago: University of Chicago Press.

Noss, Reed F., and Allen Y. Cooperrider. 1994. *Saving Nature's Legacy*. Washington, DC: Island Press.

O'Neill, Onora. 1986. *Faces of Hunger*. Boston, MA: Allen & Unwin.

Ortega y Gasset, José. 1972. *Meditations on Hunting*. New York: Charles Scribner's Sons.

Pacala, S., and R. Socolow. 2004. "Stabilization Wedges: Solving the Climate Problem for the Next 50 Years with Current Technologies." *Science* 305/5686: 968–72.

Parfit, Derek. 1984. *Reasons and Persons*. Oxford: Oxford University Press.

Parry, Martin L., Nigel W. Arnell, Anthony J. McMichael, Robert J. Nicholls, Pim Martens, R. Sari Kovats, Matthew T. J. Livermore, Cynthia Rosenzweig, Ana Iglesias, and Gunther Fischer. 2001. "Millions At Risk: Defining Critical Climate Change Threats and Targets." *Global Environmental Change – Human and Policy Dimensions* 11/3: 181–3.

Passmore, John. 1974. *Man's Responsibility for Nature: Ecological Problems and Western Traditions*. New York: Charles Scribner's Sons.

Pauly, Daniel, Villy Christensen, Sylvie Guénette, Tony J. Pitcher, U. Rashid Sumaila, Carl J. Walters, R. Watson, and Dirk Zeller. 2002. "Towards Sustainability in World Fisheries." *Nature* 418: 689–95.

Pimentel, David, and Marcia Pimentel. 2003. "Sustainability of Meat-Based and Plant-Based Diets and the Environment." *American Journal of Clinical Nutrition* 78: 660–3.

Pluhar, Evelyn B. 1995. *Beyond Prejudice: The Moral Significance of Human and Nonhuman Animals*. Durham, NC: Duke University Press.

Pollan, Michael. 2006. *The Omnivore's Dilemma: A Natural History of Four Meals*. New York: Penguin.

Rachels, James. 1990. *Created from Animals*. New York: Oxford University Press.
    2003. *The Elements of Moral Philosophy*. New York: McGraw Hill.

Railton, Peter. 2003. *Facts, Values, and Norms: Essays Toward a Morality of Consequence*. Cambridge: Cambridge University Press.

Regan, Tom. 1982. *All That Dwell Therein: Essays on Animal Rights and Environmental Ethics*. Berkeley: University of California Press.
    1983. *The Case for Animal Rights*. Berkeley: University of California Press.
    1985. "The Case for Animal Rights." In Peter Singer, ed., *In Defense of Animals*. Oxford: Basil Blackwell.

Rodman, John. 1977. "The Liberation of Nature?" *Inquiry* Spring: 83–145.

Roemer, Gary W., and Robert K. Wayne. 2003. "Conservation in Conflict: the Tale of Two Endangered Species." *Conservation Biology* 17/5: 1251–60.

Rolston III, Holmes. 1988. *Environmental Ethics: Duties To and Values In the Natural World*. Philadelphia, PA: Temple University Press.

Rosa, Humberto D. 2004. "Bioethics of Biodiversity." In Charles Susanne, guest ed., "Societal Responsibilities in Life Sciences." *Human Ecology Review* Special Issue 3/12: 157–71.

Routley, Richard. 1973. "Is There a Need for a New, an Environmental Ethic?" *Proceedings of the XVth World Congress of Philosophy* 1/6: 205–10.

Routley, Richard and Val. 1980. "Human Chauvinism and Environmental Ethics." In *Environmental Philosophy*, ed. Donald S. Mannison, Michael McRobbie, and Richard Routley. Canberra: Research School of Social Sciences, Australian National University: 96–189.

Ryder, Richard D. 1975. *Victims of Science: The Use of Animals in Research*. London: Davis-Poynter.

Sagoff, Mark. 1991. "Nature Versus the Environment": *Report from the Institute for Philosophy and Public Policy* 11/3: 5–8.

Sarkar, Sahotra. 2005. *Biodiversity and Environmental Philosophy: An Introduction to the Issues*. New York: Cambridge University Press.

Scarre, Geoffrey. 1996. *Utilitarianism*. London: Routledge.

Schlosser, Eric. 2001. *Fast Food Nation: The Dark Side of the All-American Meal*. Boston: Houghton Mifflin.

Schumacher, Eric F. 1973. *Small Is Beautiful*. New York: Harper & Row.

Schwartz, Thomas. 1978. "Obligations to Posterity." In Brian Barry and Richard Sikora, eds., *Obligations to Future Generations*. Philadelphia, Temple University Press: 3–13.

Sen, Amartya. 2006. *Identity and Violence: The Illusion of Destiny*. New York: Norton.

Sibert, John, John Hampton, Pierre Kleiber, and Mark Maunder. 2006. "Biomass, Size, and Trophic Status of Top Predators in the Pacific Ocean." *Science*, Dec. 15: 1773–6.

Singer, Peter. 1990. *Animal Liberation*, 2nd edn. New York: New York Review of Books. (First edn. 1975.)

1993. *Practical Ethics*. 2nd edn. Cambridge: Cambridge University Press. (First edn. 1979.)

Singer, Peter, and Jim Mason. 2006. *The Way We Eat: Why Our Food Choices Matter*. New York: Rodale.

Smith, Michael. 1994. *The Moral Problem*. Oxford: Blackwell.

Snyder, Gary. 1990. *The Practice of the Wild*. Berkeley: North Point.

Sober, Elliott. 1986. "Philosophical Problems for Environmentalism." In *The Preservation of Species: The Value of Biological Diversity*, ed. Bryan G. Norton. Princeton: Princeton University Press: 173–94.

Sorabji, Richard. 1993. *Animal Minds and Human Morals: The Origins of the Western Debate*. Ithaca, NY: Cornell University Press.

Stevenson, Charles L. 1944. *Ethics and Language*. New Haven, CT: Yale University Press.

Stone, Christopher. 1972. "Should Trees Have Standing? Toward Legal Rights for Natural Objects." *Southern California Law Review* 45: 450–501.

Taylor, Paul. 1986. *Respect for Nature: A Theory of Environmental Ethics*, Princeton: Princeton University Press.

Toulmin, Stephen. 1948. *Reason in Ethics*. Cambridge: Cambridge University Press.

Turner, Jack. 1996. *The Abstract Wild*. Tucson: University of Arizona Press.

van den Bergh, Jeroen C. J. M., and Harmen Verbruggen. 1999. "Spatial Sustainability, Trade and Indicators: An Evaluation of the 'Ecological Footprint.'" *Ecological Economics* 29/1: 63–74.

Varner, Gary E. 1998. *In Nature's Interests? Interests, Animal Rights, and Environmental Ethics*. New York: Oxford University Press.

Vitousek, Peter M., Paul R. Ehrlich, Anne H. Ehrlich, and Pamela A. Matson. 1986. "Human Appropriation of the Products of Photosynthesis." *BioScience* 36/6: 368–73.

Vitousek, Peter M., Harold A. Mooney, Jane Lubchenco, and Jerry M. Melillo. 1997. "Human Domination of Earth's Ecosystems." *Science* 277/5325: 494–9.

Volk, Tyler. 2005. *Gaia's Body: Toward a Physiology of Earth*. Cambridge, MA: MIT Press.

Wackernagel, Mathis, and William Rees. 1996. *Our Ecological Footprint: Reducing Human Impact on the Earth*. Gabriola Island, BC: New Society.

Wapner, Paul, and John Willoughby. 2005. "The Irony of Environmentalism: The Ecological Futility but Political Necessity of Lifestyle Change." *Ethics & International Affairs* 19/3: 77–89.

Warnock, Geoffrey J. 1971. *The Object of Morality*. London: Methuen.

West, Henry. 2003. *An Introduction to Mill's Utilitarian Ethics*. New York: Cambridge University Press.

Westman, Walter E. 1990. "Park Management of Exotic Plant Species: Problems and Issues." *Conservation Biology* 4: 251–60.

White, Lynn, Jr. 1967. "The Historical Roots of Our Ecologic Crisis." *Science* 155/3767: 1203–7.

Wiggins, David. 1998. *Needs, Values, Truth*, 3rd edn. Oxford: Oxford University Press. (First edn. 1987.)

2000. "Nature, Respect for Nature, and the Human Scale of Values." *Proceedings of the Aristotelian Society* 100: 1–32.

Williams, Bernard. 1995. *Making Sense of Humanity*. Cambridge: Cambridge University Press.

2006. *Philosophy as a Humanistic Discipline*, ed. Adrian Moore. Princeton: Princeton University Press.

Williams, Bernard, with J. J. C. Smart. 1973. *Utilitarianism: For and Against*. Cambridge: Cambridge University Press.

Wood, Allen. 1998. "Kant on Duties Regarding Nonrational Nature." *Aristotelian Society Supplementary Volume LXXII*: 189–210.

Woods, Mark, and Paul Moriarty. 2001. "Strangers in a Strange Land: The Problem of Exotic Species," *Environmental Values* 10: 163–91.

World Commission On Environment and Development. 1987. *Our Common Future.* New York: Oxford University Press.

Zamir Tzachi. 2007. *Ethics and the Beast.* Princeton: Princeton University Press.

Zeki, Semir, and Hideaki Kawabata. 2004. "Neural Correlates of Beauty." *Journal of Neurophysiology* 91: 1699–705.

Index